A Case of

LIFE
AND
LIMB

A Case of

LIFE
AND
LIMB

SALLY SMITH

RAVEN BOOKS
LONDON · OXFORD · NEW YORK · NEW DELHI · SYDNEY

RAVEN BOOKS
Bloomsbury Publishing plc
50 Bedford Square, London, WC1B 3DP, UK
Bloomsbury Publishing Ireland Limited
29 Earlsfort Terrace, Dublin 2, D02 AY28, Ireland

BLOOMSBURY, RAVEN BOOKS and the Raven Books logo
are trademarks of Bloomsbury Publishing Plc

First published in Great Britain 2025

Copyright © Sally Smith, 2025
Map © Liane Payne, 2025

Sally Smith has asserted her right under the Copyright,
Designs and Patents Act, 1988, to be identified as Author of this work

This is a work of fiction. Names and characters are the product of the author's imagination and
any resemblance to actual persons, living or dead, is entirely coincidental

All rights reserved. No part of this publication may be: i) reproduced or transmitted in
any form, electronic or mechanical, including photocopying, recording or by means of any
information storage or retrieval system without prior permission in writing from the publishers;
or ii) used or reproduced in any way for the training, development or operation of artificial
intelligence (AI) technologies, including generative AI technologies. The rights holders expressly
reserve this publication from the text and data mining exception as per Article 4(3) of the Digital
Single Market Directive (EU) 2019/790

Bloomsbury Publishing Plc does not have any control over, or responsibility for,
any third-party websites referred to in this book. All internet addresses given in this
book were correct at the time of going to press. The author and publisher regret
any inconvenience caused if addresses have changed or sites have ceased to exist,
but can accept no responsibility for any such changes

A catalogue record for this book is available from the British Library

ISBN: HB: 978-1-5266-6877-6; TPB: 978-1-5266-6876-9;
EBOOK: 978-1-5266-6878-3; EPDF: 978-1-5266-6881-3

2 4 6 8 10 9 7 5 3 1

Typeset by Integra Software Services Pvt. Ltd.
Printed and bound in Great Britain by CPI Group (UK) Ltd, Croydon CR0 4YY

To find out more about our authors and books visit www.bloomsbury.com
and sign up for our newsletters

For product safety related questions contact productsafety@bloomsbury.com

For Roger

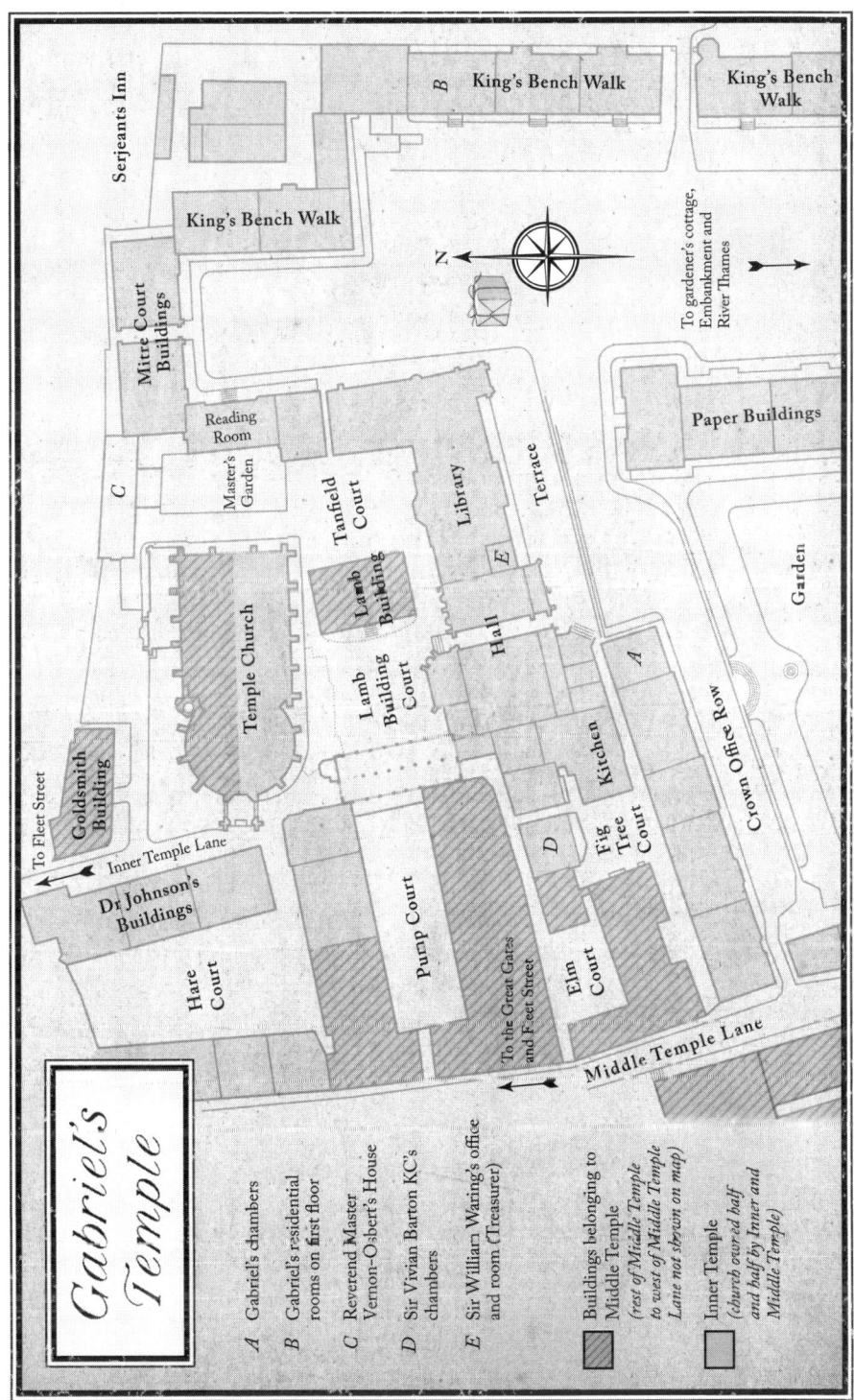

I

No hint of the horror to come was discernible in the pure snow. It lay pristine on every ledge and roof of the ancient buildings and drifted into the doorways and around the old gas lamps and water pumps. No whiff of corruption in the perfect scarlet berries that hung from the holly bushes in the gardens. No discordance in the robins' song. Through the windows, the soft glow of oil lamps illuminated desks, their occupants deep in studious concentration. Smoke drifted peacefully from the crooked chimneys.

It was Christmas Eve. The Michaelmas term of 1901 had recently concluded. The Temple, that cloistered little area of London in which the lawyers live, huddled together in the ancient chambers that line the passageways and squares around the Temple Church, was slowly emptying. Save for the residents and for the industrious few who faced big trials in the New Year, barristers were leaving for Christmas at home.

The whole scene, thought Sir Gabriel Ward KC, as he picked his way across Inner Temple Terrace, was the very embodiment of a three-dimensional Christmas card. It needed only a few choirboys. As if on cue came that unmistakable sound, the ringing yet muffled swell of joy that is children liberated into snow. A group of small boys, in the innocence of red gowns and white ruffs and the determination of stout boots, tumbled from their rehearsal onto the smooth white lawn of Inner Temple garden and within seconds defaced it with frantic feet and scrabbling hands.

The smallest of the pack hung back and watched the snowballs flying with trepidation. On impulse Gabriel crossed the Terrace and, heedless of his immaculate black kid gloves, scooped up a very soft bundle of snow and shied it gently through the railings at the child's back. He started and turned, and Gabriel removed his top hat and bowed.

'I fear,' he said in his precise way, 'that I have assaulted you. I beg your pardon.'

The little boy smiled, fairly sure this was a joke, and at the sight of that characteristic wide smile that seemed to link ear to ear, Gabriel made a discovery. 'Are you one of Sir Vivian Barton's sons?' he asked.

'Yes, sir; Bertie, sir. The third one, sir.'

'In that case, Master Barton Tertius, as the son of an eminent lawyer, you know that if you are assaulted, you are entitled to damages.'

And Gabriel extracted sixpence from his inner waistcoat pocket and handed it through the railings. The other boys had kept their distance. Gentlemen barristers walking along the Terrace between the Dining Hall, the library and the Temple Church were an unpredictable bunch. It might be a penny and a pat on the head, but equally it might be a telling-off and a demand to know where your papa's chambers were. But now they gathered round, neck ruffs askew and mittens caked in snow. Sixpence!

'It is for you all to buy toffee,' said Gabriel. 'But remember, Master Barton is in charge of it.'

They tore off in a breathless chorus of thanks; Gabriel noted with satisfaction that Barton was now in the lead.

From his elegantly curtained study window, Sir William Waring, Master Treasurer, head of the Inner Temple, watched the scene with strong disapproval and a complete lack of appreciation of its subtlety.

Really, he thought to himself disagreeably, sometimes I do wonder about Sir Gabriel Ward KC. Throwing snowballs! A lawyer of his seniority and distinction. One of our King's Counsel! In public! I shall speak to him.

He looked at his pocket watch. Time was getting on. Gertrude had visited earlier in the afternoon, heavily veiled for a quick Christmas assignation, and now he was soon to go home to his beautiful house in Chelsea, a testament throughout to Lady Waring's immaculate taste and efficient management of the servants. And Christmas Eve dinner with the family. Dear Amelia and Harriet... both as pretty as pictures, thank God, and their futures thus assured. Indeed, Amelia was to announce her engagement that very evening, and as for Raymond, the Bar was beckoning: a real chip off the old block. A credit to Sir William. None of the nonsense that other men had with their sons. But there, he'd been brought up from an early age to understand his duty to his parents. Waring looked at himself in the mirror above his chimneypiece, smoothed back his already smooth hair and straightened his already straight shoulders. Getting on a bit now, but not bad; Gertrude had no complaints anyway. He sighed with deep complacency.

There was a knock at the door.

'Come,' Sir William barked peremptorily. A maid entered holding a Christmas box of the most attractive kind. Exactly a foot square in all dimensions, it was immaculately wrapped in thick green paper and tied across both ways with a shining red ribbon that finished in a glossy bow.

'This was left on the doorstep for you, Sir William,' she said.

Sir William looked gratified. He would take it home to adorn the top of the already towering pile under the family tree. But even as he resolved this, a doubt entered his mind; it was a rather feminine looking present. Gertrude was a long-standing feature of his domestic life, with a family of her own and a mania for discretion. She had made no mention of sending him a present earlier and he knew she would not expose him to the embarrassment of taking home something more suitably opened alone. All the same, perhaps…

Nodding dismissal to the maid, he put the parcel on the table, pulled the bow with a satisfying slither, and tore off the paper. Inside was a plain brown cardboard box. When he lifted off the lid, he found enticing layers of tissue paper. Sir William unwrapped them to reveal the contents.

So great had been the expectation of something expensive and good to look upon, that his mind seemed for a moment unable to adjust to what it was seeing. He stared as though paralysed. Then a wave of panic rolled over him. A sharp reflex action caused him to slam back the lid, and he staggered to his chair with a shudder of horror.

2

Hovering on the snowy Terrace, the choirboys a distant tumult heading for the gates, Gabriel saw that now all the cracks between the paving stones that he had so assiduously trained himself to avoid had been obliterated by the fast-falling snow. It was with a surprising sense of freedom from his usual ritual that he embarked upon his route back to his chambers in 1 Crown Office Row. He thought with anticipation of the brief awaiting him on his immaculately ordered desk. It posed a legal problem requiring just the kind of mental gymnastics he most enjoyed, and he looked forward, as happily as any choirboy in the snow, to wading through the arcane statutes and regulations that might hold the answer.

Gabriel was known in the Temple for his liking for solitude. The only child of an ancient dynasty, he had showed no interest in the running of his family's estates and this had led to his disinheritance in favour of a bucolic cousin. Alone, he had realised his ambition to study the law and had built his reputation as one of the finest minds within that discipline, always wholly absorbed in the next impenetrably difficult case sent to him. Cocooned in the security of his residential rooms and professional chambers within the Temple, Gabriel was utterly content in his own company, bound by the self-imposed little habits and rituals that were to him not the bondage that they might seem to others, but the comfort that made his life liveable.

As he turned towards his chambers, indistinguishable figures drifted slowly past him in the luminous darkness of the snow, like ships in fog; silent, shadowy, their breath hanging in the still air. One of these shapeless figures, seeing Gabriel, approached: a large man, heavily overcoated and muffled.

'Barton,' said Gabriel, identifying him through the gloom, 'I have just had an encounter with your youngster; rather overwhelmed by his fellow choirboys' snowballs, I fear.'

Sir Vivian Barton KC looked fond. 'Our Bertie is the smallest in the choir, though he has a voice like a little angel.'

'Well,' said Gabriel, 'I know what it is to be small. And he does not have one of these,' he patted his top hat, 'to help.'

'He'll grow,' said Barton from the comfort and confidence of his six foot one inch. This kindly insouciant optimism characterised him. The two men, friendly colleagues out of the courts, old sparring partners within them, could not be more different.

Barton, devoted father to seven children, happily and uncritically married to his companionable wife, glided cheerfully through the practical and emotional demands of his large family and his demanding practice at the Bar. Gabriel resented all practical intrusions into his time and found emotional demands nothing short of terrifying. He could not begin to imagine how it was that Barton could combine the concentration required to conduct a trial with getting home to read to his children before they went to bed. Every ounce of energy, intellectual and emotional, that Gabriel possessed was channelled into his work. He did not think he had anything left to give.

They had grown to know one another's strengths and foibles. Vivian Barton privately called Gabriel a dear old pedant; Gabriel privately thought that if Barton, a good lawyer, had a weakness, it arose from a propensity to take short cuts. Both men were considered to be among the most able barristers in the Inner Temple, though it was generally felt, by the solicitors and clients who instructed them, that Barton's easy-going charm made him the more approachable. Gabriel's sternly cerebral attitude to his work could on occasion seem a little intimidating.

Barton, his gadfly attention now on other things, was fishing from his pocket the kind of newspaper not customarily read by gentlemen members of the Bar, already folded onto an inside page.

'Look at this. I saw it in Fleet Street and couldn't resist the headline.'

It was hard to miss: SUE US IF YOU DARE, TOPSY! blazoned across it. Gabriel looked blank.

'Who is – er – Topsy?' he asked.

'Really, Ward,' said Barton, 'even you must have heard of Topsy Tillotson?'

Gabriel shook his head rather shyly, well aware of his reputation for unworldliness.

'She was a chorus girl at the Drury Lane Theatre who caused a tremendous stir and is now their leading lady in *A Girl Like Me*. Face like Helen of Troy, voice like a nightingale, figure...' Barton trailed off. Suddenly the conversation seemed unsuitable for his audience. In a curious way he felt as protective of Gabriel as he did of young Bertie. But he had underestimated his listener's classical education.

'...like Aphrodite?' said Gabriel helpfully, and Barton laughed.

'Exactly so. But it wasn't her personal charms that made me buy the newspaper. Any litigation in which she is involved will be the sensation of the decade. By Jove, it will be a plum of a case for two lucky barristers! She seems to be threatening to bring proceedings against the newspaper. Look at this.'

Gabriel, squinting in the dim light, read the opening paragraph.

'*Miss Topsy Tillotson threatens to sue the* Nation's Voice *for damages to her – yes, to* her *– reputation!!!*' There were then several lines heavily redacted by a bold black bar of type before the article continued. *'On the advice of our lawyers we will refrain from repetition until we prove it in court!! Sue us if you dare, Topsy!'*

Ever the lawyer, Gabriel considered the article seriously. 'I should have thought that the three exclamation marks, and the words *'yes, to* her *reputation'*, could in themselves be said to be defamatory by innuendo.'

Barton laughed. 'If they had put twenty-three exclamation marks, they could have defended it,' he said. 'I've seen that young woman performing. I imagine,' he added rather wistfully, 'the Tillotson brief will go to Hopkins.'

Sir Edward Hopkins KC was famous for his shameless pursuit of publicity. 'No doubt it will, unless the *Nation's Voice* offers him a bigger fee,' said Gabriel drily. 'Well, he is welcome to either. There is nothing I dislike more than cases in which the purity of legal debate is sullied by sensationalism.'

'Give me sensationalism and some juicy newspaper reports and a fat cheque,' said Barton cheerfully. 'I have a family to support.'

The two men plodded on through the deepening snow, the tall burly figure, top hat at a jaunty angle, and the short slight one, his hat a model of symmetrical precision, both silhouetted by gaslight against the white backdrop. They had nearly reached the end of the Terrace when Gabriel, recalling an errand, turned back to Sir William Waring's doorway close by.

Sir William Waring, still huddled in his chair, had not been able to bear to look again at the ghastly contents of the box to verify what he thought he had seen. He had never before experienced, quite literally, an inability to believe his own eyes. Torn between a horrible desire to hurl the box away and a compulsion to look again, he did not know how long he had been sitting there, his horrified gaze transfixed by it, before the tentative knock on his door. It opened before he could respond.

Sir William had always found Gabriel Ward odd. He did not think men should be happy to live in solitude. And then he was so damned clever. There was no virtue in being that clever. He did not recognise that what he really disliked in Gabriel was his self-sufficiency, the quality that made him immune from the manipulations of power so dear to Sir William's own heart. Though ruthlessly ambitious, Sir William was not self-sufficient. He was too vain and liked admiration too much for that. And therein lay his weakness.

'Do forgive me, Sir William,' said Gabriel apologetically. 'I saw you had not yet left for home and I wondered if I might retrieve the paper I lent you in connection with the Inner Temple manuscripts?'

He advanced in his hesitant, unassuming way towards the table.

Sir William gave a strangled yelp. 'Do not...' he cried. 'Do not touch it!'

Gabriel looked startled. 'Do not touch the table?' And then, looking at him more closely, 'My dear Sir William, are you all right? Do you feel unwell?'

Sir William gesticulated wildly towards the table. 'There is something ghastly in the box!'

Gabriel began to look a little alarmed. 'In the box, Sir William?'

'Yes, yes, man! In the box, for Christ's sake! In the box!' shouted the Treasurer.

Gabriel's own emotions were habitually restrained, and he found the lack of such restraint in others almost indecent. Sir William's raised voice and distraught demeanour seemed to him disproportionate to any event that Gabriel could imagine.

'I do not know what has so upset you, Sir William, but I am unable to help you unless either you tell me what it is or I look for myself,' he said reasonably.

The Treasurer shuddered. 'It is horrible, Ward,' he said, 'beyond description.'

'Nothing is horrible beyond description,' said Gabriel, his inner lawyer – ever alert to inaccuracy of vocabulary – challenged by this observation. 'Words are all we have. Everything is describable, however terrible. Look at *Medea*; look at the *Book of Revelation*; look, for that matter, at *Dracula*.'

Sir William could not look at any of these since he never read anything but the *Law Reports*; but this scholarly analysis calmed him a little and he gestured to the box with a despairing acquiescence.

Gabriel cautiously lifted the lid. Emanating from the box was a faint sweet smell he could not place. He removed the tissue and peered at the contents. There was a pause.

'Yes,' he said at last, slowly. 'It is indeed horrible, but not beyond description. It is a human hand, severed at the wrist.'

There it lay, a wizened nightmare. Palm up, the fingers slightly curled as though beckoning. The desiccated brown flesh was beginning to flake from the palm; the nails were horribly cracked and pulling away from the sides of the outstretched fingers. The stump, once attached to a living agile wrist, was stringy and decayed. Revulsion and astonishment struggled with Gabriel's forensic instinct. As always, forensic instinct won.

'What is that sweet smell?' he said.

Sir William shuddered.

'It is decay,' he said.

Gabriel shook his head doubtfully and looked a little closer.

'I am no expert in these matters, but I think it is very clear this is far from fresh, Sir William.'

Waring grimaced with horror as Gabriel, peering still closer, saw the corner of a white card tucked down one side of the box and extracted it. He gave his characteristic little snuffle of mirth.

Can I give you a hand? read the writing on the card.

Gabriel handed it to the Treasurer. 'I think the sender has a warped sense of humour, Sir William. And, it must be acknowledged, a certain dexterity with words.'

'Disgusting,' said Waring fiercely. 'This dreadful crime must be investigated and the perpetrator brought to justice.'

'I am not sure,' said Gabriel slowly, his interest aroused as always by obscurity in the law, 'that it *is* a crime.'

'Cutting bits off people? Of course it is a crime! It is – it is a malicious wounding!' Sir William's voice rose in indignation.

'Not if the body was dead before the bits were cut off.'

'Then it is – a desecration of a body!'

'Not necessarily, Sir William. And even if so, it is a long-dead body and we do not have that body as evidence.'

'But the hand must have belonged to a body!'

'Certainly, it must once have been attached to one,' said Gabriel cautiously.

'And the body must have belonged to someone!'

'Certainly, when it was alive, it belonged to the person who inhabited it. But not now it is dead. You will recall from your pupillage days, Sir William, the old legal principle that a dead body belongs to no one. No one can claim to own it.'

Sir William searched the dusty recesses of his legal training. 'There is certainly a duty to bury a body; I remember it very distinctly being taught to me when I was a pupil barrister.'

'No general duty,' said Gabriel, dogged though apologetic in the face of Sir William's indignation. 'A duty only if you have a specific responsibility, Sir William; as the parent of a child for instance; or perhaps as the administrator of the Poor Laws. But even in those special circumstances, there is no duty of which I am aware to bury all parts of the body intact with it.'

The grinding of the wheels of Sir William's never very considerable and long-forgotten legal learning was almost audible.

'All right then, what about body snatching? That is a crime, isn't it?' he said triumphantly.

'Yes,' said Gabriel, 'but that is because it is a removal of an entire body from the custody of someone who *does* have a duty to bury it, or it is the disinterment from consecrated ground of an already buried body; there is no evidence to suggest that either situation has arisen here.'

Even at his best, Sir William had never been a subtle lawyer.

'It must be *something*,' he shouted, as people have always shouted when the law does not fit with their expectations. 'You can't just send people body parts! It is— It is— Outraging public decency!'

'I would agree with you, Sir William, had it been left in the street, but this parcel does not seem to have come through the post. Nothing suggests it has been in the public domain.'

Baulked, the Treasurer glared at him. Then there appeared in his eyes the determined gleam that always preceded his juggernaut tactics for getting his own way.

'This outrage cannot be known outside the Inner Temple,' he said firmly. 'It requires discretion and sensitivity. It is a direct insult to me, as the head of this institution. It must be investigated by one of our most senior and trusted members. You must find the culprit.'

'*Me?*' said Gabriel in alarm. 'But I couldn't possibly. I have a very important case—'

'Oh, you always have a very important case. You have an interest in forensic detection, have you not? This would not be the first time you have saved us the public humiliation of the presence of policemen in the Inner Temple!'

'Oh, dear, I have an interest in everything,' said Gabriel miserably, 'but it is only intellectual interest. Really, I have no natural aptitude at all… Sir William, I do feel you should call in the police.'

The Treasurer's voice took on a hectoring edge. 'On no account! I forbid it. You know very well, Ward, that the City of London Police can only enter our gates with consent. We are an Ancient Liberty. They have no rights here. I forbid it, I say! And anyway,' he added, more reasonably but not without a note of triumph, 'you said yourself: it might not even be a crime.' Waring shuffled the papers on his desk with hands that shook, and under the bluster Gabriel saw the signs of shock in his white face.

He said more gently, 'I am sure we can somehow get to the bottom of this, Sir William, after the Christmas festivities have concluded.'

And with that ill-considered 'we', he was committed.

3

The Treasurer, in an uncharacteristic display of vulnerability, buried his sleek dark head in his hands. 'The timing of all this is most unfortunate. It has made me feel quite unwell when my son Raymond is down for Christmas after a highly successful term, and my daughter Amelia is to announce her engagement tonight. We are to have a big family dinner.'

Gabriel, who found vulnerability hard to deal with, cast his mind back hastily to his only encounter with the Treasurer's family, the previous year at the Inner Temple garden party. Attending as a matter of duty, hovering by the hydrangeas, as far as possible from the noisy conviviality, he had been stumbled upon by Sir William who had brought his family to admire the borders.

Lady Waring had been large, handsome and rather formidable, he recalled, dressed – one might almost say upholstered – in mauve lace. There had been a young girl and a slightly older one and a son, Raymond, an almost identical younger version of his father both in looks and, more unfortunately, in manner. The self-satisfaction, irritating enough in Sir William, was insufferable in a boy of nineteen or so. Gabriel recalled thinking, most uncharacteristically for him, that had he been a younger man (not to mention a rather larger one) he would have wanted to kick him. But the older girl, Amelia, he recalled with great approval. A very engaging young woman, he had thought, with eyes bright with intelligence and humour under what was really a very pretty hat, who had taken an interest in the history of the Temple and giggled in the right places at his mild jokes.

'I am happy for them,' said Gabriel politely, if, in Raymond's case at least, insincerely.

Sir William thawed and recovered his usual rather smug expression, diverted from present horrors by this opportunity for complacency. 'Raymond is up at Cambridge and due here to read for the Bar next year. And Amelia is to marry a most suitable young man. A newly qualified barrister who is destined for the highest political office. He is the son of Sir Leopold Gibson, the last Home Secretary but one. Gibson of the banking family, you know; and Sir Leopold has had a safe seat in Parliament for thirty years, which it is hoped and believed will one day be that of his son. Lady Waring and I are delighted. We have known young John's family for many years and this union has long been both families' dearest wish.'

He recalled the present with a jolt. 'Now,' he concluded briskly, 'we must turn to the matter in ha—'

Gabriel suppressed a snuffle of mirth and Sir William, hearing him, revised the sentence hastily to, '—that we have to deal with.'

'It seems to me, Sir William, that there are two issues of equal importance to consider here. One, why was this sent to you? To warn you? To frighten you? To convey a message of some kind?'

'A message?'

'Yes. Have you, for instance, requested assistance, a hand, so to speak, with some task recently?'

'I am always requesting assistance from members of the Inn,' said Sir William stiffly. 'We are governed, as you know, by committees of our senior members.' Here he glanced meaningfully at Gabriel, who remained imperturbable. Both he and the Treasurer knew that nothing would ever induce Gabriel to join a committee, with the forced camaraderie, the inevitable sloppiness of collective thought, the need for compromise and co-operation. That was not why he had chosen the fiercely independent life of the barrister.

Sir William abandoned a subject he knew to be hopeless. 'You said two issues?'

'The second: where did the sender obtain the body part? From a live person or a dead one? And in either instance, was it the result of foul play? And where is the body? It seems a trifle unlikely that either body or parcel has come from outside the Temple, given the vigilance of our porters,' said Gabriel. Though even as he said it, he was forced to acknowledge to himself that just as unlikely was the idea of a corpse, or indeed parts of one, secreted within the Temple's peaceful grounds. Either, in truth, seemed as improbable a theory as the other. Both, he supposed, must be entertained.

'How did you receive this parcel?' he asked.

'A maid brought it. It did not come through the porters. She said it had been left on the doorstep.'

'Which points, tentatively at least, to someone within the Temple having delivered it to you. Where they obtained the contents must of course remain an open question.'

Sir William scowled.

'Well,' said Gabriel philosophically, 'there is little we can do on Christmas Eve. After the festivities are concluded, if you wish, I will make a few gentle queries within the Inner Temple, to see if I can ascertain the answer to either of these two questions.'

'If this parcel was sent by a member of this institution, the perpetrator must be found and he will have me to answer to. I simply cannot think of anyone,' Sir William sounded repressive, 'who could have the slightest desire to distress me in so dreadful a manner. However, I wish you to make such discreet enquiries as you think appropriate. But the word is: discreet.

On no account must anyone be told the reason for them. And remember, above all else, no word must reach Fleet Street and the outside world.'

This, Gabriel knew, mattered more to Sir William than anything else. It was more important than the dreadful shock inflicted on him, more compelling than the question of whose body had been defiled, more significant than the outrage itself. The vital requirement was to protect the Inner Temple from exposure in the popular press. Sir William lived in terror of the ever-present threat of the newspaper offices of Fleet Street so close by, so potentially intrusive, so ungentlemanly, like a pushy neighbour just the other side of the hedge whom he did his best to ignore but to whom, occasionally, he felt obligated to extend hospitality.

Once a year, representatives of the press were invited to Evensong in the Temple Church followed by High Table dinner, in the fond hope that the distinction of the Inner Temple traditions and kitchen and cellars might buy a little loyalty in times of trouble. The newspapers, all conscious of the tantalising impregnability of the Temple, accepted the invitations in the fond hope that they might be able to wring a nasty story out of this privileged access. Occasionally dragooned to attend High Table dinners, Gabriel now had a vague recollection that one of these was planned for the New Year. Tentatively, he reminded Sir William of the fact.

Sir William blanched. 'The invitations have gone out,' he said. 'I cannot cancel without raising interest and suspicion. And we are inviting those — those *ferrets* into the Temple at a time when you tell me there may be a body somewhere with parts missing? Not to mention that there appears to be a maniac on the loose.'

'Really, Sir William,' said Gabriel with his usual dry logic, 'I do not think you should worry too much about that. The chance of either body or maniac being present on such an occasion is vanishingly unlikely; as is any opportunity for the – er – ferrets to discover this occurrence about which only you and I know.'

It was not until much later that Gabriel, to whom accuracy was a god, became aware that this statement had contained a number of errors.

4

Coincidentally, it was at this same moment, in his attic office high above Fleet Street, that Mr Lionel Sullivan opened a letter embossed with the Inner Temple Pegasus emblem. He and one employee were invited to a dinner in the Inner Temple on 2 January.

Sullivan had always said that what success he had achieved in life lay in the fact that, on first meeting him, people thought he was a bishop. This was a delusion. No bishop would have been seen dead in Sullivan's vulgar waistcoats nor have spoken in his peculiar blend of self-conscious refinement and cockney. But it was true that his round, benign face, rosy cheeks and white eyebrows were a little ecclesiastical in appearance and belied the malignancy of his character. He did not look like what he in fact was: proprietor and editor of the *Nation's Voice*, a shameless daily newspaper that traded in a toxic mix of cheap sentimentality and the exploitation of human misery.

'It's for two of us,' he said morosely to Frank Holloway, his most favoured reporter, who had just walked through the doorway. 'You'd better come too. I'll need a bit of company. I hates that lot.'

He walked over to his window and glowered down onto the tangled, turreted rooftops of the Temple. There lay the two Inns of Court, the Inner and the Middle Temple, two learned societies of lawyers, each with its chambers and library and great dining hall and gardens, united by the honeyed stone of the round Temple Church. Snow was everywhere and the great trees stood out as frozen skeletons guarding the ancient squares and alleyways. But Sullivan was untouched by the romance of the spectacle.

'Perish the thought that the *Nation's Voice* should ever report on any breath of scandal in their precious Temple. Not that we would even know if there was any; they keep it all tight in their own little world, they do. Never have I heard such a thing,' he said wistfully. 'Just think of the headlines we would have if I did. Our readers would love them lot to have a fall. But all the news we get is of their garden parties and royal visits and fancy dinners with them snobby judges.'

Frank Holloway was an unprepossessing young man. Despite a neat grey suit worn with his habitual bowler hat, he still managed to look a bit scruffy. His mousy brown hair defied frequent trips to the barber and always looked as though it needed a good trim. His face was sallow and, although in fact robustly healthy, he somehow looked sickly. He walked with a limp from a childhood injury and, despite his best efforts to stop, he bit his fingernails. His expression since a small boy had seemed to fall naturally into one of indifference. He was quite unmemorable.

He had heard Sullivan on this particular hobby horse many times before. The tantalising impregnability of the Temple with all that it implied – exclusivity, superiority, entitlement – was a red rag to Sullivan's populist philosophy. Holloway was well aware of the kudos he would get from delivering to his employer some salacious tale of wrongdoing in the Temple's hallowed grounds. If only it were that easy.

He threw his hat onto a chair and fished his notebook out of his pocket.

'The verdict on the Lawnmower Murder is in,' he said.

Sullivan looked indignant. 'I reckoned on that trial lasting at least another week. That lovely gruesome death… and now the trial all over in the blink of an eye? I dunno what is happening to English justice; more efficient, more expeditious, altogether more businesslike. I hates it. Bring back the good old days, I say. When I was a lad on the paper like you is now, a good murder would guarantee headlines for days on end whereas nowadays, you...'

Holloway had heard all this before as well.

'Guilty,' he said briefly.

Sullivan looked more cheerful. 'When will they be hanging him?' he asked hopefully. 'That'll be good for a few days.'

Holloway made a rapid calculation. 'Three clear weeks after conviction, no hangings on a Monday. Do you want me to cover it?'

'Of course I want you to cover it, you fool! Start as soon as tomorrow is over. I hates Christmas. Waste of time and money. Get the murderer's letter from the condemned cell to his old mother.'

'How do I do that?'

'Get round her, boy – and if that don't work, bully her,' said Sullivan shamelessly. 'And sniff around the prison, interview the prison chaplain.'

'I can't question him, unfortunately. It's against prison regulations.'

'Offer him money.'

'I've tried that before. No luck. He's incorruptible.'

'I hates that word,' said Sullivan petulantly. 'You'll have to do what you can, Holloway. We needs them headlines. Our circulation is going down. Too much competition and too little of the right kind of news. We need more and worse, boy. More blood, more gruesome violence, more defiled innocence, more disasters. Even a fatal train crash,' he concluded wistfully, 'would help.'

Holloway knew that what he had to say next would fan the flames of Sullivan's wrath.

'Talking of defiled innocence... About the Topsy Tillotson case – you know she wrote to us, requesting an apology, and we printed a challenge: sue us if you dare...'

Sullivan's cherubic countenance turned purple.

'...well, she is,' finished Holloway laconically.

'Is what?'

'Going to sue us. She's taking her case to court.'

Very slowly, Sullivan twisted the cord of the blind at the window until the cracked old wooden acorn splintered in his fat fingers.

'Let her,' he said. 'Reputation, my Aunt Nellie! Just let her try it. We'll crush the little tart.'

The reporter got up to leave but as he reached the door, Sullivan called him back.

'Holloway, I trust you, lad. Are you sure of your source on that story?'

'Yes, sir. Dead sure. I hang around the stage door now and again, to see what I can pick up. The Honourable Frederick Sewell told me himself he'd succeeded with her. A week or so ago, apparently. And he will give evidence to that effect.'

'Well, the word of a toff like him is good enough for us to report the story, but if it comes to court proceedings, can we back it up at the hotel in question? Just to be certain.'

'Happened in a cab, he said,' said Holloway succinctly.

Sullivan grinned nastily. 'And very nice too,' he said. 'But all the same, I'd feel happier, if we are going to court, having a bit of crob— codrob— what's that word?'

Frank Holloway tried not to look superior. He'd had no more formal education than the newspaper proprietor, but he always was good with words.

'Corroboration.'

'That's it. I'd feel happier with some of that. See what you can find to support Sewell's story. And while you're at it, have a sniff around Topsy Tillotson's past. Though she is only nineteen, isn't she? Not much time to have done very much.'

'You'd be surprised,' said Holloway cynically. 'Plenty of time for what that type can get up to. I'll do some digging.'

Sullivan looked a little uneasy. He felt he never really knew Frank, even after the best part of ten years. No one could deny he was loyal and good at his job. And he got results all right. But sometimes Sullivan wondered just how he got them. The proprietor's own ethical code was sketchy to say the least, but he valued his membership of that organisation he affected to despise, the National Association of Journalists. He had been around newspapers for forty years. Laughable as it might be to his more respectable colleagues in Fleet Street, he liked to call himself a gentleman of the press. And as a result, while he was perfectly at ease with speculation, innuendo, and indeed gross exaggeration, he drew the line at flat-out lies.

'Well,' he said, 'you do your digging and good luck to you, boy. But don't you forget what I've always told you. We peddle the truth. As dirty as you like. In fact, the dirtier the better. And get it however you can. But it must be the truth.'

And then again, he said, 'Crush her. You'd better inform Brown and Boyd.' They were the *Nation's Voice*'s faintly disreputable solicitors. 'Tell 'em to get Sir Edward Hopkins KC as usual. And snap him up quick as they can, before Topsy Tillotson goes to him. I don't like to think what will happen if we lose this, Holloway. We can't handle the damages award, not on this we can't. You'll be out on the street, lad.'

Frank Holloway felt a familiar sick feeling in his stomach. The fortunes of the *Nation's Voice* were of the utmost importance to him, and Sullivan had been making references to its labouring finances more and more frequently. Arriving in London aged eighteen, determined to become newspaper reporter, Frank Holloway had found that the Fleet Street pavements were lined, not with gold, but with queues of aspiring journalists: young curates and schoolmasters and barristers with decent educational backgrounds; older men who had scaled mountains or fought military campaigns and had stories to tell; ladies who had fallen on hard times and had the charm of novelty. The lucky ones with permanent positions in Fleet Street had contacts or experience on local newspapers, even sometimes university degrees. Frank had none of these. The only thing he had was a fierce ambition for money and success.

He had been nearly twenty, scraping by on piece-rate writing jobs that grew ever-more elusive and close to starvation, when he at last gave in and applied for a job as a post boy at the *Nation's Voice*. In that position he would have remained had it not been for Lionel Sullivan identifying him as having the two qualities he most prized in a journalist: he was clever with words and he was desperate. Sullivan had given Frank a modest wage and validation, and Frank had repaid him with years of hard work and unfailing loyalty.

He knew that Sullivan peddled trash; but nonetheless he defended the newspaper to outsiders with such fervour that he had now begun to believe what he said. When the then Prime Minister Lord Salisbury had said of the halfpenny press that it was 'written *by office boys for office boys*', Frank had shrugged in contempt. He had been an office boy. So what? Time the nobs realised that office boys were the future. The public liked scandal and he, Frank Holloway, would give them what they liked and make his own fortune in the process. And if that little trollop Topsy Tillotson thought she was going to ruin the newspaper then she would have another think coming.

5

The snow was deeper on Christmas Day, drifting against the Great Gate that led to the outside world so that the Temple was closed to all vehicles and only the most athletic pedestrians could wriggle past. In the strange muffled silence, the seclusion seemed more profound, worldly considerations utterly distant, the idea of a severed human hand lying on Sir William Waring's polished Pembroke table even more preposterous.

Late on Christmas morning Gabriel prepared, a little reluctantly, to leave his snug sanctuary, and his tottering piles of books. Books on all sides, shelves of them, walls of them and covering most of the floor; books on everything – children's books, priceless books, obscure and useless books loved by him for their familiarity – his world between their covers. The snowy day seemed more attractive seen from inside, framed by the faded blue silk curtains at the long sash windows, the room warmed and lit by the gentle glow of the fire.

But nonetheless he closed his front door upon this haven, pressed it three times to make sure it was securely locked then made his way to the Reverend Master's house.

'Happy Birthday!'

Hugh Vernon-Osbert, Reverend Master of the Temple Church, beamed benevolently at Gabriel and raised a glass of sherry in his shaky old hand. It was the traditional prelude to Christmas Day luncheon at his house.

Gabriel's life contained many eccentric little singularities, uncharitably referred to by Sir William Waring as 'affectations'. But not even Sir William could suggest that Gabriel had played any part in the fact that Christmas Day was also his birthday. Along with all the traditional festivity, Vernon-Osbert's housekeeper, Mrs Jenkins, always marked the occasion with a birthday candle on top of the Christmas pudding, and Vernon-Osbert himself with the very best his cellar had to offer.

'After all,' Gabriel would say every year, 'it is a good day to be born. Remember, I share it with Pope Pius VI and with Isaac Newton. As well as, of course,' he would add with a chuckle, 'with your chap.' And timid old Vernon-Osbert would smile, long accustomed to Gabriel's irreverence.

It was always a joyous and decorous occasion, although this year, Christmas 1901, it began with a small note of drama. Everything was as it always was at first when Gabriel arrived, uncharacteristically pink from his cold walk across the snowy Temple. Mrs Jenkins, thin, wispy and deceptively deferential, admitted him.

She had been Vernon-Osbert's cook-housekeeper for twenty years. The 'Mrs' was honorary. Mrs Jenkins' fierce devotion was expended entirely on her employer. She ran her small household, consisting of herself, two maids and Reverend Master Vernon-Osbert, with great efficiency. The Reverend Master's house was kept in a perpetual state of glory; the furniture shone, the linen was stiff with starch and every room smelled of beeswax. Within its walls she reigned with authority. This was enhanced by the fact that her status as the Reverend Master's housekeeper brought with it access to a certain kind of knowledge. Vernon-Osbert was responsible for the care and cure of the souls of all who lived and worked in the Temple. Many of them came to his door in states of distress and exultation and all the emotions in between, and Mrs Jenkins liked to convey her resultant superior understanding of the personal lives of the Temple residents. Loyalty precluded the dissemination of anything she knew; but that did not prevent her from pulling a particular expression, lips histrionically pursed, eyebrows raised, whenever she wished to convey that, *had* she wished, she could have recounted gossip of the most astonishing nature about almost everyone in the Temple.

Any energy remaining from her duties was expended on a twenty-year rivalry with Mrs Bugg, the Inner Temple cook. Mrs Bugg, at least twice Mrs Jenkins' physical size, was a master of her art. The 'Mrs', in her case, was not honorary, but conferred on her by Mr Bugg and reinforced by a daughter and by a son-in-law, who worked in the Inner Temple gardens. And the huge Inner Temple kitchens over which she presided were of central importance to many aspects of the running of the institution. Quite apart from the everyday meals served to the barristers who worked there, the High Table dinners were of great social significance. Historically, those who wished to be called to the Bar were required to eat their dinners in the body of the Hall as part of their qualification.

Compounded by the fact that, with the exception of lesser beings such as the laundresses who cleaned the buildings, they were the only women in the Inner Temple, they had each acquired considerable status within the Inn. Now they vied for supremacy – Mrs Jenkins like an indignant squirrel; Mrs Bugg like a kindly but patronising bulldog.

Christmas Day luncheon was invariably attended only by Gabriel and by Vernon-Osbert's beloved Persian Blue cat Delphinium. But this year, when Gabriel was ushered into the drawing room, he found a newcomer. In addition to Vernon-Osbert in his best velvet smoking jacket, and the enormous Delphinium curled on the rug emitting a noise resembling in quality and volume that made by a small traction engine, there was a young and unknown man, lanky and dark-haired with intelligent eyes in a thin sallow face.

The man unfolded himself from a chair by the fire, stood politely, and trod hard on Delphinium's tail, stretched out like a thick furry rope across the floor. Pandemonium ensued. By the time order had been restored, a lengthy business entailing not only the placating of Delphinium, a prima donna at the best of times, but also the soothing of frail old Vernon-Osbert, the calm, apologetic young man felt to Gabriel like an ally. An introduction seemed almost superfluous.

At last, Vernon-Osbert remembered his duties as host and made it.

'You may not yet have met my young guest, Sir Gabriel. This is Rupert Brandish. He is to stay with me until he has found his feet in the Temple.'

Gabriel bowed. 'Are you to begin a pupillage here?' he asked politely.

'No,' said the young man. 'I have a degree in jurisprudence, but then, when I found the law was not where my heart lay, I became a clergyman. I am to be the new Reader in the Temple Church, assisting Reverend Master Vernon-Osbert.'

'Indeed?' said Gabriel, his interest piqued as it always was by any detail of the Temple's unique history. 'A most historic and fascinating role. I believe it has its roots right back in the days when the Knights Templar occupied the Temple, does it not? And I am pleased your vocation has not taken you away from the law entirely.'

'No indeed. The spirit of the law is ever-present in the Temple Church; and Reverend Master Vernon-Osbert has been kind enough to offer me a home here, in the heart of the Temple, at least for the time being.' He glanced around the exquisitely proportioned room, its panelling glowing in the snowy light. 'I am very fortunate. This is a wonderful house.'

'I am the fortunate one,' Vernon-Osbert interposed. 'Youth about my house. Such a joy and privilege, Sir Gabriel.'

Gabriel smiled politely. He had not personally felt the need for this particular joy and privilege to ruffle the scholarly calm of his days. His eye caught that of Rupert Brandish and he sensed from the sudden twitch of the young man's long humorous mouth that he knew exactly what Gabriel was thinking. Gabriel began to think he would like Rupert Brandish.

'And furthermore,' said Vernon-Osbert, 'he has given me a most pleasing present.' Extricating a cardboard box with some difficulty from behind his chair, he removed from it, leather-bound, romantically aged and battered, four volumes of Burn's *Ecclesiastical Law*.

'I bought it in a second-hand bookshop in an alleyway off Fleet Street,' said Rupert Brandish. 'Just a very lucky find.'

'Most interesting,' said Gabriel politely. But an astute observer might have noticed that, uncharacteristically for him, his attention was caught not so much by the books as by the box containing them: it was made of plain brown cardboard and was exactly a foot square. It seemed to Gabriel that along with the glorious musty tang of old leather was another, sweeter, smell, so elusive he could not define it.

Gabriel's positive impression of the young cleric continued over luncheon. Brandish was a charming and cultivated young man, with ideas of his own and the courage to express them. He was as widely read as it was possible for a young man to be without becoming insufferable. He was eager to hear the ideas of his elders, deferential to Vernon-Osbert's age and Gabriel's intellectual distinction. He had a quick sense of humour.

Conversation across the white linen and crystal and silver of Vernon-Osbert's dining table meandered with a scholarly ease. The history of the Inner and Middle Temple, some niceties of canon law, the special ingredient that made the Temple cook

Mrs Bugg's egg custards so irresistible, the ongoing Boer War, the incorrigible grumpiness of the Temple gardener's son Joe.

'He should attend church as all the other Temple servants do,' said Vernon-Osbert sadly, his mind never far from the care of his flock. 'But he has done so only very intermittently for years and I cannot prevail upon him to attend regularly. I will try again after Christmas.' He sighed, and then his usual geniality returned.

'Well, well,' he said, rising from the table. 'Enough of shoes and ships and sealing wax...'

'Of cabbages,' said Brandish.

'And kings,' finished Gabriel, and they smiled at each other, united, old and middle-aged and young, by Lewis Carroll.

The lamps were lit and coffee was carried through to the drawing room where Delphinium, too replete even to purr, had flung herself like a great furry rug over an ottoman, thereby securing the pole position by the fire. Brandish prepared to depart for his own room.

'It has been a great pleasure,' said Gabriel, 'for us at least. But we must find you some younger companions. There are plenty of young barristers whose company you will find more enlivening than ours.'

'They could not be more enlivening,' Brandish said politely, 'but I look forward to meeting them. One I know already. An old friend, from my Cambridge days. John Gibson.'

'Gibson? The previous Home Secretary's son?' said Gabriel.

'Yes indeed,' interposed Vernon-Osbert, 'about to begin his pupillage with us; although whether the Bar is quite the right—' He changed the subject rather hastily. 'He has announced his engagement to our dear Treasurer's daughter, Miss Amelia. Such a joyous occasion the wedding will be for the Temple Church.'

'A delightful young man,' said Gabriel, when Brandish had gone.

'Yes,' said Vernon-Osbert. 'Did he remind you of anyone?'

There was a short pause. 'He reminded me of Simon Rawlings,' said Gabriel. 'The same quick mind. What a very charming young man Rawlings was. With what the Greeks call charisma. Indefinable, but unmistakable when encountered. It was a loss to the Bar. Such a dreadful waste of promise.'

Vernon-Osbert leaned forward and put another log on the fire. 'Yes indeed, the saddest of mysteries. But there is always hope. His grandmother comes every year to say a little prayer with me on the anniversary of when – when it happened.'

'Yes,' said Gabriel, for Vernon-Osbert had often told him this.

Vernon-Osbert sighed. 'There seems to me no greater suffering than that caused by uncertainty.'

'It is time for our Christmas game of chess, is it not?' said Gabriel, very gently.

It was early evening when at last the game finished and Gabriel took his leave. Mrs Jenkins, responding to the summoning bell, led him to the darkened hall and retrieved his hat and coat. Gabriel hesitated on the step.

'An idle question, Mrs Jenkins. But do you happen to know where Mr Brandish obtained the box containing Reverend Master Vernon-Osbert's Christmas gift?'

A wave of scarlet flooded up Mrs Jenkins' sharp squirrel-like countenance.

'I couldn't say, I am sure, Sir Gabriel.'

And she closed the door firmly, leaving him alone on the snow-covered doorstep.

The expression on her face, Gabriel thought, had not been that usual look of knowing superiority. It had been one of confusion; almost of fear.

6

Sir Edward Hopkins KC was the next victim, on the Monday after Christmas, when the Temple was slowly coming back to life.

Sir Edward was used to death. Murder was his bread and butter, the more horrible the better. The brevity of the Lawnmower Murderer's trial had been as much a disappointment to him as it was to Sullivan. Hopkins had hoped that this sensational trial, running at ten guineas refresher a day in addition to the large brief fee, would go on for a very long time. Arising from the butchery inflicted with one of the newfangled steam-powered lawn-mowing machines on the body of an aristocratic lady by a gardener mad with lust, the case had grabbed every headline in the country. It was one exactly suited to Sir Edward's talents and as always, now it was over, he was missing the limelight.

Even his detractors would have admitted that Sir Edward was an exceptionally handsome man. From his Irish mother he had inherited his black hair and startlingly blue eyes and from his father his great height and distinctive Roman nose. The glamorous patrician result was every lady novelist's dream and the impact of his physical appearance was frequently invoked as one good reason why the introduction of ladies for jury service would be detrimental to the administration of justice.

Sir Edward was also a charismatic orator. He blustered and yelled his way around court, haranguing and cajoling his way to the result he sought. No cliché was too obvious, no sentiment too emotional, no leap of logic too fanciful once Sir Edward Hopkins got going. Every case in which he appeared entailed an injustice to his client never paralleled in an English court. Juries loved him. His colleagues distrusted him. Sir Edward's obedience to all the time-honoured unwritten rules of conduct that governed the Bar was at best opportunistic, at worst non-existent.

He was sitting in his opulent chambers reading the brief that had arrived from the *Nation's Voice* requesting his opinion as to the conduct of their defence in Miss Topsy Tillotson's anticipated defamation action, when his clerk came in bearing a square box, exactly one foot in every dimension...

'This was left on the doorstep, sir,' he said deferentially, and Hopkins, without thanks, waved his hand towards his desk, where the box was accordingly placed.

Sir Edward was feeling rather wistful. Certainly, it was gratifying to be instructed for an enormous fee in the case that would be the sensation of the decade, discussed when the Lawnmower Murderer was long forgotten. But he was aware that one of his colleagues would be getting Topsy Tillotson as a client with a brief fee just as enormous and with all the prestige attendant on displaying the most beautiful actress in England on his arm. Sir Edward rather liked the picture conjured up had it been *his* handsome manly arm. He wondered to whom the brief had gone. He had always felt it was a pity he could not be on both sides of every sensational case. He consoled himself with the thought that the next best thing to portraying himself as knight in shining armour to a wronged and innocent girl, would be exposing that same girl in court as the abandoned little hussy she no doubt was.

By the time he had finished reading the brief he had whipped himself up into his usual frenzy of self-righteousness on behalf of his client. This newspaper, pledged to tell the truth in the public interest, custodian of the opinions of the decent men of this country, clean-living Englishmen like you members of the jury... this newspaper was being sued for damage to the reputation of a young woman who disported herself on a public stage, scantily clad, and sang lewd songs that no gentleman would allow his wife and daughters to hear. Reputation! What reputation?

His speech composed itself gratifyingly in Sir Edward's head and it was not until an hour later that, running out of indignation, he turned his attention to the box. It was unwrapped and unadorned. He opened the lid and was conscious of a faint sweet smell.

And then, disclosed to his horrified eyes was a human foot. It was leathery and tanned, the flesh in dry ribbons, the middle toe missing, the metatarsal bones half revealed, severed jaggedly at the ankle. And tucked in beside it was a card, the writing clearly visible. *Don't put your foot in it*, he read.

Unlike Gabriel, Sir Edward Hopkins, barrister though he was, did not appreciate word play. At the grisly sight that confronted him, a wave of nausea rolled over him and he was promptly sick on his prized Turkish carpet, bought in Sotheby's only a week before. Recovering himself, he slammed the lid back and, grabbing the box, left his chambers to head for the Treasurer's office, yelling to his clerk to clean up the mess as he passed.

Gabriel, gazing out of his window in 1 Crown Office Row, saw his colleague's precipitate rush across the Terrace. Accustomed to the drama extracted by Sir Edward in relation to the most minor vicissitudes of life, he would have ignored him had he not seen the box he was carrying. Made of cardboard, exactly a foot square in all dimensions. Seeing that ominous portent, Gabriel made his unhurried way out and intercepted Sir Edward on the Terrace.

Without salutation or introduction, Sir Edward Hopkins tore the lid off the box and shoved it and the accompanying note under Gabriel's nose.

'Look at this! Who has committed this outrage? Who will bring this monster to justice? Where lies the innocent man whose body has been defiled?' he demanded in his finely modulated voice, pitched to reach the public gallery of any court in the land.

'Really, Hopkins,' said Gabriel mildly, 'please do not treat me like one of your juries. These are matters of which I am fully cognisant. You are not the first recipient of such an item. Sir William Waring himself received one, just before Christmas. That is why I came to speak to you, when I spotted the box and your – er – demeanour.'

'What! He has received the other foot?' cried Edward Hopkins in horror. 'And has taken no action? Where is this footless man? Who has committed this horrible crime?'

'Not a foot. A hand,' said Gabriel repressively. 'Just before Christmas. And it is arguable whether any crime has been committed. In law, no one can—'

'—own a dead body. We all know that. And what have *you* got to do with it?' demanded Hopkins.

'I happened to come upon Sir William when he had just made the discovery. He is very anxious that word should not be spread about these incidents either inside or outside the Temple, and so, since I had stumbled upon the matter, he has asked me to investigate.' He gestured to his own chambers doorway. 'Shall we discuss this somewhere a little more private?'

It said something about Gabriel's disapproval of Hopkins that in all the years they had been neighbours, this was the first time he had been inside Gabriel's chambers in 1 Crown Office Row. He looked around him at the crooked old panelling, its contours almost obliterated by centuries of paint, the uncurtained windows with their shutters pulled back to reveal the ivy creeping closer, the immaculate desk, the old oak grandfather clock, the sink with its dripping tap housed in a cupboard in the corner.

And he thought of his own opulent room. Of its elaborate wallpaper and heavily tasselled curtains. Of the piles of briefs, some long completed, but nonetheless remaining there to give the right impression of his enormous practice. Of the museum-quality mahogany furniture and the red velvet chaise-longue. Of the guns and bottles of poison and silk garrottes, all in glass cases, memorabilia from every murder case he had ever done, and of the framed press cuttings hanging in any remaining gaps on the walls. His lip curled contemptuously. It did not seem to him that Ward was making much money, for all his reputation for intellectual distinction.

'Now,' said Gabriel equably, well aware from the eloquent curl of that lip of the thoughts now running through his fellow KC's mind, 'may I discuss this matter with you on Sir William's behalf?'

'I suppose so,' said Hopkins ungraciously.

'Sir William, too, received a note. "*Can I give you a hand?*" it read. We have no idea where the body parts come from although they are plainly very far from fresh. Have you?'

'Of course I haven't! The whole thing is an absolute disgrace. If I were a weaker man, the shock could have killed me.'

'Then the only thing we have to go on is the identity of the two recipients. Sir William Waring. You. "*Can I give you a hand?*" "*Don't put your foot in it.*" Is there any enterprise you have both been involved in where such – er – phrases might be apposite?'

Sir Edward Hopkins looked self-righteous. 'I see a great deal of Sir William. I hope I know my duty to the Inner Temple. I am Master of the Wine and Master of the Silver. Sir William will tell you I am his right h—' he caught himself up at Gabriel's involuntary smile '—am his able lieutenant in the running of the Inn.'

'Has anything happened recently when you might be said to have – er – put your foot in it?'

Hopkins glowered ferociously at him. 'Certainly not.'

Realising that this was a suggestion that a man of Hopkins' overweening self-confidence would be bound to reject, Gabriel rephrased his question rather hastily.

'Forgive me. Perhaps it would be better to ask, have there been matters of any particular sensitivity that you have had to deal with?'

A little mollified, Hopkins hesitated. 'There are always such matters in an institution like ours. Staff to supervise, financial issues, all the day-to-day running of the Inner Temple. Of course,' he added, echoing Sir William, 'you would not be aware of all that.'

'Staff to supervise?' queried Gabriel, ignoring this dig.

'Yes, I am frequently requested by Sir William to intervene. Simmonds, of course, is the perfect head porter. But not everyone understands as well as he does how to know their place and to address their betters. On occasion I have had to rebuke one or other of the under porters for impertinence. And Joe Brockley has been insolent on more than one occasion to Sir William, and both Sir William and I have had to speak to him. And I have had to give warnings to both Mrs Bugg and Brockley Senior. They are both getting too old,' said Hopkins brutally.

Gabriel thought of all the octogenarian members of the judiciary with their unchallenged right to occupy their exalted positions regardless of state of mind and body.

'Too old for what?' he said.

'Oh, unwilling to take on new ideas. Sir William suggested to Mrs Bugg that she attempted one of the new Battenberg cakes, but she simply scoffed at the notion. Said she couldn't be bothered with all those fancy squares!'

He carried on, heedless of Gabriel's snuffle of mirth.

'And the Reverend Master's garden... proud though Brockley may be of it, it has not been without its shortcomings over the years. Sir William felt at one time, a good while ago now, that it would be nice to train a climber up the front of the Reverend Master's house. He instructed Brockley to plant a vine. It died, so he told the gardener to put in a climbing rose. That died too. When Brockley was quite properly reproved, young Joe Brockley was downright rude about it and Sir William feels that Brockley Senior is losing his touch. And then, last year, all the rhubarb died. Oh, of course Vernon-Osbert sticks up for old Brockley, but we all know for that matter that the Reverend Master himself is getting more and more decrepit. The gossip in the Temple is that his heart is very fragile now. And who will his successor be?'

Gabriel felt a pang he tried not to show. 'The new Reader, Reverend Brandish?'

'Too young,' said Hopkins inconsistently. 'Anyway, I am merely using these as examples of the many administrative matters with which poor Sir William has to contend. And I cannot stay here all day talking. This evil act must be investigated. I trust you will find the corpse and the culprit as soon as possible. Meanwhile I shall go and report this to Sir William.'

As he rose to go, he cast an inquisitive eye towards Gabriel's open brief, its pages exactly aligned, the pink ribbon with which it had been bound neatly coiled beside it.

'Anything interesting?'

Gabriel smiled for the first time since their interview began.

'Indeed yes. *Most* interesting. My client, the Plaintiff, has acted to his detriment on the basis of an implied promise by the Defendant. All very complex; there is an 1877 case—'

'Good God, man, you are welcome to it,' interrupted Hopkins, and made for the door with a snort of contempt. 'The only thing I am interested in is who is acting for Topsy Tillotson. Someone will soon be having some fun with that little trollop.'

Without comment, his face stiff with disapproval, Gabriel opened his door for Hopkins to leave.

As he did so, Hopkins dug him in the ribs. 'Hope her eye will alight on you, eh, Ward? I should leave her to one of the men.'

And he swung away jauntily down the steps.

Concentration broken by the encounter and spirits ruffled, Gabriel turned to the solace of his daily (clockwise) walk around the garden.

The pristine white lawns, the great skeletons of the plane trees and, in the distance, the turbid swell of the winter Thames, all soothed him. On his return, as the familiar doorway of his chambers came into view, he saw to his astonishment that standing quite alone in front of it, staring at the boards on which the names of the members of chambers were painted, was a young woman. Dressed in the very latest fashion, her Titian hair tumbling in luxuriant ringlets down her back, she was strikingly beautiful, with the face of Helen of Troy and the figure of Aphrodite.

Tabitha Mary Tillotson's father had been the first to call her 'Topsy' when she was a baby, rolling over and over in her cradle. 'She is a little Miss Topsy-Turvy,' he said fondly, and the name had stuck. She had been on the stage since she was fifteen. There had been an advertisement for chorus girls in the newspaper: 'My teacher says I sing and dance lovely,' Topsy had said to her mother. 'I'm going to give it a try.' Mrs Tillotson had been very anxious, but she knew from experience that opposition was unwise when her Topsy had got the bit between her teeth. 'Anyway,' she had said comfortably to Topsy's father, 'they'll never take her. She's far too young.'

The management at the Drury Lane Theatre had taken one look at her copper-gold ringlets, extraordinary topaz eyes and exquisite little figure, and engaged her on the spot. When they discovered she could indeed sing and dance lovely, they could not believe their luck. Her parents had been very alarmed at this turn of events but in the end Topsy had had her charming, determined way. 'Wraps them round her little finger,' said the censorious neighbours to each other.

From the very beginning, Topsy had dominated any show in which she took part, adding to her singing and dancing that indefinable quality that made audiences adore her. That had been four years ago. The chorus had long been left behind; she had made more money than she had ever imagined was possible, and now her name featured on a big painted board outside the theatre.

Despite all the ambition and bravado she had displayed, she had nonetheless been very innocent when she began life on the stage. 'You will be a good girl, Topsy?' her mother had said anxiously, over and over again; and although she was not at first sure what her mother meant, Topsy was. She genuinely had not known why everyone laughed and cheered when, dressed in a demure maid's outfit and proffering a giant tray of jammy biscuits, she had sung: 'Would You Like a Nice Little Tart for your Tea?' Or why she had brought the house down when, carrying the adorable kitten provided by the management, she sang: 'Love Me, Love My Pussy'. She was just pleased that the management had let her adopt the kitten after the show had run and take it home with her.

She had grown up since those early days, of course. The other girls had seen to that. And she would have had to be stupid not to understand that men found her attractive. Topsy was very far from stupid and she knew what she wanted from her life. It was not one of the young men who congregated nightly in their evening clothes and top hats, bouquets of roses and lilies in their arms, entitlement stamped upon their foreheads, waiting to ask the girls out to supper after the show. Lots of the girls thought they might find a husband amongst them; but then, Topsy noticed, they always settled for less. First of all, for the champagne and fancy dinners; then the jewellery; then if they were lucky, they exchanged the chorus line for the flat in Shepherd Market and the lady's maid. And then came social ostracism.

None of that was what Topsy wanted. She wanted the deep satisfaction she got from her increasingly accomplished performances to continue for a few more years. She wanted fame and money and admiration; she was only nineteen; there was time for a few years more of that. But then, ultimately, she wanted a loving, loyal family all her own. Of just the kind she had grown up in. She wanted a kind husband and her own little boy and girl, and she would bring them up as she had been brought up. And then she met George and all these careful plans were thrown into utter – though delightful – confusion.

But all that was before this dreadful humiliation inflicted by The Honourable Frederick Sewell and the *Nation's Voice*, this fabricated and unimaginable insult. She had written to the newspaper. The response had been the headlines that had piqued Barton's interest in Fleet Street, and the article had brought all her happiness tumbling down.

Topsy had sworn vengeance. 'Who is the cleverest barrister in England?' she had asked the lady next door whose son was a solicitor's clerk, and the lady next door had promised to find out. 'Sir Gabriel Ward KC,' had been the reply. Then he was the one Topsy wanted.

The Temple, so close to the theatre in which she performed every night, was nevertheless unfamiliar to her. She knew it existed, that it was where the barristers were to be found, but she had had no reason to go inside its gracious gates until now. Sir Gabriel Ward's name, dropped nonchalantly to the dazzled porters, had gained her admittance. Now she was astonished at this extraordinary little world, just a gateway from the noise and dirt of Fleet Street, with its ancient buildings and alleyways and gardens and a cloistered quiet that seemed almost magical. The weight of history was palpable, diminishing the spectator. Somehow, she felt smaller. Not the celebrated Miss Topsy Tillotson at all, but a shadow slipping unobtrusively in and out of narrow passageways and squares. She wandered on, entranced, until eventually she found her way to 1 Crown Office Row. Peering up at the names written on the boards outside the door, uncertain as to which bell to ring, she looked around for someone to ask.

The approaching figure seemed strangely reluctant, she thought. She had the impression he was measuring with his eyes the distance between her and the doorway, as though he hoped he might still slip through without being seen. Topsy was unused to men wanting to avoid her. She stood her ground. Trapped, the approaching figure raised his top hat.

'May I help you?' he said, very cautiously, in a quiet, precise voice.

'I am looking for Sir Gabriel Ward KC.' Her friendly voice was as close to a purr as it was possible for a human being's voice to be: low, husky, its East End tones softened though discernible, infinitely attractive.

'I am Gabriel Ward,' he said reluctantly. And again, 'How may I help you?'

'I have come to ask your legal advice,' said Topsy firmly.

Gabriel's neck retracted like that of a startled tortoise returning to its shell. 'My dear young lady, you cannot possibly do that!'

'But I thought you were a barrister.'

'Precisely so. You cannot consult a barrister. You must ask a solicitor to do so on your behalf.'

Topsy digested this. 'Why?' she demanded.

Gabriel was rather taken aback. He was not at all accustomed to the company of young women but surely they were not usually quite so challenging as this one? He could not recall that anyone had ever asked this penetrating question before and was obliged to acknowledge, to himself at least, that it was not without merit.

'Because,' he said, rather repressively, 'that has been the way barristers have conducted their profession for centuries, and it is unlikely to change now.'

He was conscious his answer was unsatisfactory. It was clear that the girl thought so too. Avoiding her unnervingly hard stare, he opened the door to his chambers. 'Now may I ask my clerk to obtain a hansom cab for you?'

Chapman was doing his accounts. Lifting his head from his ledger, he took one look at the visitor and leaped to his feet, jaw dropped and eyes popping.

'Chapman,' said Gabriel, ignoring this behaviour, 'this young lady has come here under an unfortunate misapprehension. Perhaps you would be kind enough to arrange a hansom for her?'

And with that, he proceeded across the hall to his own room and settled down to the obscure legal problem, so despised by Hopkins, that awaited his learned opinion. Not for him, thank God, those showy cases upon which his colleagues thrived. Chapman could point out as often as he liked the money and prestige involved. Both were immaterial to Gabriel. He checked his desk; was his inkwell placed so that the hinges on the silver top were precisely aligned with the edge of the perpetual desk calendar that stood next to it? Was his gold pencil (with the lead pointing towards the window) tucked away in the shallow tortoiseshell case that housed it? He gave no further thought to the encounter on the doorstep.

7

Police Constable Maurice Wright of the City of London Police was feeling both shy and curious, the latter emotion predominating. It was some months since his glorious collaboration with Gabriel in relation to the mysterious death of the Lord Chief Justice. Settled back into life on his beat, he had thought wistfully that never again would the need arise for him to penetrate the secure environs of the Temple and experience the unexpected pleasure he had gained from glasses of sherry and close consultation in Sir Gabriel Ward's tranquil rooms.

This invitation to meet Sir Gabriel, issued by his clerk Chapman, had been completely unexpected, therefore, and was deeply mysterious. It requested Wright to name a time when he was off duty, to ensure he was non-uniformed, and to meet Sir Gabriel at the Great Gate in order to accompany him to St Bartholomew's Hospital. This last request was the only one that made any sense; Wright was aware that even St Bartholomew's, all of ten minutes up the road, would be for Gabriel quite an intrepid journey. But the remainder of the request was a complete mystery to him.

Standing expectantly at the gate next Tuesday morning, the last day of 1901, in his civilian cloth cap, old tweed Ulster and purposeful boots, Wright had only a few moments to wait before Gabriel, small and immaculate in his top hat, unmistakably Savile Row overcoat and galoshes, came hurrying up Middle Temple Lane. Under his arm he balanced two cardboard boxes, both of which he gratefully relinquished when the young policeman held out a helping hand.

On the walk to St Bartholomew's, Wright listened with mounting astonishment to the horrible story of Sir William Waring's unwelcome Christmas present and the similar box subsequently delivered to Sir Edward Hopkins KC.

'…And so, I hoped, Constable Wright,' concluded Gabriel, 'that you might be persuaded to assist me. In this instance,' he added, 'I am quite convinced, from previous experience, that our two heads will be better than my one.'

It was an old joke between them. Wright went very pink and beamed bashfully. But doubt followed quickly on. He hesitated.

'Is this official like, sir? I mean, if you'll pardon me, sir, it is a funny old place, the Temple. Will they – er – *let* the police investigate?'

Wright was only too aware of the obscure and independent status of the Temple, quite different from anywhere else in London, a closed community, free from the jurisdiction of the City of London, run by its own parliament and policed by the City of London Police only by consent and in collaboration with its own porters.

'It is very *un*official, Constable Wright. Indeed, Sir William Waring has had a fit at the suggestion that the police should be involved at this stage. He wants the culprit found and the whole thing hushed up. Hence my request to meet you when you are off duty and not in uniform.'

Wright glowed at the conspiratorial tone but sounded unconvinced.

'I have a duty to report crime, even if committed in the Temple, sir. Detective Inspector Hughes—'

'At present, there is a good argument for saying there has been no identifiable crime.' Gabriel recounted the reasoning he had expounded on to Sir William Waring.

The young policeman looked doubtful.

'If you say so, sir. Though it all sounds very rum to me. And if we were to discover the body, I should have to tell Detective Inspector Hughes. At once.'

'The very instant,' said Gabriel solemnly, 'that we find a body, Sir William Waring and Detective Inspector Hughes shall be the first to know.'

Wright cheered up. 'Well then, sir, for now, there is no reason why, when I am off duty, we should not talk; and then I have most of Tuesday off, sir, and could come about with you a bit then, non-uniformed, just as friends, you know.'

He blushed as soon as the words were out of his mouth. 'Well, not *friends* exactly. I don't mean to… I beg your pardon, sir. I just meant… I meant…'

'I am honoured, Constable Wright,' said Gabriel. 'And where would you begin?'

'With the parcels, sir. And I suppose, the – the body parts?' He had already guessed what the boxes he was carrying contained.

Gabriel nodded.

Wright shuddered. Ever since Gabriel's story had begun, he had tried not to think about the contents of the two boxes, shifting ominously in time with his tread. 'Horrible, sir,' he said. 'I fish a corpse out of the Thames or find one down an alleyway now and again, but somehow this – this is more horrible when you dunno where the rest of it is.' And for some unaccountable reason, he felt the urge to look behind him.

'Well,' he said practically, dismissing the urge firmly, 'first we need to know if the body is a man's or a woman's. And how old they were when they died. And how old the body is. That would give us a start.'

Gabriel nodded approvingly. 'Exactly, Constable.'

They had reached the snow-capped stone gate pillars of St Bartholomew's Hospital.

'And hence my request you accompany me here. I know the very man to tell us.'

They entered the huge hallway and were ushered to two of the hard chairs with which it was lined.

Whilst they waited, Gabriel told Wright about the smell he had noticed when he had first inspected the boxes and the same smell in the box in which Vernon-Osbert's books had arrived.

'Did you ask where that box came from?'

'I asked Mrs Jenkins the housekeeper. She either did not know or was not going to tell me. I wanted to see what else we could find out about those boxes before I – asked Brandish.' For a moment, he realised, he had almost used the word 'confronted'.

He drew from his pocket the anonymous cards that had accompanied the parcels.

Wright read them and grinned as the double meanings dawned on him. 'A bit of a joker, sir.'

'Quite so, Constable Wright,' said Gabriel approvingly. 'A subtlety lost on Sir William Waring. The handwriting might be identifiable, I suppose, though it looks unremarkable to me. And we have nothing and no one to identify it with.'

'Professor Humphries is ready to see you now, Sir Gabriel,' said an approaching clerk.

The room to which they were shown was a congenial one, heavily panelled in dark mahogany. The once conventional furnishings had acquired an overlay of what was plainly a singular personality. Beside the cheerful coal fire, disconcertingly at home, sat a skeleton in a leather armchair. The windowsills were lined with a collection of particularly repellent cacti, plainly lovingly tended. An astonishing collection of pictures, ranging from sentimental oil paintings of country cottages and kittens to human anatomical drawings of the most graphic kind, covered the walls. The vast desk, dominating the centre of the room, was thick with dust and cluttered with papers, books, a dismal aspidistra in a pot, a bird cage containing a stuffed parrot, overflowing boxes of slides and a brass microscope.

In the midst of this chaotic yet curiously cohesive interior, on a tall stool, hunched over the microscope, was the legendary Professor Gilbert Humphries MB, BCh, Oxon, FRCS, as robust and red-faced as a farmer, jacketless, his ample front scarcely contained by his braces and open bulging waistcoat. The son of a bank clerk, with no social or educational advantages, he had, thirty years earlier, overcome the raised eyebrows and only half-hidden smiles at Christ Church, Gabriel's own old college, and emerged with a blazingly triumphant first. Having trained as a surgeon, and with skills in both anatomy and pathology, he was now greatly in demand as unofficial Home Office pathologist, called as the expert witness in all the great murder trials of the day. Over the decades, occasionally invited to Inner Temple dinners, he had always sought out Gabriel, never forgetting the kindness of one aristocratic young undergraduate who had displayed, all those years ago, a complete indifference to social divides and a mind as incisive as his own.

Now he greeted Gabriel as an old friend, and looking round for a space to put his top hat, placed it on the skeleton's head, thereby adding a bizarre touch to the already eccentric room.

'This is off the record, Humphers,' said Gabriel firmly as he and Wright put the boxes on the desk. 'We want to know anything you can tell us to help with identity.'

The doctor looked at him sharply from under thick brows and without comment lifted the lids. Seeing the contents for the first time, Wright suppressed an involuntary shudder.

Humphries on the other hand gave no reaction other than a silent whistle.

'In my professional opinion this is a hand and a foot, old boy. Usually found in pairs, attached to wrists and ankles.'

Constable Wright felt quite shocked by this levity. Professor Humphries' august name was of course known to him, and he had expected a high degree of scientific sobriety. Catching his disapproving eye, Humphries grinned like a schoolboy.

'Don't mind me, young man,' he said. 'Couldn't do my job if I took it too seriously. Now how did you get these?'

'Shall we say,' murmured Gabriel, 'that we came by them in, er, confidential circumstances?'

Humphries picked up a fine scalpel 'May I?' On Gabriel's assent, he carefully sliced some more of the tattered dry flesh away, exposing the metacarpal and metatarsal bones.

'Well, I can tell you these are the hand and foot of a sturdy woman or a slight man. And I can tell you from the epiphyseal lines that the woman or man was a young adult. And the remains are desiccated so must have been left in some very dry, very warm environment.'

'For how long, sir?' broke in Constable Wright eagerly.

Humphries shook his head. 'I cannot answer that with any precision. It depends on the exact nature of the environment in which they were kept. But certainly, for several years.'

'And were the remains cut from a dead or a living body?'

Humphries gave Wright another of his sharp looks from beneath the shaggy brows. 'I haven't the faintest idea. Though I might be able to tell starting from the other end, so to speak. For that, you will first need to find the body.'

'And were the foot and the hand taken from the same body?'

Humphries began to assume that slightly superior air that doctors put on when they do not know the answer.

'Probably but not certainly,' he said. 'And if you want a better answer, you must wait for the advancement of science, my boy, or alternatively consult a clairvoyant, not a doctor.'

He picked up the hand and foot with an air of casual familiarity and replaced them in their boxes. 'Speaking of the advancement of science, we can't get enough of these,' he said wistfully. 'Oh, we get bodies from the prisons and workhouses and hospitals if they are unclaimed for forty-eight hours after death. But not nearly enough of them.'

Wright looked at him in horror. 'Forty-eight hours, sir! But how do their families even know they are dead?'

Humphries frowned, all geniality gone. 'Few have anyone to care, young man. And of those that do, well,' he shrugged, 'we are not the body snatchers of the last century, you know. How will medicine ever advance if my young medical students cannot get subjects to learn on? Do you imagine the rich will ever donate the bodies of their families and risk their immortal souls? No,' he said, answering his own question grimly, 'they simply make sure they benefit from the scientific advances we make by dissecting the bodies of the destitute.'

Out on the pavement again, Wright was silent.

'What is it, Constable Wright?' said Gabriel.

'I-It is all so complicated, sir. I've never thought — I don't know if it is right or wrong. Is it right to use the bodies of the poorest to help us all? And to use them when their loved ones have little chance of preventing it if they want to? But then again, it is right that doctors should learn all about human anatomy, isn't it, sir?'

'It is indeed. Humphries is a good man but ruthless in his pursuit of medical development. So, he makes moral choices, in which the law supports him. He has a statutory licence to do what he does.'

'But just because it's legal, sir, does that make it right?'

Gabriel nodded approvingly. 'You have identified perhaps the greatest question in jurisprudence; that is, in the study of the philosophy of the law, Constable Wright. And I do not know the answer.'

Wright was slowly becoming a little braver with Gabriel. He grinned. 'I thought you knew the answer to everything, sir.'

Gabriel chuckled. 'Touché, Constable Wright.'

They began to pick their way back along the icy pavements. 'Quite apart from receiving a lesson in morality, we are now a small step further on the way to solving our mystery,' said Gabriel. 'Our hand and foot belonged to a young person or possibly persons. A slightly built male or a more robust female. And they were somehow preserved for several years, somewhere very warm. Where is it very warm?'

'Hell?' said Wright, cheerfully. And both men suddenly looked sober. The word, so lightly spoken, seemed more apposite than Wright had intended.

The two of them walked on in silence, conscious again of the horrors lurching about in the boxes Wright carried, horrors once attached to a body that had been living and breathing before being desiccated by some infernal heat.

'I wonder, sir,' said Wright at last, 'if there might be someone in the Temple who has disappeared mysteriously? I realise we do not know precisely when, but we can assume several years ago at least, and the rest of the body must be somewhere, sir. And if there have been any disappearances over the years, there cannot have been too many. The person who sent the remains to Sir William and Sir Edward is most likely to be connected to the Temple, so isn't there a chance that the body they came from was as well? Could we ask around, so to speak?'

'Exactly my view,' said Gabriel. 'And we can certainly try, starting today.'

8

On the same morning that Gabriel and Wright had been walking down Fleet Street, with the cardboard boxes, to seek assistance from Professor Humphries at St Bartholomew's Hospital, Frank Holloway of the *Nation's Voice* was walking down the same street, in the opposite direction, in search of the corroboration demanded by his editor. Holloway saw Sullivan's point; the word of a toff was good enough for a newspaper story, but he had a feeling a judge might expect a bit more.

Tipping his bowler hat to one side, cigarette hanging from one corner of his mouth, he was going to do what he liked doing best: ferreting. His thin overcoat was ineffective against the freezing air, and his gloveless hands with their bitten nails were blue with cold. Holloway never really noticed the cold. He felt on top of the world. Fleet Street had picked itself up from Christmas and Holloway felt a buzz in the air with the prospect of the New Year that began the next day.

There were people scurrying everywhere, people of all sorts, living rich and varied lives. And it seemed to him that they were mere puppets, living those lives just so that he, Frank Holloway, puppet master, could set them dancing to his tune, to explore and expose and exploit at his will. Vans were crowding down the busy street and the steaming piles of horse manure were growing, despite the crossing sweeper's best efforts. The news sellers were shouting the headlines of the morning's editions, hot off the presses in the Fleet Street basements. There was the buzz all around of infinite possibilities and of news. How he loved news;

always fascinating, always changing, always – well – *new*; there to be grabbed and manipulated.

As Holloway walked towards the Aldwych, a rat emerged from a doorway and hesitated, nose aloft, whiskers trembling, before it shot nimbly across the pavement and into a nearby drain. Down, Holloway supposed, into the Fleet River, closed over for a hundred and fifty years now. He liked history. He liked to think of that torrent of brown water down there, still running the course it had always run, a secret road underneath the one he knew so well. He rather liked rats too. Nosy, hungry, vicious, competitive; in *control*. A bit scruffy. He had never really analysed why he liked them.

While he walked, he exchanged greetings with the shopkeepers and publicans, the news sellers and road sweepers, in his laconic unenthusiastic voice. Everyone knew him. He made it his business that they did. And as a result, he always knew where to start his investigations. In this case, what he wanted to find was the hansom cab in which Sewell said Topsy had lost her virtue. But he was not going to begin at the innumerable cab ranks that littered the area around the Drury Lane Theatre. Too many of them, and anyway the turnover of cabmen waiting was constant. No, it was at the little green-painted cabmen's shelters where all the gossip was to be found. They had sprung up over the past twenty-five years all over London and it was in these locations, where the cabmen sought relaxation and companionship and warmth, that Holloway had got some of his best stories.

In his mind he ran through the nearest shelters. Temple Place, St Clement Danes, Embankment Place. He made for Temple Place first. Too experienced to barge in, he hung around the door. Above it a sign read: *No drinking. No gambling.* Frank pulled a face at it. He was glad he was not a cab driver. He did both those things whenever he could in some of Fleet Street's least-savoury public houses. He thought if he waited awhile, he would know someone well enough to be invited in; and indeed he did, after a few men unfamiliar to him had gone in or out.

'Morning, Holloway. What you nosing after?' said a genial little man with bright eyes and a strong cockney accent. He was wrapped in the traditional cabman's uniform of thick greatcoat down to his ankles, muffler and bowler hat. 'Fancy a cuppa?'

Holloway followed him into the dark snug interior and was hit by a warm fug of smoke and brewing tea and frying onions. Only seventeen feet long, the little cabin was just wide enough for benches on either side, enough seating for up to ten men sitting hugger-mugger, clutching their steaming tea mugs, their knees almost meeting, glutinous onions on slabs of bread and dripping in various stages of consumption on the narrow tables in front of them. The eight already there shifted up, not unwillingly. This was far from the first time. Holloway was often a good source of a shilling or two in exchange for information.

'What is it you want this time?' said his companion knowingly.

Holloway did not beat about the bush.

'Topsy Tillotson? Anyone know anyone who has driven her anywhere recently?'

There was a collective whistle.

'Oh, my word,' said a fat cabman at the other end of the bench. 'I'd drive her wherever she wanted to go, my stars I would.'

There was a general howl of derision.

'She can do better than you,' said Holloway's companion to the fat man. And, turning to Holloway, 'In fact, I read in your rag that she *has* done better? A real nob, eh?'

'Well,' said Holloway, 'it's about that story. The little trollop is threatening us with the law. My editor wants a bit of back-up evidence.'

There was a regretful silence. No one there knew anything.

Emerging from the sweltering atmosphere, he made his way to the identical little hut at St Clement Danes. This time, since there were only two cabmen inside, buried in newspapers, he penetrated it without invitation. Neither newspaper, he noticed disapprovingly, was the *Nation's Voice*. The answer to his query was immediate. 'Stan,' one cabbie said at once. 'Was in here only yesterday and he told us—'

Holloway was not interested in hearsay. 'Where do I find Stan?' he asked sharply, shoving a shilling across the table.

'At the rank outside the Savoy,' was the answer, 'unless he's off on a job.'

Holloway made his way there.

'Stan?' he said to the massed muffled drivers, standing stamping their feet against the cold, by the heads of their patient horses.

One of them stepped forward, bear-like in his greatcoat.

'That's me.'

'I hear you had Topsy Tillotson in your cab. And that you have a story to tell?'

Stan said cautiously, 'I dunno for sure it was Topsy Tillotson. I never said so. I only said I thought it might be. Young couple hired me. It was dark and snowing and they were huddled up, oh, very cosy like, under an umbrella. All I saw was the girl's hair. Long and red down her back with all them ringlets. They hopped in and he called up the address through the roof hatch and I took 'em to Hackney.'

'A good long way.' Holloway took a shilling casually from his pocket and fingered it thoughtfully. 'What did they get up to?'

The cabman looked wooden. Holloway took out another shilling.

'Couldn't see nothing. They drew the leather curtains mighty quick.'

'Hear anything?'

'Couldn't hear nothing neither. What with the harness jangling and the horse's hooves on the cobbles and the wind.'

Holloway looked a little deflated.

Stan leered. 'You ain't asking the right questions, matey. I didn't see nothing nor hear nothing, but I felt something all right.'

'Felt it?'

'Shook the cab they did. Swaying it was, from side to side like. Oh-ho, I thought, I knows what you two is up to. And very nice too,' he added, unknowingly echoing Lionel Sullivan and looking expectantly at Holloway.

He handed over the money. It wasn't conclusive evidence, he knew, but it would do. He turned to leave.

The cabman timed it nicely, so that Holloway was about to cross the road.

'O' course,' he called out complacently, 'I never forgets an address.'

Holloway turned back. Stan stood, silent and expectant. Holloway got out another shilling, the last the newspaper had supplied him with for the purpose. He handed it over.

'Well now, I took 'em to Roundpark Lane, Hackney. Number forty-three.' He looked smug. 'I never forgets a number. Out his little Valentine hopped, and takes out her key and lets herself in, and he stays in the cab and then up he shouts to me through the roof, "South Rising House, Mayfair."'

Holloway looked at him narrowly. 'Would you swear to all that, so to speak? If it's worth your while?'

Stan nodded and winked and turned away.

It was with all the customary buoyancy back in his step that Holloway flung himself onto a passing omnibus, bound for Hackney. This was corroboration if you like: 43 Roundpark Lane, Hackney would turn out to be Topsy Tillotson's home address. He would put any money you liked on it.

By six o'clock that evening he had confirmed Topsy's address, visited, he reckoned, every shop and public house in Hackney, and was back in Fleet Street, sitting at a corner table in the Old Bell. In front of him, on the stained deal top, was a pint of porter, a copy of the *Sporting Life*, and his shabby black notebook. The latter contained six closely written pages recording all the gossip he had picked up about Topsy. Irrelevant, grubby, unsubstantiated most of it might be; but he thought it would be enough to enable Sir Edward Hopkins KC to make mincemeat of Miss Topsy Tillotson. It had been a good day.

Back in the Temple, Gabriel had started his own investigations that afternoon, accompanied by Wright, still discreetly dressed in civvies. They first made their way to the Inner Temple kitchen, cavernous and as always buzzing with activity. The air was full of the enticing smell of hot scones.

'And how was your Christmas dinner at the Reverend's, Sir Gabriel?'

This seemingly innocent question from Mrs Bugg the cook was, Gabriel knew, nevertheless charged with significance. He answered it with all the diplomacy of which he was capable.

'It was a very happy occasion as always, Mrs Bugg.'

She sniffed and wiped her floury hands on her ample hips. 'I'll be bound Eliza Jenkins did not give you the dinner I would have cooked you. A housekeeper is not the same thing as a cook, to my mind, and never will be.'

Gabriel was not to be drawn onto this dangerous ground. Instead, he declared the nature of his visit.

'People who have disappeared, Sir Gabriel? Whatever do you mean, bless you?' Gabriel had recognised long ago that these constant benisons from Mrs Bugg were intended to convey affection as much as was the perfect hot scone she now placed before him with a flourish. After a moment's doubtful glance at Sir Gabriel's unlikely-looking companion, burly in his Ulster and boots, she put one in front of him too.

'You have your ear far closer to the ground than I do, Mrs Bugg. I fear I am deficient when it comes to taking any more interest in my fellow man than is strictly required. It is just a little matter I am looking into for Sir William. He is checking back, you know, on people who have left our community, so that we may learn from the past where we might have gone wrong with those who serve us. And Mr Wright here is a gentleman I have asked to help me.'

It sounded weak to him, this pre-prepared and mendacious excuse, but uncritical Mrs Bugg seemed to find no fault with it. True it was that Wright did not comply with her notions of a gentleman, shaped and settled by her thirty years among the privileged occupants of the Temple, but there, if Sir Gabriel vouched for him, it was not for Mrs Bugg to question the classification. She shook her head complacently. 'A happy place, the Inner Temple, I am glad to say, Sir Gabriel. When the staff come here, they stay.'

Here Meg the scullery maid, gleaming with curiosity at the presence of Sir Gabriel's young and personable companion, intervened helpfully, calling from the Belfast sink in the scullery, 'There was the one you told me about, Mrs Bugg. Ivy?'

Mrs Bugg frowned. 'Be quiet, Meg, and speak when you are spoken to. If Sir Gabriel wants to hear from you, he will ask you.'

Gabriel peered through the short passage to the scullery. 'Good afternoon, Meg,' he said. 'I did not see you through the steam.' And turning to Mrs Bugg, 'Ivy?'

'I told Meg about her,' said Mrs Bugg severely, 'as an example. Here about ten years ago, she was.' She lowered her voice. 'No mystery about it, Sir Gabriel. Sir William Waring told her he was letting her go at the end of the week and she flounces away that night without telling anyone. No better than she ought to be.'

Although Gabriel's inner lawyer, who demanded precision of speech at all times, baulked at this meaningless expression, his real self knew exactly what the cook intended to convey.

'What happened to her, Mrs Bugg?' Wright asked respectfully, brushing the remains of his scone from his chin.

'What happened to her,' said Mrs Bugg awfully, 'was exactly what you might expect. She had gone wrong and so she went the way of all hussies. Other than that, I cannot tell you.' She patted her stomach and looked meaningfully at Meg.

'She was only sixteen. Same age as Meg now. I wasn't sure at first. She wasn't a slip like Meg. Sturdy and buxom, Ivy was. But as time went on, no doubt about it, and Sir William said she must go. Let that be your lesson, I say to Meg.'

Simmonds the head porter, snugly protected from the cold in his gatehouse beside the Great Gate at the top of Middle Temple Lane, was in an expansive mood, responding to Gabriel with his usual elaborate deference and conveying his disapproval of his companion by studiously ignoring Wright's presence.

'We have just appointed a new young chap, sir. Though not because anyone has disappeared. The work here seems to grow, and if the gentlemen are to be kept happy, I need another pair of hands. Can't think of any disappearances... well, not since Durrant,' he said in answer to Gabriel's tentative question. 'Must be about ten years ago now. You probably won't remember him, sir. A slight dark man? Not quite right for us, sir, didn't last that long; upped and went one night; did his shift and then he wasn't seen no more, money owing him and all. Mind you, he might not have been too worried about that. Sir Edward Hopkins, the Master of the Silver, mentioned to me some time later that a pair of silver salts disappeared around then.'

'Did you report the theft to the police?' asked Wright, his professional interest roused. But this was quite the wrong thing to ask. Simmonds drew himself up in offended dignity.

'I don't report to no police. I am the head porter of the Inner Temple. I keeps the peace and upholds the law here and I reports only to Sir William Waring. And as for the silver salts, I only investigate if the Treasurer asks me to.'

Gabriel nodded approvingly. 'Very proper, Simmonds, and I thank you.' He hesitated. He did not want to arouse the man's curiosity. But at last he said, 'By the by, has anyone entered the Temple recently bearing a parcel? Anyone, I mean, other than the usual errand boys?'

Simmonds shook his head. 'No one comes in here with parcels, Sir Gabriel, who isn't known to us. Or if they tries, they are questioned.'

'One last thing. How old was Durrant?'

'A young 'un, is all I can tell you, sir,' said Simmonds. 'And a wrong 'un.'

Seeing that the potting shed was open, Gabriel made his usual clockwise progress around the garden towards it, Wright in tow. Inside the shed was Brockley. A tall wiry figure with the permanently stooped back of the habitual gardener, he was among the older servants of the Inner Temple, with a long knowledge of its occupants and its history.

He straightened up with the little groan that was part ache, part affectation. A habitually gloomy man, he felt that it did his employers no harm to know that he suffered in the cause of the all-round glory of the Inner Temple gardens. Nigh on an acre, as he was fond of pointing out, not to mention the vegetable garden that supplied the kitchen and the separate flower garden that lay beside the church and enhanced the beauty of Reverend Master Vernon-Osbert's eighteenth-century house, and never a leaf out of place nowhere. And no help neither except from his son Joe and Mrs Bugg's Ruby's Fred to scythe the lawns.

He tipped his cap. During their occasional exchanges in the garden, he had gained the impression that Gabriel knew his plants and had no airs and graces. He accepted Wright's presence without curiosity.

'Come you in, sir,' he said in the Norfolk burr that twenty years in London had not obliterated. 'I am just sorting the autumn bulbs left over from the planting. They'll do for another spring.'

'A hopeful job,' said Gabriel hopefully, for he knew Brockley's gloom of old.

Brockley ran true to form. He sighed heavily. 'A big job. Getting too much for me this is.' He had been saying this for at least fifteen of the twenty years he had ruled over the gardens.

'Do not let me hear you say that, Brockley,' said Gabriel as he was expected to say. 'What on earth should we do without you?'

Brockley sighed. 'Joe will take over one day. And God help the hydrangeas then. They only grow for me.' He looked justifiably complacent. The hydrangea border was one of the triumphs of the garden.

Brockley had come to the Inner Temple as a widower, moved into the Gardener's Cottage tucked away at the end of King's Bench Walk, and had transformed the gardens. With him had come Joe and Benny, his sons then aged nine and seven, who had flourished and grown with the gardens, trundling wheelbarrows twice their size, raking the leaves, and graduating to the planting and pruning and propagating in which their father was an expert.

'Does Joe hope to spend his working life here?'

'That he does,' said Brockley. 'Loves the garden, though he and Sir William sometimes have their spats. But Joe is a good hard-working learner. Apart from the hydrangeas,' he added lest anyone should detect pride or praise in his voice.

The men gazed across the gardens to the distant figure, wrapped up against the cold so heavily that his silhouette against the white seemed more animal than man, shovelling snow from the paths.

'I can vividly remember those two little shrimps of lads playing chase round the trees...' said Gabriel reminiscently, and then trailed off, suddenly conscious of Brockley's flinch in response.

The gardener turned back into the dark shed and his soil-covered hands began to fumble amongst the bags of bulbs.

'I often think on that, Sir Gabriel. We miss Benny, Joe and me.'

'Do you often hear from him? How does he get on?'

Brockley shrugged. 'Messages from all over foreign parts. He seems to go on all right. They are like plants, children, Sir Gabriel. You feed 'em and water 'em and love 'em, but if the conditions aren't right, they won't thrive. I know that. I dunno why he never told me it was the sea he wanted.' He hesitated. 'He always loved the garden so; used to say, him and Joe would always live here and tend it.' He shook his head. 'I suppose he said it because he knew it was what I wanted to hear. And he had a real talent. Green fingers, if you like. Joe is a good practical gardener, but Benny, he had magic in his hands, ever since he was a little boy with a patch I give him for his first daisies. They say it's wrong to love one child more than another. But Benny was... well, he was Benny. But there,' he straightened himself, 'he is happy and that is what matters.'

Almost petulantly, he thrust a bag of bulbs at Gabriel. 'What is the name on these? Joe writes 'em on for me. We've daffs of all kinds.'

Gabriel peered at the scruffy label. 'Good old King Alfreds, Brockley. The bravest spring show.'

Re-circling the garden he and Wright encountered Joe, sweating with exertion, huge iron shovel in hand, his strong bulky figure moving rhythmically as he laboured over the impacted snow on the path.

'A hard job,' said Gabriel sympathetically.

Joe shrugged. 'Not so bad with Father's old spade. They knew how to make things to last when he was young. But it's a waste of time bothering, with the snow keeping on falling. If only Sir Vivian Barton had not taken it into his head to walk round the garden and slip and fall. Told Sir William, he did, and then I have Sir William telling Father we must clear it today or else.'

'I fear,' said Gabriel in his gentle way, 'that I may have distressed your father, Joe, by tactlessly mentioning Benny. He plainly finds the subject difficult.'

The young man's face darkened. 'He does that,' he said rather curtly. 'I reckon we both do. Though no reason for it. My brother has gone his own way, though he keeps in touch with Father now and again.'

'Has he never been back to see you both in all the years?'

Joe shook his head. 'He's all over the world. He's a grown man. No reason to come back to what he ran from. But there,' he said, and there was a sudden bitter tone to his voice, 'no denying Benny was Father's favourite. "Why didn't he tell me he wanted to leave?" Father says to me afterwards. But Father sets such store by gardening. "Benny is the one's got true green fingers," he says to me. But the sea was what he always wanted and Father never would have let him go, whatever he says now.'

Joe bent once again to his task, and they left him.

Trudging back across the snow-covered lawn, Gabriel deliberately stepped where no one had previously trodden and derived from the exact neat imprint of his feet the same sharp pleasure he had felt since he was a schoolboy. He recalled the emotion in Brockley's face. It had not been the moment to pursue his enquiries. Thank God he had been spared the pain of emotional commitment; the involvement in someone else's life, which meant giving some of your own in return, the exchanges of desire and selflessness that added up to compromise, the love that went hand in hand with loss. On that cold winter afternoon he thought of the sanctuary that awaited him in his rooms in King's Bench Walk, of the joy of self-sufficiency and of the pleasure he was deriving now from seeing his solitary footprints in the pristine snow. His life seemed to him infinitely preferable to one confused by human entanglements.

They had reached the garden gates, and while Wright made his way back to police headquarters, Gabriel walked on across the Temple through the now thickly falling snow. He wondered fleetingly with whom Ivy had 'gone wrong'. It was not a subject with which he felt comfortable and he tucked it away rather hastily at the back of his mind. He must speak to Hopkins, as Master of the Silver, he supposed, about the missing salts and the possible role of Durrant the porter who had disappeared. He could not think what else to do with regard to the staff and turned his mind to consideration of the Bar.

The ancient buildings of the Inner Temple were cauldrons of ambition and dashed hopes and very public successes and humiliations, of resignation and aspiration, of vicious competition and covert kindnesses. Young men came and sometimes left. Gabriel, serenely at the top of his profession for many years now, shielded by Chapman from any administrative demands, resolutely uninvolved with the running of the Inner Temple committees, was not disturbed by these comings and goings and they had made little impression on him. Over the years he could recall none in which there had been any lingering sense of mystery save for one. But that one had lingered long in the consciousness of the Temple. One of their most promising young men. Simon Rawlings.

On impulse, he waded through the snow accumulating in the narrow alley between his own chambers and those of Sir Vivian Barton in Fig Tree Court, and with the comfort of long habit, tapped on the frost-encrusted window through which he could see Barton in his habitual pose, sitting back from his chaotically laden desk, feet resting upon it, wedged between piles of paper and textbooks, cigar between his fingers, his genial balding head surrounded by the gentle wreath of its smoke.

9

Without moving from his supine position, Barton beckoned Gabriel into the room, stretched out his arm to fling another log on his fire, proffered the cigar he knew would be refused, and extracted from the cupboard in his desk the sherry he knew his colleague would accept.

'Thanks for coming, my dear fellow,' he said with his customary easy warmth. 'It was good of you to obey my anguished summons when no doubt you are busy.'

'Summons?' said Gabriel. 'I have been out all day. I received no summons.'

'Oh? Then it is a lucky chance. I sent one round an hour ago. Ward, I have had a most distressing incident. Quite frankly, I did not know what to do. Then I thought of your wise head, old boy.' He bent laboriously under his desk.

With a sinking heart, and a deep sense of déjà vu, Gabriel knew what he would see. Barton placed upon the desk a familiar-looking brown cardboard box, a foot square in all dimensions.

'I warn you...' began Barton.

'I am afraid I can guess.' It was Gabriel who lifted the lid to release the haunting sweet smell and to reveal, tucked under tissue paper, a human toe that lay, obscene and sausage-like, the nail corroded into the flesh surrounding it like a blackened scab.

The accompanying card read: *Toe the line.*

Barton shuddered and replaced the lid. 'I could not believe my eyes, Ward. Where the devil does such an obscenity come from?'

'How did it arrive here?'

'It was found on the doorstep of my room by my clerk. I thank God it was here and not at home. What if one of my little scamps had opened such a thing? Or my wife?' He hesitated and then said ruefully, 'I don't mind telling you, Ward, it has shaken me up. Oh, not just the horror of the thing but the fact that it has been sent at all. You know me. I am not the sort to make enemies. Why should anyone do such a thing?'

'If it is any comfort,' said Gabriel, 'you are not alone.'

'You too?'

'No,' said Gabriel, and it occurred to him that he had not in fact given any thought to this fact. Why not him? He tucked the question away for later consideration and told Barton of the ghastly parcels sent to Waring and to Hopkins.

'Good God. Good God. And that is why you came to see me?'

Gabriel hesitated. 'Yes, indirectly. I wanted to talk to you about Simon Rawlings.'

Barton straightened sharply from his friendly slump and pitched his cigar stub into the fire. Standing up, he hobbled to his window. 'Lame as the devil,' he grunted. 'That damn' young fool Joe Brockley didn't sweep the paths and I came a cropper yesterday morning. I am the Master of the Garden too! Sir William expects me to keep an eye on it and the gardeners. "What do we pay them for?" I said to him.' He threw open the sash so that freezing air poured into the room.

'I smoke too damned much,' he said. 'God awful fug in here, old boy.' And then, still with his back to Gabriel, 'Wasn't there enough unhappiness about Rawlings at the time without digging it up again now?'

'I am afraid that expression may be only too apt.'

Barton turned to look at him in some astonishment. 'Expression? What expression?'

'Consider for a moment: where did these body parts come from? I am advised they are several years old. It – it is my fear that they may indeed have been *dug up*.'

A look of revulsion came over Barton's genial face. He returned to his desk and sat down heavily once more in his chair.

'I hope I am wrong,' said Gabriel slowly, 'but I have a growing suspicion that the body they came from is within the Temple. There is a local feeling about the whole affair. Of course, the parcels may have been imported from elsewhere but they were apparently delivered by hand, sent with personalised messages. And the Inner Temple is, as you know, an internalised little world. I have made extensive enquiries; the parts came from the body of a young person. We are looking at a period at the earliest several years ago. We are a small community. I can only discover two members of staff who have disappeared without trace in that timespan. Both, as it happens, about ten years ago. Both had obvious reasons for doing so. But Rawlings... Could you bear to recall the circumstances for me? If only so that I may eliminate him? You cannot deny that he disappeared without trace. And it was also some ten years ago, was it not? And he was the right age.'

'I do not have to recall it, Ward,' said Barton. 'I live with it. The boy was my pupil, and a quite exceptional one at that. He was well on the way to being the most wonderful advocate. He came to me and told me he had had an unfortunate liaison. He didn't say any more and I didn't ask. I told him if he had behaved like a fool, he must go home and tell his grandfather and hope that he and Sir William Waring could keep the matter quiet. He was quite collected when he left me. I heard afterwards he went home and then later came back to the Temple. Vernon-Osbert saw him on his knees in the church, in some distress. He did not want to talk. Walked out, apparently in the direction of the Embankment. Then the lad was never seen again.' Barton sighed. 'He was an orphan as you may know; there were three of them, brought up by their grandparents. My God, the utter waste of a promising young barrister over some minor sexual misdemeanour. I do not know any of the details, I am afraid. No trace of him was ever found. I always assumed the Thames took him, poor lad. You must apply to the family for further information.'

Gabriel nodded soberly. 'I am sorry, Barton.'

There did not seem anything left to say. Picking up his top hat, he prepared to depart.

As he crossed the room Barton said, 'Ward, believe me, I uttered no word of condemnation to the boy that night. I just gave him the advice I would want a man to give to one of my youngsters in similar circumstances. But now I reproach myself. He was in despair. Young men take things hard. They have not learned that life goes on.'

'Indeed yes,' said Gabriel, and to both men's surprise as he passed the desk he patted Barton's shoulder.

Walking back slowly to his chambers, Gabriel felt the deep discomfort he always did when brought face to face with reality; with the hypocrisy of apparently good people, with love and tragedy and loss, with the whole crazy patchwork of human emotions. He pushed the feeling away from him. He would go back to 1 Crown Office Row and check that his desk was in order, although he knew that it was, and then go home and pull down his drawing-room blinds in just the way he always did, with his right hand and with the thumb folded inwards. And then he would close the faded blue silk curtains. He would close out the dark of the night, and reality. He would read an old friend.

10

The next day, the very first day of the New Year, he had promised himself a full day writing a difficult opinion relating to an obscure provision of the Settled Land Act 1882. Though as it turned out, he found it difficult at first to apply his usual fierce concentration to it.

Last year had been for Gabriel a significant one and this first day of the new one caused him to be in a reflective mood. It was not so much his involvement in the detection of the murderer of the Lord Chief Justice of which he thought, but of the consequences to his own inner life. Somehow his role as a detective had thrown him off the metaphorical bank on which he had stood for so long; not into the mainstream, but so that he was at least paddling in the shallows of life; something he had previously only observed. He wondered, very cautiously, if he might grow to like the sensation. He was not at all sure. He turned with a sigh to the comforting challenges of Section 5 (The Transfer of Encumbrances) until Chapman's deferential knock aroused him from thought.

'I have agreed that you will give some urgent advice, sir,' he said. 'To Mr Brindle and a client.'

Fussy, meticulous Arthur Brindle, of Brindle, Wade, Brindle & Wade, had the great personal misfortune to be a dreadful bore. But he made up for this unfortunate characteristic in industry and integrity and a large clientele, and was therefore a valued instructing solicitor of chambers. Urgent requests for advice were not uncommon, though generally preceded by some form of written instructions.

'Papers?' said Gabriel hopefully.

'No, sir. No time. I have said you will make allowances and consider the problem now in consultation with Mr Brindle and the client.'

Gabriel nodded resignedly and shrugged himself into his tail-coat. He was wearing his favourite wire-framed spectacles with one earpiece secured by a paperclip. Gabriel, usually averse to change and innovation, was rather pleased to have been introduced by Chapman to paperclips, a new invention for which he had discovered numerous purposes other than that for which they were intended. But now he replaced the spectacles with a more respectable tortoiseshell pair.

'Mr Brindle,' announced Chapman sonorously, 'and Miss Topsy Tillotson.'

Trapped, Gabriel cast a deeply reproachful eye at Chapman, who met it with a look in which defiance and sheepishness were combined and who withdrew rather hastily.

'How do you do?' Topsy Tillotson removed a small hand from a very large muff. Her sultry, husky voice betrayed no indication that she had ever met Gabriel before. She sounded very solemn, but he saw that her eyes were dancing with triumph.

Transfixed for a moment like a rabbit in front of a stoat, he peered short-sightedly across the immaculate surfaces of his desk as this vision settled herself into his client's chair. To him, the sultry voice, the tumbling tawny tresses, the improbably hazel eyes so light they were almost topaz, the lush curves, evoked a sensation not of allure but of suffocation. But he noticed with approval that she had a rare quality of stillness. Once settled, she sat quietly, her remarkable eyes fixed thoughtfully on him. He was suddenly rather relieved that he was not wearing the spectacles with the paperclip.

Brindle, bald, bespectacled and prosperous-looking, tumbled immediately into anxious speech.

'Your Chapman asked me to see Miss Tillotson. I have already told her that this is close to madness, Sir Gabriel, but she insisted upon my firm arranging this consultation. She is determined to sue the *Nation's Voice* for defamation of her character and she will not listen to reason. I have told her the letter of the law is against her, the jury will be against her, the cost will be exorbitant and that she will lose.'

Gabriel gave the characteristic little snuffle that meant he was amused.

'That is certainly comprehensive,' he said. 'And clear.'

'But wrong. And surely unjust. I thought the law was about justice,' said Topsy Tillotson. The topaz eyes blazed at him across the desk. Gabriel could not think of whom they reminded him.

She spread open the news sheet that lay on her lap. The purring voice shook with indignation as she read aloud.

'"*Miss Topsy Tillotson the music hall belle is living up to at least part of one of the songs that made her famous*:

'"*"Keep a good hold of your prince when you find him/they are few and far between…*'

'"*We are reliably informed by the lucky gentleman in question that Miss Tillotson's 'prince', The Hon. Frederick Sewell, elder son of Lord Somerton, has already stormed the citadel and conquered 'The Unconquerable'! We fear that in her enthusiasm she may have forgotten the song's last lines:*

'"*"Make him buy you a ring when you find him/without one you'll never be Queen."''*

'I suppose by "stormed the citadel" they mean to suggest I have become his mistress, don't they?'

Here Brindle intervened.

'The Honourable Frederick Sewell, as you may know, Sir Gabriel, is a young man about town of impeccable lineage. His father, Lord Somerton, Seventeenth Earl of Mapleford, is a member of the House of Lords and owner of a vast acreage and of South Rising House in Mayfair, while Lady Somerton is one of society's most prominent hostesses. Frederick is generally thought to be a very personable young man of great charm. And, if I may say so, the ladies certainly consider him handsome. He is sole heir to his family's fortune. I believe young Frederick is also known to be a... a keen theatre-goer.'

Topsy sniffed. 'I know what that means,' she observed.

Gabriel retreated into the comfort of a formal exposition of the law relevant to her case. 'Miss Tillotson,' he said, 'it seems to me that there is no doubt this is an imputation upon your chastity. It is defamatory if what it conveys, if only by innuendo, is untrue. However, if what The Honourable Frederick Sewell told the newspaper is true, and if they have accurately reported it, then it is not defamatory for them to make it public and they will plead the defence of justification. I fear, if I am to represent you, I must therefore ask you an ungentlemanly question: is there any truth in what they suggest?'

Topsy showed no hesitation. 'Certainly not! I do not even know him! It is a lie! And it dirties my name and ruins my reputation!'

'Miss Tillotson,' said the solicitor severely, 'when you speak of your reputation, I am constrained to point out that you have achieved your famous name by appearing on the public stage, scantily clad, while singing songs riddled with double-entendres of the most vulgar kind. I have seen you perform and, if you will forgive me for saying so, was shocked. Remember, some of the gentlemen on the jury will have seen you on the stage too. I cannot think they will have any difficulty in deciding where the truth lies.'

Ignoring this diatribe, Topsy Tillotson leaned across Gabriel's desk and addressed him earnestly. 'I was fifteen when I was first given those songs to sing, Sir Gabriel. That is my job. I am paid to perform the part I am given. I do not mean it. It does not reflect *me*. Why should people be allowed to think that it does?'

Brindle snorted again.

But for Gabriel her words were an echo that seemed to resonate back through the cavernous decades of his professional memory; *that is my job. I am paid to perform the part I am given.* And with that echo came another and another. All his clients over all the years, the good and the bad, the mad and the misjudged, the innocent and the guilty. The speeches he had made on their behalf with no belief whatsoever in the veracity of what he was saying. The indiscriminate, detached representation of anyone with the money to pay him to say what they wanted said. *I do not mean it.*

And then into his mind came an image of those three insolent challenging exclamation marks that had followed the reference to Topsy Tillotson's reputation; and this image was followed by one of Mr Lionel Sullivan, editor and proprietor of the *Nation's Voice*, in all his cynical populism.

And he knew that Topsy Tillotson had found her barrister. Because it was his job to do it. Like her, he was for hire. But also, because he understood her.

This latter fact, however, did not blind him to the already obvious difficulties of her case.

'Miss Tillotson,' he said, 'if I may sum up: a newspaper has apparently been reliably informed that you have committed an indiscretion with a young man of good family. That young man says that you did – er – succumb. You say that you do not know him from Adam. I am used to arguing opposed positions, but don't you feel that that is a rather extreme example? One or the other of you cannot merely be mistaken. One or the other of you is a liar. I would not be doing my duty as a lawyer if I did not point out to you that perjury is a very serious offence indeed and carries an inevitable sentence of hard labour in prison.'

The topaz eyes looked boldly into his.

'Tell that to The Honourable Frederick Sewell,' she said firmly.

11

When he returned home that evening, Gabriel found the hallway outside his rooms in 4 King's Bench Walk was piled with belongings, and teetering perilously on a stepladder in the midst of them was the Temple carpenter and signwriter, painstakingly writing a new name above the lintel of the residential rooms opposite Gabriel's own. *John Gibson, Esq.* it read.

'Good evening, Sugden,' said Gabriel. 'Am I to have a new neighbour?'

Sugden, the oldest member of the staff, now a bit wobbly on his ladder but with a hand still as steady as a rock, had done this job for fifty years, and the leather apron he had worn all that time was stained black from painting up the names of a generation. When a barrister joined his professional chambers, and when he moved into a residential set of rooms, Sugden painted his name on the board beside each door. When he became Queen's or King's Counsel, or a judge, it was Sugden who embellished that name with the latest honour or amended it as appropriate when the monarch died. And when that barrister himself died, it was Sugden who, with the same respectful hand, first removed his old cap and then painted out the name to make room for the next inhabitant. Little went on that Sugden's kindly, cynical old eyes did not see while recording the living history of the Inner Temple. Sugden had an affection for Sir Gabriel Ward, whose name he had painted up over thirty years ago.

Now he observed drily, 'You are indeed, Sir Gabriel. He's moving in this week in time for the commencement of the

Hilary term. Mr John Gibson is a very junior member of the Bar to have been allocated residential rooms in the Inn. But such it is to be our Master Treasurer's soon-to-be son-in-law.'

Their conversation was interrupted by the thump of boots on the stairs and, turning, Gabriel saw two young men staggering under the weight of a trunk. One was sturdy, fair-haired, bespectacled and dressed in the traditional black coat and pinstriped trousers of the young barrister. The other, dog-collared and lanky, was Rupert Brandish.

While Gabriel exchanged greetings with Brandish, the young fair-haired man, negotiating around Sugden and his ladder, opened the door opposite Gabriel's own. In the inner hall stood five brown cardboard boxes of unusual symmetry, exactly a foot square in all dimensions. They were unpleasantly familiar. Gabriel peered uneasily at them. The cube, always equal, always based upon itself, invariably just in its proportions, usually so satisfying to his tidy mind, was now imbued with another and more sinister significance.

The young man turned, smiling, to Rupert Brandish who was now balancing the trunk on the top step.

'Can I give you a hand?' he said.

In spite of himself, Gabriel jumped.

Brandish, misinterpreting the jump and remembering his manners, tumbled into speech.

'I should introduce you, Sir Gabriel, to my old Cambridge friend John Gibson, who is to be the new tenant here. I mentioned him, you will recall, at Christmas luncheon. I am helping him move in.'

'Indeed, yes,' said Gabriel, recovering himself hastily. 'My new neighbour. And I believe congratulations are due?'

The young man looked blank. 'Congratulations?'

'Why, yes,' said Gabriel. 'Upon your engagement to Miss Amelia Waring. You could not have a lovelier setting for your wedding than the Temple Church. When are your nuptials to be?'

'Oh, well,' said John Gibson, 'I d-d-d-d—' He stopped talking and swallowed convulsively. 'I d-d-do not think there is any hurry.'

There was a brief silence. Gabriel, already preoccupied with the significance of the boxes, was aware of a social embarrassment now on two counts: the marked stammer was surprising in a young man aspiring to be a barrister, even with the connections this one apparently had; and the remark, by a newly engaged young man, a strikingly odd one.

Gibson himself seemed to realise something was lacking in his response.

'I am to settle into the rooms for a little while, sir, whilst I b-b-begin my career. P-p-perhaps it will b-b-be b-b-b-best to leave any arrangements ab-b-bout my marriage until after the Hilary t-t-term,' he trailed off.

Brandish put an affectionate hand on his friend's shoulder and gave it a little shake.

'He is hopeless, Sir Gabriel; head in the clouds, always the same. If it were not for me, he would be sitting there with his precious collection, no thought of a kettle or bedsheets or even a chair to sit in.'

'Collection?' said Gabriel cautiously.

But John Gibson had retreated inside his rooms, Brandish had turned his attention to the trunk, and Gabriel had an engagement to keep.

It did not matter whether anyone who knew Gabriel saw him sitting in the circle for that night's performance of *A Girl Like Me*, since they would, quite simply, have been unable to believe their eyes.

There was a time, he acknowledged to himself, when he would have been unable to bring himself to emerge out of the Temple gates and down crowded Aldwych to the Drury Lane Theatre, so cradled had he felt in the security of the Inn. But over the last year, after his enforced involvement in the tracking down of the murderer of the Lord Chief Justice, he had learned that he could venture out if necessity demanded it and if the expedition was hedged around with careful precautions. Precautions against what? He did not know. He knew only that the self-imposed rules made the unknown tolerable to him. He walked very carefully, avoiding the lines on the pavements as he always did in the Temple, but now with the added requirement that the ferrule of his umbrella should be placed precisely in the centre of the next stone.

Through the crowds of people, their varied sociable lives so different from his own, a small isolated entity, he progressed doggedly to the theatre, murmuring repeatedly to himself as he did so: '*Step over the line, Gabriel, ferrule in the middle.*' He bought his ticket and programme and settled himself, quite without self-consciousness, in his seat. It did not occur to Gabriel that he was a singular figure at a show such as this and he was unaware of the curious glances of his jovial neighbours.

The curtain went up and his senses were assailed by the noisy climactic chorus that led to Topsy's first entrance. Her own song was titillating, her costume extremely revealing, and the jokes vulgar. But it was very clear, as the show went on, that she held her boisterous audience in the palm of her hand and, even for him, the trite storyline and easy popular tunes seemed transported by the purity of her voice and the precision of her movements, into things of irresistible charm. She was warm and winsome and yet, somehow, she remained aloof as a goddess from the vast wave of adulation and lust that she must surely have found almost palpable, all directed at her slight figure on the faraway stage.

Here indeed, thought Gabriel, was a personality to be reckoned with. When at last the show reached Topsy's final and iconic song, 'A Girl Like Me', amidst the ear-splitting applause and the rain of flowers flung at the stage, he was so engrossed in thought that he forgot to clap, a small still centre of concentration in the midst of the tumult. He had finally realised of whom Topsy reminded him. The precision, the perfectionism, the topaz eyes alive with a wild innocence, the willingness to accept homage combined with that curious personal withdrawal. Her effortless power over her admirers. It was Delphinium, Reverend Master Vernon-Osbert's cat.

When the performance was over, Gabriel made his way through the throngs of admirers to the open stage door and addressed the burly man who seemed to fill the doorman's cubicle set beside it.

'I should like to send a message to Miss Tillotson.' He felt in his pocket for his card case only to find he had left it at home.

The man looked weary. 'Ho, yes, hof course,' he said with heavy irony. 'You and the rest of the male population of London, why not? And now you can scarper off, my friend.' He peered more closely at Gabriel. 'And wot's more, you should be ashamed of yourself. Nineteen, she is. You push off before you are pushed off!'

Gabriel stood his ground. 'In that case,' he said politely, 'I wonder if I may speak to a member of the theatre's management?' The man gave him a nasty look. '*I* am half the management. You can speak to the other half if you dare.' He flung open the door behind him with a flourish.

'Who shall I say?' he asked with sarcastic courtesy.

'I am Gabriel Ward KC.'

The man gestured him in. 'Mr Gabriel Ward-Casey, Vera,' he yelled. 'And I can't get him to go away.'

To Gabriel's astonishment, from behind a desk upon which lay a half-consumed fried dinner, an immense woman got to her feet. She wore a shapeless tweed jacket over a no less shapeless serge skirt, her hair was cut as short as a man's, and between her stained fingers she held a cheroot. Her expression was hostile.

'What do you want, Mr Ward-Casey?' she said. Her cracked voice reflected a lifetime spent in smoky backstages and a strong liking for gin.

'Forgive me,' said Gabriel in his polite way, 'I did not make myself sufficiently clear. I am Gabriel Ward, King's Counsel. I am a barrister. I—'

The woman roared with laughter and stubbed the cheroot out in her congealing fried egg.

'You are an ass, Perkins,' she said. 'This is Topsy's brief!'

Fastidiously, Gabriel averted his eyes from the horrid sight of the plate and gingerly took the greasy hand she offered him.

'I am,' he said, 'and you and your husband, I think, must be the management?'

'I am Vera Perkins, impresario, Sir Gabriel, and very pleased to make your acquaintance. Perkins out there is my brother. Very worried, I have been, about our Topsy. "Topsy," I said to her, "if you must bring this case, you go to Sir Edward Hopkins KC and ask him to represent you." A very big name he is. In the Old Bailey, in all the big trials and all over the newspapers. And sometimes waits at the stage door for my girls, too… nothing but champagne at the Savoy will do for him and the lucky one he asks, so we all know him. Oh, a charmer if ever there was one! And handsome! You may know him yourself, Sir Gabriel?'

Gabriel bowed without comment. He was tempted to quote Nanny: *handsome is as handsome does*, but his inner lawyer baulked at it. What *did* it mean? That was the infuriating thing about Nanny's sayings, he reflected. One knew at once when they were apposite even when they did not make sense.

Vera Perkins was continuing.

'But no. Our Topsy said, "I don't want the likes of him, I want the Real Thing." "What does that mean?" I said. And *she* said, "I want Sir Gabriel Ward KC." "Never heard of him," I said, begging your pardon Sir Gabriel, and she said, "I don't want some show-off, I want him. He is the Real Thing." Done her research, she had. She's a clever girl, our Topsy.' Vera Perkins looked sharply at Gabriel. 'And a good one. If you take my point.'

'Well, Miss Perkins,' said Gabriel in his tranquil way, 'that of course is the crux of the matter. I fear that the *Nation's Voice* will be scouring for evidence to prove otherwise. And, of course, Mr Frederick Sewell does indeed say otherwise.'

'Scum,' said Vera Perkins briefly. 'I don't believe a word of it. Like a daughter to me is Topsy. So are they all, come to that. I know what is said about chorus girls, Sir Gabriel, and when they begin, Perkins and me, we coddle them like eggs and guard them like lions. But we can't keep them in cotton wool forever—'

Dreadful mixed metaphors, thought Gabriel's inner lawyer.

'—and, well, they must choose their own way in the end. For some of them it's a bad way, there's no denying it. But not all of them. And not Topsy.'

'I felt it was a little discourteous not to tell her I have been to see her performance; I would not wish her to feel she was being... spied upon in any way. So, I intended to send in my card, only to discover I have brought none. I wonder if you would be kind enough to convey the message instead?'

'I'll take you backstage, ducky,' said Vera Perkins decisively, and before Gabriel could protest, he was ushered out.

Backstage was darkness and dust and garish backdrops propped perilously against walls and labyrinthine corridors lined with doors from which yells of laughter issued and shouts of anger. A piano tinkled out a repetitive tune and a violin shrieked at its mishandling. There were boots and bags on the floor, coats piled into vast humps on small hooks, dead flowers brimming from a bin and the all-pervasive smell of food and greasepaint.

No order. No quiet. Gabriel tensed miserably against the onslaught. He followed Vera Perkins' back to a door through which he hoped there would be a respite, and she opened it and ushered Gabriel into hell. The colour and the noise were a physical assault; his ears and eyes hurt. There were girls everywhere, in fewer clothes than Gabriel had ever seen a woman wearing. He averted his eyes from bosoms and encountered legs; he looked away from the legs and met enormous kohl-encircled eyes and bright scarlet lips.

He turned in panic to the door behind him but it closed on its swing hinges as he did so. Vera had abandoned him here. And then he realised one pair of kohl-lined eyes was looking at him and the scarlet lips were speaking directly to him.

'You're in a right state,' she said. 'Sit down, dearie.' And she pulled forward a chair.

Why a right state? said his inner lawyer. Surely it should be a wrong state. Where had the idiom come from? It was used in so many contexts. A right mess, a right idiot, a right palaver... palaver, now there was an interesting word. Portuguese, of course, in origin, from the Latin *parabola*... His mind meandered down the labyrinths of his learning until, with a start, he came back to the present and discovered that his heart had resumed its usual steady beat and he was able to respond quite calmly.

'Thank you,' he said, peering myopically around. 'I wonder, is Miss Tillotson amongst you?'

'She has her own room,' said the feather-clad vision before him, nodding to an inner door. 'She's the star and we are the chorus, dearie. I am Rosie Bunch.'

She grinned at Gabriel's expression. 'I know,' she said. 'But it really is – my mother called us all names to fit with Bunch. My poor brother is Rowan. Who are you?'

'I am Miss Tillotson's, er, brief.'

The chorus immediately clustered round him. Boas tickled his cheek, the smell of Attar of Roses was overpowering, and voices from shrill to melodic were raised in an anthem of praise to Topsy's unimpeachable virtue.

'Leave him alone, can't you?' said Rosie Bunch proprietorially. But her earlier warmth seemed very much diminished. She looked at him sharply. 'I know all about the Temple and KCs, dearie. You want to watch your step with our Topsy.' And she hauled him out of the chair into which she had so recently thrust him, gripped his arm and propelled him towards the inner door.

12

Topsy was seated at her dressing table with her back to him. Standing at the door, Gabriel saw her vivid face and tumbling tresses reflected in the mirror, and in the background his own slight ascetic figure. Both reflections were surrounded by the flowers that filled the room and by the dozens of cards tucked haphazardly into the mirror's gilt frame. Topsy saw him too and spun round on her dressing stool in surprise. It was as he stepped forward and hurried into explanations that he observed something else that put the formalities quite out of his head. Trickling down the beautiful face were tears; her cheeks were stained with them, and the little straight classical nose could not be described as anything but very pink at the end.

'My dear young lady, what can be the matter? You were a great success! Why, I thought the cheering would never cease.'

Topsy dug frantically and unsuccessfully in her dressing-robe pocket and then rubbed her beautiful nose with the back of one hand.

Gabriel sighed. His immaculately starched handkerchief was plainly in jeopardy. He extracted it and handed it over, wondering as he did so whether kohl was eradicable from white linen.

'I should tell you, Miss Tillotson, that I came to watch your performance, to see for myself why your solicitor was expressing concerns about your case. I would have sent in my card, but I had forgotten them, and Miss Perkins, er, took over.'

Topsy smiled rather tremulously. 'Yes,' she said, 'she does.'

'And I witnessed what was plainly a triumph and now find you in distress. Is it anything I can assist you with?' He wondered what the girl would say and hoped it would not be some embarrassing personal revelation. But what she did say surprised him a great deal.

'I'm lonely,' said Topsy. Her musical voice resonated with pathos.

Loneliness was not an emotion that Gabriel ever felt personally, but he made a soothing noise as he looked around the charming little dressing room that to him radiated warmth and adulation. She seemed to see through his eyes the flowers and cards, the fur stoles and striped hatboxes, all the rich clutter, and she flushed.

'Oh, I know I sound ungrateful, Sir Gabriel. I am the luckiest girl in London. All of this is lovely. And, as you say, the show is a success. The audiences are wonderful to me. And lots of people want to be my friend.'

'But?'

'They're not real friends. I've realised that they all want something. The other girls – they – sometimes I think they only like to be – to be seen with me.' She bent her head and fumbled with Gabriel's handkerchief. 'And the men – well, they want something too; they say they admire the show and my singing and dancing, and tell me I am wonderful, but – but— And even Mr and Miss Perkins, they are so kind to me, but in the end, I know it is because I am earning money for them. And then, quite recently, I met a real friend who did not want anything bad and everything was different. And now he has disappeared.'

The last word held a horrid significance for Gabriel.

'Disappeared?' he said cautiously. 'When was this?'

'A week ago. On Christmas Eve,' said Topsy miserably, and Gabriel relaxed. Not the disappearance he was concerned with, at any rate. 'After the newspaper had blackened my name. I am afraid he saw what they wrote, Sir Gabriel, and thought I was a bad lot.'

She buried her face once more in his handkerchief. 'And now I have lost him,' she said, and the beautiful voice broke piteously.

'My dear child, no one is simply lost,' said Gabriel firmly.

'We were to meet after the show,' she said. 'He always came. But then he did not.'

'Have you sent a message?' asked Gabriel, practical as ever. He had no personal experience of love and loss. But he had read stories of passion and betrayal repeated throughout literature, and he had heard them over and over in the Law Courts. How many love stories, he thought, were encapsulated in those few words? *He always came. But then he did not.* He sighed. Thank God, he thought, I am spared that. But looking at Topsy's unhappy, trusting face, he felt a tremor of something he dimly recognised as protectiveness.

She looked confused by the question. 'I can't send a message,' she said. 'I don't know where to send it to. I only know his name – George – and that he lives with his mother somewhere near Smithfield Market. That is all. We met in the street three weeks ago. They all wait outside the stage door, Sir Gabriel, the men. A big crowd of them, in their top hats and silk evening scarves, with their flowers and their smirks. I hate them. Won't even look at them. I bow my head, push through them. And sometimes I'm just wading through bouquets. I hate it. The more I say no, the harder they try. Then, when the newspapers began to call me The Unconquerable, it made it even worse. And now they say I *have* been conquered and that I am a – a – that I am like the girls in my songs.'

'Well,' said Gabriel, 'it is my job to help with your case against the newspaper. But do you wish to tell me anything more about your lost friend?'

And Topsy, comforted, as clients of his so often were, by Gabriel's soothing kindly indifference, confided her little story.

It happened one night, three weeks before Christmas, when she came out of the stage door. It was raining quite hard and very cold; the crowd of men was smaller than usual. On the other side of the road one young man stood alone, rivulets of rain running down the peak of his cap and his shabby overcoat. As she drew level with him, he did not speak but smiled at her, and his smile was so wistful that she responded to it.

'Have you been to the show?' she said.

The young man nodded. 'Up in the gods. My third time. You— You were a *joy*, Miss Tillotson.'

'Thank you,' said Topsy rather primly as she hopped into her hansom. But despite her familiarity with lavish praise, she felt warmed by the simplicity of the tribute.

Looking back through the rear window, she saw him still standing there in the rain.

After that, he was there every night for a week.

And then one night it had rained again and a deep puddle had separated Topsy from her waiting hansom cab. The young man was there, in what she was beginning to think of as his usual place.

'I would throw down my coat,' he said, 'like we were told at school Sir Walter Raleigh did. But I expect he had another. This is the only one I've got.' And they had both laughed.

'I wish I could ask you to have supper,' he said wistfully. 'But I could not afford the kind of places you are used to.'

'I don't like places the nobs go,' said Topsy firmly. 'Give me good plain food like my mother cooks any time.'

'Pie and mash?' he said, and that had been the beginning. Looking back, Topsy thought she had fallen in love over that pie and mash. He told her his name was George and he lived not far from the theatre in Smithfield with his mother. He was a printer's apprentice in Fleet Street. There was just enough money to go round if he was careful. Topsy had liked hearing about the world of printing, so different from that of the theatre. He was ambitious. One day, George said, he would like to be rich.

'What will you do then?' asked Topsy.

George said he would buy evening clothes and a top hat and kid gloves and a bunch of roses and lilies and come and meet her at the stage door.

'I hope not,' said Topsy.

A day or two after that first pie and mash, they went for a walk in the park one afternoon, and on a couple more occasions they had supper, not in the glitter of the Savoy Grill, but intimate little places in Soho backstreets where the food was cooked by the owner's family and the steamed-up windows and anonymous clientele offered the very recognisable Topsy a degree of privacy. Only three more little outings over those magical two weeks.

And then there had been that horrible article. And George did not come to meet her that night.

She was sobbing again. Gabriel sighed. It might indeed be the case that the salacious nature of the article in the *Nation's Voice* had driven a decent young man away, particularly since it told of an infidelity with Frederick Sewell. His first thought, as always, was for the forthcoming litigation. If the libel case was to be effectively conducted, her mind must be concentrated upon it – and upon combatting the searing cross-examination she would undoubtedly have to face from Sir Edward Hopkins KC at his most self-righteous – not on her broken heart.

'How can I try to find him?' she sobbed. 'Everyone knows who I am. If I go and ask in Fleet Street, those men will put me in the newspaper and make it worse.'

This, thought Gabriel, was only too true. And realised with a shudder the impact it would have on the case if Miss Topsy Tillotson's name were linked with that of another man. He cast around for inspiration. And then it came to him in the form of a pink honest face under a policeman's helmet.

'Will you leave it to me?' He picked up his top hat and suppressed the temptation to retrieve his handkerchief. 'And trust me to do my best?'

She nodded, comforted. And then said wistfully, 'Please tell me honestly what you thought of the show? And please do not just say "you were wonderful".'

'You *were* wonderful,' said Gabriel, with his little bow. 'But I think that your material did not do you justice, Miss Tillotson.'

That night, looking from his window before retiring to bed, as always, at exactly half-past midnight, Gabriel gazed out over the dark paved area of King's Bench Walk across to the looming bulk of the library clocktower. Somebody crossed in front of it, and Gabriel watched incuriously the progress of the figure whom he assumed to be the night watchman. But then he saw another emerge from the shadows and the two figures meeting, and as they walked away together, for an instant, they were clearly illuminated by the gas lamp over the library entrance. One, tall and lanky, was Rupert Brandish, and the other, shorter and stocky and fair-haired, was John Gibson. Close together, the two men turned out of sight, and their demeanour as they did so, keeping in the shadow of the building, sidling along close to its wall, could not have been described, by even the most uncritical, as anything other than shifty.

13

The next day, the second of the New Year, Gabriel put on full evening dress with extreme reluctance and dutifully made his way to the Temple Church for Evensong.

The service was to be followed by the Treasurer's dinner for the press, and every member of the Inner Temple community had been dragooned into attending church by Sir William Waring. The sole exception was Mrs Bugg, given leave to remain in her kitchen where the succulent dinner was in its last stages of preparation. When it came to a choice between a good dinner or godliness, Sir William's priorities were unhesitating. But all the other servants were there, including, Gabriel noted, that reluctant worshipper Joe Brockley. He looked rather surly. Presumably Hopkins and Vernon-Osbert had had a word to some effect.

Amongst the laundresses, the maids, the porters, the garden and kitchen staff, Gabriel spotted two new faces; one, a small pale girl, stood as close as she could to Meg the scullery maid, awestruck and bewildered in the new world in which she found herself. Meg, self-important, whispered instructions. It seemed that she was no longer at the bottom of the pecking order, thought Gabriel with satisfaction. He had a very soft spot for Meg. The other newcomer, a slim dark young man, far from being awed, looked merely bored. Gabriel guessed he was the new porter to whom Simmonds had referred. Judging from his expression, Gabriel thought that Simmonds might have his work cut out inculcating his own particular brand of subservience into this young man.

After the service, the staff dispersed to their duties and the Bar and their guests made their way to Hall. Its cavernous Gothic architecture was accentuated by the light of dozens of candles on sconces on the walls and in candelabra on the white damask-covered tables. Crystal and silver gleamed. Hothouse flowers tumbled luxuriantly. And from the panelled walls the painted faces of judges, yellowed with layers of restorative lacquer and kippered by the smoke of centuries of cigars, peered down from their gilt frames at those who had followed after them.

The distinguished members of the Inner Temple filed in to take their places at High Table, interspersed by their guests from Fleet Street. About to go to his seat, Gabriel spotted Meg's shadowy figure just visible though the serving hatch that opened onto the service lift to the basement kitchen. He made his way across the Hall, ignoring the Treasurer's disapproving glare.

'Good evening, Meg,' he said. 'Have you been promoted from the scullery?'

She nodded proudly. 'We have a new girl. Pearl.'

'And is she one?' Gabriel said.

Meg giggled. 'Too soon to tell, Sir Gabriel. But from now on I am to help Mrs Bugg in the kitchen and Pearl is to be at the sink.'

'Well done, Meg.'

'I shall be in trouble with Mrs Bugg if I do not get on with serving the soup.'

'And I shall be in trouble with the Treasurer if I do not prepare to drink it.'

Gabriel made his way back, oblivious to the raised eyebrows of his colleagues; really, Ward sometimes carried his eccentricities a little too far.

Sir William prided himself on his personal attention to seating plans. As in every aspect of his life, he always began with himself. Next to him, on either side, he had put the editor of *The Times* and one of that newspaper's journalists. Conservative, unionist, imperialist, these were men with whom he could spend a convivial evening. Then came representatives of the *Telegraph*, perhaps a little middle-class but sound enough. Further away he had placed the *Daily Chronicle*, a Liberal (and liberal) newcomer in Fleet Street of which he disapproved. And so, down the long sides of the table, the seating progressed in line with Sir William's view of the journalists' quality. Nearing the foot was the *Daily Mail*, regarded by him as unacceptably populist, followed by the sensationalist *Illustrated Police News*. At the very end he had put Mr Lionel Sullivan, editor and proprietor of the *Nation's Voice*, the most disreputable of the newspapers represented.

It was now known all over the Temple that Sir Edward Hopkins was once again to represent the *Nation's Voice*, this time in the keenly awaited litigation brought by Miss Topsy Tillotson, and so Sir William had placed him next to Sullivan. Their booming conversation, resounding with camaraderie, was already audible.

Interspersed between the newspaper men, Gabriel spotted Vernon-Osbert and thought with a pang how old he was looking, though resplendent still in the red cassock in which he had conducted the service, a snowy napkin tucked incongruously under his chin. Vivian Barton, he saw, was sitting next to the representative of the *Daily Chronicle*. Sir William did not approve of Barton's politics. Further down, also dressed in a cassock, sat Rupert Brandish. On the other side of the table, and still further away, was John Gibson, fair and sturdy, his immaculate gown, in contrast to the shabbier ones around him, betraying his junior status. Gabriel's gaze dwelled on the young man. Gibson's neighbour, he saw, wore the agonised expression of a man doing his best not to prompt any further plainly laboured conversation.

What had brought the boy to this of all professions? Gabriel wondered.

As he watched, Gibson looked up the table and, following his eyeline, Gabriel saw he was looking at Rupert Brandish. Brandish, with deliberation, removed his pocket watch and tapped the face, and Gibson nodded and looked away. Recalling rather uneasily his previous sighting of the two young men meeting in a way that seemed a little furtive, Gabriel wondered whether there was any significance to be attached to what had unmistakably been the passing of a message. Then he turned his attention to his own neighbours.

Had Sir William been aware that Gabriel had been instructed to act for Topsy Tillotson in the forthcoming libel trial, he would not have committed the impropriety of placing him next to Frank Holloway. But, since Gabriel lacked Sir Edward Hopkins' facility for self-publicising, Sir William was not aware. It now occurred to Gabriel that he had inadvertently put himself into what might be an embarrassing position, and he determined to seek topics of conversation as far as he could from the affairs of the *Nation's Voice*.

Once grace had been said and Mrs Bugg's first triumph of the evening put in front of him, Gabriel turned to his right as etiquette required.

Frank Holloway was casting a panic-stricken gaze at the rows of silver cutlery ranged to both sides of his plate, and Gabriel, following its direction, put down the sherry glass from which he was about to take a sip and instead picked up the spoon designated for the soup.

'Forgive me,' he said, 'I cannot wait to begin. Mrs Bugg's chestnut soup is one of her very special dishes.'

Holloway was torn between gratitude for the rescue and resentment that the need for it had so easily been detected. He picked up his own spoon sullenly. The chestnut soup, he discovered, was indeed wonderful.

'Is this your first visit to the Temple?' said Gabriel politely.

'Well it would be, wouldn't it?' Holloway's response was ungracious to say the least. 'You lot don't let the public in.'

Gabriel's equability remained unaltered.

'It is, after all, the home of many of us as well as our workplace; we treasure our privacy, I confess. But we endeavour to extend invitations to our neighbours occasionally and to be good hosts. And speaking of home, do I discern in your voice a trace of East Anglia?'

His genuine interest robbed the question of any of the patronising edge for which Holloway was always on the lookout. His ferrety face softened a little. 'Yes,' he said, 'do you know East Anglia?'

'Not well,' said Gabriel, 'but voices interest me and I notice them.' Welcoming a topic safely distant from the *Nation's Voice* and the upcoming litigation, he added, 'I have only been there once. I was taken to Hunstanton on the North Norfolk coast as a small boy, because it was thought my sickly lungs would benefit from sea air; I am not sure why since it was midwinter. But I recall the beauty of the grey, grey skies blending into the grey of the North Sea. And I remember seeing geese wheeling in unison above me in a great arc, which left me feeling very small. I think it was the first time that I perceived how little I mattered, watching those geese.'

He recalled now, sharply, that along with the sense of his own insignificance he had just described, had been another more private, obscure sense of conviction. He had been seven and was just recovering from the pneumonia that had delayed his going away to school for a term. Very soon, he would have to depart, leaving behind all that was familiar, and be pitched into the unknown world where big boys lived. He had previously been afraid, but in that moment had suddenly felt, standing on the shore and gazing up at the sky and the geese, a deep sense of self-sufficiency. It did not matter where he was sent. He, Gabriel Ward, unimportant though he was, had all he would ever need packed into his own body and mind, and he would always have it. He did not, and would never, need anyone else. He remembered that he had wanted to retain that wonderful solitary security. He had needed a rhythm through which to capture it, so he could recall it all his life like a musical refrain. Perhaps, he had thought, if he stepped only on the white pebbles on that beach littered with pebbles... 'Stop hopping about in that silly way and walk properly, if you please, Master Gabriel,' Nanny had said rather crossly...

Gabriel came to with a start and said apologetically to his neighbour: 'For a moment I was almost back there.'

But somehow, listening to the quiet discourse on the geese, Frank Holloway had forgotten the extreme discomfort of his second-hand evening clothes and about how he was holding his spoon, and remembered his pre-Lionel Sullivan days at home where there had been no sensations to chase nor human tragedies to exploit.

As exquisite turbot followed the chestnut soup, Gabriel's gentle, indifferent courtesy worked its magic.

'Tell me about yourself, Mr Holloway,' he said.

And Frank, to his own surprise, did. About how he had always wanted to be a journalist, about his arrival in Fleet Street and how overwhelming London had seemed, and about his father, who had been a land agent before he died. He had taught Frank to like history and gardening. His father had grown hydrangeas that won prizes in the village show. He would have loved to see the spectacular display that grew in Inner Temple garden.

'They are Brockley the gardener's pride and joy. An interesting flower,' said Gabriel. 'First cultivated in Japan. And moisture-loving as their Greek name tells us. *Hydros* – water, you know. And *angos*, vessel. So beautiful to look at it, it is hard to believe their blooms carry cyanide. Do you garden now, Mr Holloway?'

Frank Holloway shook his head. Brought back to the present day, his resentment returned. Did these nobs think the likes of him could garden in London? A fat chance of that when you lived in rooms in a backstreet in Mile End. He told Gabriel so, sharply.

'No gardening for me. The nearest I get to the country is the horses.'

'The horses?'

'The races. I like to bet. I go to the courses when I have the time.'

The turbot was replaced by the perfectly cooked beef and Gabriel turned, in accordance with etiquette, to the neighbour on his left-hand side while Frank Holloway's attention was claimed by his other neighbour, a judge senior in years though not status, and legendarily heavy-going as a dinner companion.

The long meal ended with the Inner Temple's best port and a speech from Sir William Waring of unparalleled hypocrisy, welcoming the press as their friends and neighbours with common interests in the pursuit of truth and of justice.

Released at last, Gabriel and Vivian Barton left at the same time and wandered together back through the Temple, insulated from the freezing cold by Sir William's port. Barton's cigar tip glowed in the darkness with a fluctuating radiance, like a little lighthouse, in time with his breathing.

'I heard a rumour,' he said, 'that you have landed the presently most sought-after brief in the Temple. Topsy Tillotson's libel action?'

'Yes,' said Gabriel resignedly, and with none of the triumph Barton would have felt at such a coup. 'And somewhat to my alarm, Chapman has told me that in view of the intensity of the public's interest in the wretched business, and the undesirable salaciousness of the case, the Lord Chief Justice has ordered expedition of the trial.'

'Has he though? When is it coming on?'

'In a week's time. As soon as the Law Courts open for the new term.'

Barton whistled. 'Bradley is certainly shaking things up a bit.' Lord Bradley was new in the post of Lord Chief Justice, successor to Lord Dunning, who had been tragically murdered. 'Not quite the lackadaisical old boy we were expecting.'

They had reached 4 King's Bench Walk. Barton tipped his hat. 'Well, good luck to you, old boy. But watch your step with Hopkins. He sometimes forgets he was born a gentleman.'

As Gabriel turned to mount the steps, Barton detained him. 'Any developments on the other matter?' he said hesitantly.

'No,' said Gabriel. 'I will take up your suggestion to contact Simon Rawlings' family if only to rule out any connection. But I was waiting until the festivities were absolutely over. I did not wish to trouble old people with an even older sadness. And for now, thank God, all has gone quiet.'

It was the very next day that all hell broke loose.

14

The morning was freezing cold, too cold now for snow, the ground hard with ice. A strong wind was blowing with Arctic persistence. Huddled into his thick overcoat, Gabriel made his way to his chambers. In front of him, a lone piece of paper blew, an escaped newspaper flyer from Fleet Street tumbled by the wind along the frozen paving. Gabriel bent automatically to pick it up. *Tidy habits, tidy mind*, Nanny had always said. The headline jumped out at him. So great was his surprise that he tottered for a moment in a strong gust.

GHASTLY STORY!
SKELETONS IN THE TEMPLE CUPBOARD!
SENSATIONAL ANONYMOUS PARCELS!
ONLY IN THE NATION'S VOICE!

Gabriel blinked and looked again, and consternation followed amazement.

And then whilst he was still assimilating the implications, there came into view, distraught, her apron askew, Mrs Jenkins, Reverend Master Vernon-Osbert's housekeeper. With one look at her face, all other thoughts fled and Gabriel stuffed the paper into his pocket and broke into a trot towards her. She gripped his arm, past speech, and urged him along. In silence they ran, as fast as the icy ground permitted, to the Reverend Master's house. Its front door was open, spilling light from the hall into the darkness of the morning. And, still silent, they stood panting in the hall until at last Mrs Jenkins recovered her breath and said,

'I have called Dr Newman from the Strand, and Sir William. You – you go in, Sir Gabriel. Mr Rupert is with him.'

And Gabriel, his hand on the brass doorknob of the familiar library, knew with a dual sensation of certainty and denial what he would find.

In the library, the fire had already been lit, and beside it, in his blue embroidered dressing gown sat Vernon-Osbert in his wing chair, staring into the eternity to which he had looked forward all his life. On his lap, anxious, protective, lay the enormous furry mound that was Delphinium. Beside the chair was an upturned cardboard box, one foot square in all dimensions, its lid beside it and its contents askew on the carpet. There it lay, horrible, a little shrivelled coiled piece of flesh, its shape unmistakable, and tucked in some tissue paper beside it a white card inserted so that it was plainly visible. It read: *A word in your ear.*

Rupert Brandish stood motionless by Vernon-Osbert's chair and Gabriel, seeing that he was praying, was motionless also. The silence was almost palpable, death a presence in the quiet library. The chessmen stood still upon the table. The last book lay open at a page that its reader would not turn. And then, as the clock ticked on and the minutes passed, at last the room filled with the people who brought normality to the aftermath.

The doctor confirmed what they already knew. 'Heart gave out. Very fragile but should have been good for a little while yet. The shock, you know, of that obscenity. What the devil is it all about?' He looked to Sir William. 'If this was sent by someone who knew the old man's condition, Sir William, there is only one word for it. M—'

Sir William Waring leaped into action.

'We are very grateful, Dr Newman, for your attendance at so early an hour. But there – always reliable and so valuable to the Inner Temple, always there to be called on, and equally we know you value our loyalty to you. You may leave this to us now and you must, of course, send in your full account to the Collector as always.' He added suavely, 'Your *full* account. Mrs Jenkins will see you out.'

When the doctor had gone, Sir William turned to Gabriel.

'We will discuss this in my rooms, Ward… Reverend Brandish… in half an hour.' And without a second glance at the still figure by the fire, he left.

Gabriel and Rupert Brandish stood silent for a few moments and then Brandish, visibly bracing himself, restored the grisly human remnant lying on the rug to its box and replaced the lid, and Gabriel approached the body and very gently lifted the cat from beneath the caress of the dead hands and lowered her to the floor. But Delphinium, suddenly galvanised, jack-knifed in his arms and shot up onto his chest, claws scrabbling frantically for a hold in the deep cashmere of his coat. Reaching his shoulder, she clung on, her huge furry head butting against Gabriel's thin cheek.

Under the mounds of fur, she was trembling. Her bones were sparrow-fragile. Gabriel attempted to disentangle her, but still she clung frantically, her claws extended into the fold of the collar. Gabriel sighed. He always found the vulnerability of others difficult. But at least she did not need a handkerchief.

'Very well, Delphinium,' he said resignedly, 'you may come home with me for a saucer of milk, and later we will ask Mrs Jenkins or Mrs Bugg in the Inner Temple kitchen to find you a kind home amongst the staff.'

But Delphinium knew better.

The interview with Waring began predictably.

'I need not tell you that discretion is paramount,' was his opening gambit.

Gabriel reluctantly extracted from his pocket the crumpled flyer, almost forgotten by him in the tragedy of the last hour, and put it on the desk at which the Treasurer sat. He braced himself for the onslaught.

'I fear it is too late for that, Sir William.'

Waring stared silently at the sensational headlines and then, scarlet with rage, began a diatribe of incoherent accusation. Rupert Brandish looked on with some astonishment but Gabriel had seen these tantrums before and cut incisively across the Treasurer's outburst.

'Sir William, it is extremely unfortunate but it has happened. Of paramount importance now is finding the man who is sending these parcels. If, as I believe, he is connected to this institution, he could not have been unaware of Vernon-Osbert's fragility. The doctor was correct. To send a human body part deliberately to such a vulnerable man turns these parcels from a horrible campaign into a very serious crime. Perhaps even m—'

'Do not use that word!' said Sir William.

'—murder, if it was intended to kill him. Or at the very least, manslaughter,' said Gabriel inexorably. 'If there was ever doubt that a crime had been committed, there is no longer any. And if I may respectfully say so, you must accept that this is a matter of which the police should be immediately informed.'

Rupert Brandish intervened. 'I have already done so. I sent one of the maids to find an errand boy in Fleet Street.'

Sir William Waring stared at the young cleric in enraged astonishment.

'You have done what? How dare you? What right do you have to invite the police into the Inn?'

Brandish looked bewildered. '*Invite*, Sir William? I found the Reverend Master dead in tragic and extraordinary circumstances; an apparently human body part on the ground beside him. What other course could I have taken?'

Gabriel, seeing the Treasurer's mounting wrath, stepped in.

'Mr Brandish has been with us for only a matter of weeks, Sir William. He cannot be expected to have absorbed all the arcane traditions and laws that govern our little world.' And turning to the bewildered young man, 'The Inner Temple prides itself on its independence, Mr Brandish. It is quite free from the jurisdiction of the City of London unless it chooses to submit to it. The police work here in collaboration with our own porters, and then only at our request.'

'And only on the instructions of the Treasurer,' said Waring pointedly.

There was a heavy knock on the door and, before Waring could respond, it was opened to reveal Simmonds the head porter, bursting with outraged dignity, and close behind him, Detective Inspector Hughes of the City of London Police accompanied by four policemen of varying rank and status, one of whom, looking as though he would much prefer to be elsewhere and assiduously avoiding Gabriel's eye, was Constable Wright.

Sir William, in the face of this invasion, and conscious as always of the importance of public reputation, capitulated and accepted the inevitable. Hastily turning adversity into advantage, he now greeted the intrusion of the City of London Police with a suavity that suggested they were there at his invitation. The whole story was unfolded by him, and at its conclusion, Hughes turned decisively to the policemen standing respectfully by.

'Start making enquiries.'

'Discreetly!' wailed Sir William Waring at their disappearing backs.

As the room emptied, the Treasurer gestured Gabriel to remain. Historically, Sir William picked up the flyer, tore it in two and cast it into the wastepaper basket.

'This was plainly printed before the events of this morning, or it would not have missed the opportunity to refer to the death of our Reverend Master,' he said. 'And it was printed after the dinner last night when those contemptible rats from Fleet Street drank the Inn's port and pledged eternal fellowship. God knows what they will make of Vernon-Osbert's death. It will have to be announced, of course. *Peacefully, in his library...* something of that sort. They will not know he, too, received one of these ghastly packages. Who in God's name talked last night?'

'Well,' said Gabriel reluctantly, 'I knew. You knew. Sir Edward Hopkins knew.'

'Hopkins would not betray the Inn. He hopes one day to succeed me as Treasurer.'

Gabriel chuckled inwardly at the naivety of this latter observation.

'Who else?' barked Sir William.

Gabriel hesitated, recalling Wright's anxious face. The young constable was now officially involved; no need to mention the earlier meetings. 'I had mentioned it to Sir Vivian Barton,' he said cautiously.

'Barton? *Barton?* What possessed you? What the hell has it to do with him?'

'Really, Sir William, I would prefer you to moderate your language a little. I have had no opportunity to inform you that he, too, has received a body part; a toe, accompanied by a card that reads: *Toe the line.* As I have already told you, I am becoming convinced that the body from which these parts were removed is somewhere in the Inner Temple. We have an expert medical view that they are several years old. It seemed to me logical therefore to look for any disappearances from our small community dating back several years. Statistically there could not be many. It seemed as sensible a place as any to start. Indeed, I asked you whether you had any suggestions, as I did the servants, and I am following them up. I have discovered a maid left – in disgrace it is true, but unexpectedly. A porter left and a theft was discovered thereafter. Both of them disappeared without trace. Then I thought, as indeed you did when you mentioned to me an old mystery, of Simon Rawlings...'

'Enough.' Sir William's voice was sharp with anger. 'I can tell you quite categorically, Ward, that none of these historic events is of any relevance to the present matter. When I authorised your investigations, I did not intend you to interfere in incidents best forgotten. Good God, do you want the Inner Temple's reputation to be besmirched any further in the gutter press? I wish to hear no more of any of these matters.'

'But, Sir William—'

'I said, no more. I forbid it!'

'Forbid, Sir William?' Gabriel gripped the side of his chair, and unseen, involuntarily, his finger traced a familiar little pattern on the underside, and with the pattern came confidence. He found, in the face of Vernon-Osbert's death, that he was not quite such a reluctant detective after all. And he heard his own voice, as he sometimes did in court, and wondered, as he always did, whether its quiet authority really emanated from him.

'A good man has died,' he said. 'Do not speak to me, Sir William, of reputation or forbidding. Vernon-Osbert died, after this dreadful incident, in the Temple, his beloved home. *My* beloved home. And I will make all the investigations necessary to find the man who killed him.'

There was a silence. In the course of it, Sir William recalled two things. The first was the fact that the occupancy of Gabriel's residential rooms in 4 King's Bench Walk lay in the gift of the Treasurer. He was minded, as he had done in the past, to remind Gabriel of that fact. He opened his mouth to do so. But his second thought was less helpful to him. It was not without reason that Gabriel was almost universally respected and trusted in the

Temple, as a great intellect, as a compelling advocate, and as a decent, albeit eccentric, man. If anyone could provide a balance to the presence of policemen in the Temple, it was Gabriel. Sir William reluctantly adopted a more temperate line.

'Very well, very well. I merely *request* you to confine yourself to the gentle questioning we agreed upon, to keep the police at arm's length from the private business of the Temple, and not to waste everyone's time on irrelevancies.'

Satisfied that he had had the last word, the Treasurer concluded the interview.

And Gabriel was left with food for thought. It seemed to him that Sir William had been not only angry but afraid. Why should that be? He was rather pleased to discover that, far from deterring him, Sir William's attitude had strengthened his determination to follow up these lines of enquiry. And furthermore, there was another one, relating to last night's dinner, that he had put to the back of his mind in his distress at Vernon-Osbert's death.

There was scarcely time that day for Gabriel to mourn. But running through the rest of it with all its activities had been memories of the old man; of their annual game of chess, the scholarly talks, Vernon-Osbert's gentle authority over the Temple Church, his joy in his God, of their Christmases. Yes, Gabriel thought, in sudden reluctant recognition, and, I suppose, of love. Or if not love, as close to it as I can imagine.

First of all, he had had to return to his rooms. There had been Delphinium to deal with. She was where he had left her before his interview with the Treasurer, sitting contemplatively by his fire with a now-empty Spode saucer beside her. Draped unco-operatively around his shoulders once more, like an enormous fur stole, she had seemed resigned when he deposited her with Mrs Bugg in the Inner Temple kitchens.

'Bless her,' Mrs Bugg had said inevitably, and just as inevitably offered solace with food. 'Mrs Jenkins is in no state to look after her. Quite gone to pieces and being looked after herself by the poor dear Reverend's maids. Delphinium will be all right with us. She shall have a little piece of the Treasurer's special turbot, shan't you, Delphinium?'

Delphinium had looked inscrutable.

With a quite unaccountable twinge of guilt on leaving her, Gabriel had first taken himself for a short walk. The dinner for the press seemed years before but had left him with a question in his mind.

Under the curious gaze of Simmonds, he turned right out of the Great Gate into Fleet Street and made his way slowly down, passing on his way the narrow alley which led to the seedy doorway of the *Nation's Voice* offices. He peered curiously down it and, rather to his embarrassment, saw Frank Holloway, coat collar turned up, hat low over his eyes and cigarette in his mouth, a copy of the *Racing Post* in his hand, sitting on the doorstep. On seeing Gabriel, he got up.

'What do you want with me?' he asked aggressively.

Gabriel recovered his equilibrium and raised his eyebrows, just a little. *Manners makyth man*, Nanny had always said.

'Good morning, Mr Holloway. I was merely passing and, recalling our meeting yesterday evening, glanced into the alleyway. Why should you think I want anything with you?'

Holloway grinned. 'The *Nation's Voice* has shaken the Inner Temple up a bit this morning, I imagine. I think you would like to know my source.'

Gabriel looked steadily at him, as he did at witnesses, for just long enough to disconcert.

'I am a lawyer, Mr Holloway. I do not ask your source since I would not like to give you the satisfaction of refusing to tell me. As is, of course, your right. But I confess, I am a little disappointed. I thought we had a pleasant evening together.'

If he sought to shame the man, he was unsuccessful.

'And I am a journalist,' said Holloway sharply. 'If a nob asks me to dinner and afterwards I have a good story, I will print it.'

Gabriel lifted his hat and bowed. 'I wish you good morning,' he said.

And leaving Holloway on the pavement, he continued down Fleet Street to accomplish his original mission, turning right into Bouverie Street and so down Temple Avenue to the Embankment. He recalled with nostalgia the days when he was a pupil barrister and the Inner Temple gardens had run down straight to the bank of the Thames. Was this wide road with its teeming traffic and incessant noise and piles of horse manure really what men called progress?

He walked slowly past the railings that enclosed the Temple Gardens, leading up to the loved and familiar buildings of the Inner Temple, and then into the Temple again down Middle Temple Lane. In this way he had circumnavigated the entire Inner Temple – and satisfied himself of what he had the previous night suspected. Such was the angle of its tucked away position, that not the most athletic monkey, not the tallest giraffe nor even the most determined journalist, would be able to see, from anywhere outside the Temple, Brockley's prized hydrangea border, whether dormant as now or in full bloom. There was only one possibility left, and to eliminate that Gabriel would have to wait for the right opportunity.

Thoughtfully, he returned to his chambers in 1 Crown Office Row and with the absolute single-mindedness that characterised his preparation of any case, submerged himself for many hours in the law of defamation. The Topsy Tillotson trial loomed now, a mere six days away, and the odds were against her.

15

Returning home at six o'clock, Gabriel had seen a shadowy mound on the doorstep of 4 King's Bench Walk and, hastening towards it, had discovered it to be an apparently inert Delphinium who, with a sudden and astonishing agility, shot through his door when he opened it.

It was nearly four hours later, when he was sitting by his fire and Delphinium was reclining smugly across a platform consisting of six tottering piles of the *Encyclopaedia Britannica*, that he was startled by a sharp rap on his outer door. He opened the inner one, a rather lengthy procedure since he had difficulties with all doors. They stood in his mind for conflicting things; for shutting out demons; for shutting himself in with them. For blissful security; for claustrophobic confinement.

From the other side of the outer door, he heard Constable Wright's reassuring voice.

'Only me, sir.'

The policeman could not be expected to know that Gabriel's delay was not caused by any conventional fear of a late-night guest but by the compulsive need to open the door in a ritualised way. He waited patiently while Gabriel opened the second, outer door, and came eagerly over the threshold at the gesture of invitation. In the drawing room, he spotted Delphinium.

'Have you adopted her, sir?' Wright said with a grin.

'Certainly not. I found her on the doorstep. She will return to Mrs Bugg tomorrow.'

Delphinium yawned.

'I am sorry to disturb you so late, sir.'

'Surely you are not still making enquiries for Detective Inspector Hughes at this time in the evening?'

'Oh, no, sir, we are only halfway through. Nothing much to report so far on that front. The box arrived like the others, just sitting on the doorstep. The two maids say they don't know nothing about it. Mrs Jenkins took it in to the Reverend. Apparently, he had already said he was feeling a little unwell. She thought it was something that might cheer him up. She is in a right old state now. We begin again tomorrow morning. I have been home, but then I discovered something, sir, and I just could not wait.'

He drew from his large pocket a paper bag and from it a colourful tin upon which was emblazoned *McVitie & Price of Edinburgh & London*, and underneath that *Digestive Biscuits*.

'Do you know of digestive biscuits, sir?' he asked rather doubtfully. He had learned that Gabriel's knowledge of everyday domestic items ranged from encyclopaedic to non-existent and was entirely unpredictable.

'Indeed, yes. Nanny used to buy them from the chemist when I was a small boy. Along with peppermints. She suffered very much from dyspepsia.'

'Oh, but these aren't the same,' said Wright, rather incoherently. 'These are digestives made specially by McVitie's to a secret recipe, as a sweet biscuit. They are my favourite and my mother buys them for me. She gave me two tonight with my cocoa and it suddenly came to me.'

He opened the tin and thrust it under Gabriel's nose. 'Smell, sir!'

Gabriel inhaled deeply and, after a moment, exclaimed, 'Well *done*, Constable!'

'I am right, sir, aren't I? It is the smell from the boxes.'

'It is indeed. But why? The boxes were not marked as McVitie's boxes and biscuits come in tins. Why should anybody put them in boxes?'

'I hoped perhaps you could link it in some way with the Temple?'

Gabriel shook his head firmly. 'I am quite sure that no bought biscuit would ever show its face in the Temple. All are hand-made in the Temple kitchens. Mrs Bugg's ginger shortbreads are legendary. I am not sure I have ever been served a biscuit of any other kind. But linked to the Temple or not, you are undoubtedly correct.'

'It doesn't seem to have got us much further,' said Wright, a little deflated.

Gabriel wagged a reproving finger. 'It is another little piece in the jigsaw. Psychology is all we need.' But even he could not help wondering where psychology could lead him via a digestive biscuit.

Wright knew that Sir Gabriel set store by this new-fangled word, the meaning of which he could not quite recall; something to do with people's minds, he seemed to remember. He held out the biscuit tin philosophically. 'Would you like one, sir?'

'I would,' said Gabriel. He added, 'And I can do better than cocoa. With your digestive you shall have a digestif.' And negotiating the books piled around it, he fetched from a cupboard a bottle of brandy and two glasses.

The two men sat companionably. Into the silence, and after his third biscuit, Wright gave a sigh of satisfaction. 'Almost perfect. If only someone would sell them covered in chocolate.'

Gabriel smiled. 'No doubt someone will, one day.'

The faintly conspiratorial atmosphere engendered by the lateness of the hour and by the brandy had made Wright relax.

'Thank you for not letting on to Detective Inspector Hughes that we had already done some investigating, sir.'

'What are friends for, Constable?'

The policeman's endearing blush surged up his face once more.

'How did you become officially involved?' asked Gabriel curiously.

'Well, sir, Detective Hughes is very kind to me. He knows I would like to be in the Detective Division and they wanted a few constables to do a bit of the leg work on this one. And they knew you and me had... we had...'

'Collaborated?'

'Well, yes, sir, when the Lord Chief Justice was murdered. And as a result, I had got to know the Temple a bit. So here I am, and I am to continue to investigate, sir, and now of course I can tell you what I discover. It is quite official.'

Gabriel nodded gently. He was well aware that Constable Wright liked to feel official. It made the next request a little difficult.

'There is one other matter, Constable Wright. I do realise we now have a major investigation on our hands, but I also have a client whose case is shortly to be tried. She has lost touch with a young suitor and it is causing her great distress. His name is George and he is an apprentice printer working somewhere in Fleet Street and living with his mother in Smithfield. Would it be a great imposition by me to ask you to make some discreet enquiries whilst you are on your beat?'

Wright looked doubtful. 'I don't know what Detective Inspector Hughes would think of that, sir. Police Regulations expressly prohibit gossiping. I am not on duty to help young ladies find lost sweethearts. Can't she make her own enquiries, sir?'

He wondered whether perhaps Sir Gabriel did not know about the regrettable way some young men behaved to young ladies. 'It sounds to me,' he added cynically, 'as if he may not want to be found by her if he has lost touch. I should tell her to find another one, sir.'

Gabriel shook his head. 'You underrate me, Constable Wright. I have spent a lifetime in the Law Courts and I am aware that young men are sometimes unreliable lovers. But this young woman— Well, this seems to me a little different. And she cannot make her own enquiries. She is – rather well known.'

'Well known, sir?'

'She is an actress. In confidence, Constable Wright, she is called Topsy Tillotson.'

Constable Wright behaved in much the same way as Chapman had when Topsy had entered the clerks' room. His jaw dropped, his eyes popped, he spluttered with incredulity and excitement.

'Blimey, sir! *Topsy Tillotson?* My word! She is a corker! Are you doing her case against that newspaper?'

'I am,' said Gabriel. 'And I do not wish her to be distracted from it by her present unhappiness. However, nor do I wish you to incur the wrath of Detective Inspector Hughes. Do not concern yourself about it, Constable Wright. It was merely a thought.'

Wright stumbled over his words in his rapid volte-face. Sir Gabriel's case load, previously thought by Wright to be of unmitigated dullness, had suddenly acquired glamour. 'Of course I will have a nose round! Blimey, sir… *Topsy Tillotson!* George, did you say? You tell the young lady if this George is there to be found, I'll find him for her.'

The mystery of the boxes lingered, like the sweet smell they had retained, at the back of Gabriel's mind. The next day, Saturday, anticipating his neighbour would be at home, he knocked on John Gibson's door.

'I see you have moved in,' he said courteously. 'And now you have settled, I felt I should come and say "welcome". We are such close neighbours,' he added, gesturing across the short landing to his own rooms.

The young man opened his door wider. 'Indeed yes, Sir Gabriel, p-p-please come in. I intended t to call on you t-to t-tell you that your cat was sitting on the d-doorstep all d-day. I feared she might b-be ill.'

'She is not my cat.' Gabriel said it firmly. 'She was poor Vernon-Osbert's. She is to live with Mrs Bugg in the Inner Temple kitchen. I will remind her of the fact.'

'It was very sad news,' said Gibson politely. 'I have been such a short time in the Temple, but I gather Vernon-Osbert was much loved.'

He ushered Gabriel into his drawing room.

Gabriel's attention was immediately caught by the light dancing on a display clustered on a table in front of a window. There stood a little city formed of five Wardian cases, bronze-framed, glass-enclosed, each with a square base but each different, turreted, domed or pinnacled, topped by tiny bronze finials. In each case was a miniature landscape of rocks and Gothic ruins, with crumbling walls and arches. And in each ruin, rooted in a bed of moss, was a fern, translucently green, fronded, trembling under the weight of the condensation clinging to it. This, then, thought Gabriel, is Gibson's collection. The boxes would have been an admirable fit in which to transport them.

'You are a pteridologist?'

'Yes, since I was quite a young b-b-boy.'

'They are exquisite,' said Gabriel, peering closer at the labels on each case inscribed with the name of the specimen. 'I fear my knowledge of ferns is very general. These are all filmy ferns, are they not? Hymenophyllaceae?'

Gibbons beamed. 'Yes indeed. The leaf t-t-tissue is only one cell thick. That gives them their shining quality. They look almost magical, d-d-do they not? All these are English b-b-but my d-d-dream is to travel to other parts of the world to find them.' He walked over to his desk and spun the globe that stood on it. The beam faded. 'P-Perhaps one d-d-day,' he said.

And then, abruptly, 'Are you happy b-being a b-b-b-barrister, Sir Gabriel?'

Gabriel hesitated.

'Forgive me,' said the young man. 'I d-d-did not mean to b-b-be imp-p-pertinent.'

'I did not think that. I was just about to say that I could not imagine doing anything else,' said Gabriel with his whimsical little smile, 'when I wondered if that was, in fact, an answer to your question. But it is the only answer I have, Mr Gibson.' He nodded towards the Wardian cases. 'I am like your ferns. I have had a safe little world created for me, and I could not survive outside it. Within it, I flourish.'

'I envy you, sir.' The young man looked wistfully towards the ferns. 'And them. B-b-but I d-d-do not want to b-b-be *safe*. I want to t-travel and collect.'

Gabriel hesitated; but then Gibson seemed to be asking mutely for something else. He said, 'I do not think the Bar is a happy career for someone who—'

'Stammers?' said Gibson sharply.

'I was not going to say that. I was going to say, for someone whose heart and inclinations lie elsewhere; though perhaps it is also true to say someone whose aptitudes may lie elsewhere.'

Gibson shrugged. 'Neither my heart nor my inclinations nor my aptitudes in any single respect have led me t-t-to my p-p-p-present circumstances, Sir Gabriel.'

Gabriel wondered where Miss Amelia Waring came into the story. The young man continued to spin the globe as if, by so doing, he could step into it.

Through an open door five square boxes were ominously visible. Gabriel wished that politeness did not preclude his going over and sniffing them.

'The boxes in which you transported the cases... they are a useful size. May I ask where you obtained them?'

To his astonishment, Gibson flushed a deep brick red. 'I d-d-don't know. I mean I— Rup— I mean B-B-B—' His voice became strangulated with effort and he began again. 'B-Brandish... oh, I cannot recall exactly.'

And the odd thing was, thought Gabriel when back in his own rooms, that it was the mention of the boxes that seemed to upset his neighbour so much, yet they were openly piled up in the hall. The change in his demeanour had been so striking at the very mention of them, that it must mean something. But what?

He pondered on the boxes. All identical. The box, the only one in Christmas wrapping, given to Sir William Waring just before Christmas. The one in which Brandish had given an innocent, real Christmas present to Vernon-Osbert. Those sent, after Christmas, to Sir Edward Hopkins and to Sir Vivian Barton. Those that John Gibson had used during his move. And then the one that had hastened poor Vernon-Osbert's death. And amongst Gibson's confused obfuscation had definitely been Rupert Brandish's name. The obvious person to ask was Brandish himself. Gabriel recalled with unease the meeting he had witnessed through his window a few days ago, and the message covertly conveyed between the two men at the dinner the night before. Could they mean anything?

He found that he did not want to think ill of Rupert Brandish. But nor, he was obliged to admit to himself, did he want to give him any warning about the investigation. That most charming young man, who had expressed such appreciation for the Reverend Master's house. Could the obvious admiration for Vernon-Osbert and his life that he had shown at Christmas have tipped over into something darker? Would he, young though he was, now be asked to step into the Reverend Master's shoes? And could he possibly already have been envisaging such a future at that happy luncheon? Gabriel wondered how Mrs Jenkins would react to the situation, and along with the thought came another resonance from his conversation with Wright the night before. He must find the time to visit Mrs Jenkins.

He turned in his careful mind to the question of the body. Whose had it been, and where was it kept? He was no nearer, it seemed, to resolving the mysteries, if there were any, of the three disappearances that had occurred in the Temple. They had all happened around the same time but nonetheless seemed unconnected, easily explained events. The only mystery lay in Sir William Waring's fury at the prospect of them being investigated. Was Gabriel's instinct that the body was in the Temple a reliable one?

He was jolted from his reverie by a frantic scrabbling at his door. Unwrapping himself from his tartan lap rug, he navigated his piles of books and opened it. Delphinium shot in.

'Delphinium,' said Gabriel, 'I must ask you to refrain from this behaviour. You have a satisfactory home with Mrs Bugg. You have a warm kitchen fire. You are being daily indulged with portions of the Treasurer's personal turbot. I am a busy man. At the risk of discourtesy, I wish to be left alone.'

Ignoring him, Delphinium took a flying leap onto her pile of *Encyclopaedia Britannica* and in so doing dislodged a book from the top of a neighbouring pile consisting of *Scrutton on Charterparties and Bills of Lading*, a battered copy of *Madame Bovary* and a shiny new one of Mr Rudyard Kipling's novel *Kim*. The fallen volume lay open at Gabriel's feet and, tutting, he picked it up. The volume comprised the teachings of Solon, the great Ancient Greek lawmaker. The first sentence on the open page caught Gabriel's eye. *'Analyse the unknown based on the known.'*

He sighed. 'I realise you intend to be helpful, Delphinium,' he said, 'but perhaps you could contrive to be a little less obscure?'

But nonetheless, when he resumed his reflections, he analysed what he knew. In truth, he thought, the only facts I know are unbelievable. Someone connected to the Temple had access to a dead human body; and that someone had the horrible resolve to sever from it individual parts and put them in boxes that smelled very strongly of digestive biscuits (of all things!), and send the boxes presumably with the intention of causing terrible distress. And had as a result killed Vernon-Osbert. Could he or she have foreseen this terrible consequence? And if so, what motive could they have had?

16

The whole country was agog over the sensational headlines relating to the anonymous parcels received in the Temple, and speculation raged as to the recipients. These, the *Nation's Voice* had promised, thereby ensuring the maximum number of editions would be sold, would be revealed one by one over the next days. It carried out this promise with a series of headlines, each featuring the words of the notes delivered with the parcel – *Can I give you a hand?... Don't put your foot in it... Toe the line* – followed by salacious theories as to the motives behind the messages.

A furore of public speculation mounted and it was widely agreed that this was punishment for the Temple's hubris. The Inn had always fostered its perceived pre-eminence, the privacy of its estate in the heart of London, the unrivalled beauty of its buildings and gardens. All this rendered it vulnerable. It had turned up its nose at those it regarded as the common herd; and the common herd delighted in this story of scandal within its gates. The *Nation's Voice* jumped off the news stands and once each revelation became public, it was picked up by Fleet Street at all levels from the respectable broadsheets to the most sensational rags. Sir William Waring grew increasingly enraged; newspaper reporters, many in Sir William's view very far from gentlemen, felt entitled to seek statements from him, and his beloved institution became the subject of the most lurid speculation. In what he felt was the cruellest blow of all there came a note of commiseration, from his counterpart, the Treasurer of

Middle Temple. This, whether or not it was in fact kindly meant, struck Sir William as not only a firm distancing at a time when there should be a united front, but also as little short of gloating.

However, in one regard, the Temple, Inner and Middle, both under the pastoral care of the same Reverend Master, was united and with them the poor who lived in the vicinity of its gates. Everywhere there was sadness and shock; everywhere the kind devout old Reverend Master Vernon-Osbert was grieved for; and over both the Inner and Middle Temple their flags bearing their emblems, the Pegasus of the Inner Temple and the Lamb and Flag of the Middle Temple, flew at half-mast.

No one, however, save for those present in the aftermath of the death and the City of London Police, was aware that, in addition to those reported by the newspapers, Vernon-Osbert had been the recipient of one of the ghastly parcels.

The police enquiries were continuing. Discreet questioning was conducted amongst servants and barristers alike. Little helpful information was forthcoming. Searches were made, but they revealed nothing.

Police Constable Wright, resuming his beat on the first Monday morning of the New Year, was almost relieved to be back in the familiar daily routine of patrolling Fleet Street, dull though it was. It gave him the chance to think, and so absorbed was he in the mystery of the body parts, that he was halfway through his shift when he recalled Topsy's George. He was by then in the centre of Fleet Street with newspaper offices to all sides and thought he might as well begin at once. No young man lucky enough to be walking out with Topsy Tillotson could have much motive for wanting to disappear, Constable Wright thought, not likely he couldn't! Wright rather fancied himself playing Cupid to an actress. Perhaps there had been some sort of misunderstanding and he would be the one to sort it out.

In his methodical way he began to make enquiries, plunging down the basement steps to the vast galleried rooms that held the printing presses of the Fleet Street newspapers. Here amidst the deafening rattle, barging his way past men wheeling teetering piles of paper on trolleys and others in ink-stained overalls, he yelled at each foreman above the din, 'Got any Georges working here?'

Later he reported back to Gabriel.

'I found six Georges among the Fleet Street printers, sir.'

'Oh, dear. I fear you must have had a lot of trouble chasing them all up.'

Wright grinned. 'Not really, sir. Three of them were over sixty. Of the remaining three, one had complications set in when he lost three fingers in an accident with one of the presses and has been in hospital for some weeks. One is married with three youngsters, and although of course that does not rule him out as Miss Tillotson's suitor, he doesn't seem that type at all, very shy and steady like, and no oil painting neither. Lives out in Kent and travels in and out every day so all in all, sir...'

'Indeed yes. And the last one?' Gabriel asked hopefully.

'The last one sounds a good bet, sir. A young man, only works at the print room on Saturdays and Sundays, goes in to sweep the floors apparently. And lives with his mother in one of them alleys beside Smithfield Meat Market. Good-looking young lad, dark hair, blue eyes, would charm the birds off the trees, the foreman said. He gave me an address. I will go and look him up, sir.'

'Thank you,' said Gabriel thoughtfully. 'That certainly sounds as though it might be our man.' Smithfield Market was very close to St Bartholomew's. His recent visit to the hospital made him feel reasonably comfortable about another excursion in the vicinity. Although he thought wistfully of his immaculate trial notes open upon his desk, he said, 'I think perhaps I had better go myself. I fear there will be some explaining to this George that only I can do.'

And then, unable to resist Wright's expression, which put him forcibly in mind of a dog denied a walk, and gladder of company than he cared to admit even to himself, Gabriel added, 'As Nanny would say, no time like the present. Perhaps you would care to accompany me, Constable Wright?'

They went that afternoon to the address Wright had been given: a dark alley lined with the back entrances of public houses and shops, and with the mean front doors of tiny dwellings wedged between them. Dustbins and barrels lined the narrow walkways and washing hung from upstairs windows. A smell of blood and offal from the nearby market pervaded the air. Wright checked his notebook.

'Number nine. Must be the other end.'

Number nine was dingy but respectable. An attempt had been made to scrub the step, and the tiny basement area, unlike some of its neighbours', was clear of rubbish.

'Somebody tries a bit,' observed Wright. He knocked hard and almost before he had finished, the door opened.

A young woman stood there, an apron over her low-cut dress. She was incongruously and heavily made up and her luxuriant, improbably golden hair was pinned up on the top of her head. Her sleeves were rolled up to reveal shapely arms covered in bracelets and soap suds.

She looked sharply at Wright in his uniform but then her glance went past him to Gabriel, standing behind, and her face lit up with recognition.

'Well, I never!' she exclaimed. 'It's you again from the other night, isn't it, dearie?'

Wright felt a burning mortification wash over him followed by a sense of disbelief. There was only one way a gentleman met a woman like this and Wright knew all about it. The degradation, the suffering, the police courts and all. The young policeman turned to Gabriel looking as bewildered as a child whose trust is suddenly fractured.

'It is Miss Bunch, is it not?' said Gabriel, and Wright saw, with a rush of relief, that he was raising his top hat and giving his characteristic little bow with his familiar imperturbable courtesy.

'Miss Rosie Bunch appears in Miss Tillotson's show, Constable Wright.'

Rosie Bunch had recovered from her surprise and now looked cautiously at Wright.

'Is Topsy all right?'

'Indeed yes,' said Gabriel.

'Has George been doing something he shouldn't?'

'Not at all,' Gabriel assured her. 'Although it is George we have called about.' He peered carefully at Rosie. It was hard to tell under the make-up, but she did not look old enough to be George's mother. 'He is your brother perhaps?'

'My brother? George? He's my sister's boy. This is her house. I'm just visiting.'

She opened the door wider and gestured them into the kitchen, directly off the street. The tiny room was sparsely furnished with a cheap deal table and chairs. It seemed spotless although, despite the faint glow from the range, soulless. The walls were bare of pictures and the wooden floor of any covering. The whole scene was redolent of poverty.

'I wonder if we might have a word with him?' said Gabriel.

'With George? He's at school.'

It was Wright who broke the ensuing puzzled silence with a comfortable chuckle. 'Well now,' he said, 'there has been some misunderstanding, miss. We are looking for a George who works at the *Capital Daily* printing press.'

'He sweeps up there on a Saturday and Sunday to help his mother a bit,' said Rosie.

'How old is he?' asked Wright.

'Ten.'

Wright's grin grew broader. 'I just asked for a young man called George, so I suppose I cannot blame the foreman. I don't know if he misunderstood or was pulling my leg. I'm sorry you have been troubled...'

As he spoke, there emerged from the back room a young woman. Like Rosie she wore an apron but the dress beneath it was worn and old. Her shoes were trodden down at the heels. She was far too thin for her sturdy frame. Her pale face, although with features similar to those of her vibrant sister, spoke of deprivation and of disillusionment. Her listless gaze ran over Wright to Gabriel standing behind him, immaculate in his dark overcoat, top hat in hand.

'Get out,' she said. The strength of the words was in such a contrast to the quiet defeated tone in which she uttered them that for a moment both men simply gaped at her.

Rosie Bunch put her hand on the other woman's arm. 'Hang on, Ivy,' she whispered, 'this is Topsy Tillotson's brief from the Inner Temple...'

'I don't care who he is,' said the woman flatly. 'I heard him asking for George. I don't want any *gentleman* from that place or anywhere else coming near my boy. I want him out of my house.'

'This is all a misunderstanding,' said Wright soothingly. 'Your George hasn't done nothing wrong. He is not the George we are after at all, miss.'

'Out,' she said, still in that expressionless tone, and opened the street door.

Gabriel, closest to it, stepped out onto the pavement and replaced his top hat. Wright would have stayed to proffer further explanations but Gabriel gently took his arm, and smiled and nodded to Rosie Bunch before he led the way back down the alley.

'Blimey, sir,' said Wright when they had emerged into the main street. 'What on earth was that all about?'

'Can't you guess, Constable Wright?'

'No,' said Wright frankly. 'I am in a complete muddle, sir. It was just a case of mistaken identity. That little lad obviously wasn't Miss Tillotson's George and I am sorry I led you on a wild goose chase. But why was the woman in such a stew about it?'

'Well, Constable, don't you think this assists us with our other enquiries into unexplained disappearances? Think about it. A young woman called Ivy with a son of about ten. Who, when she saw me, plainly a member of the Bar, became very upset.'

Light dawned on Constable Wright. 'Oh! Ivy! The maid what Mrs Bugg told us got into trouble and was dismissed?'

'Precisely so.'

'But where does Miss Bunch come in to it, sir?'

'I thought at first it must be the sheerest coincidence that Ivy is Miss Bunch's sister. And that Miss Bunch is in the chorus of Topsy Tillotson's show. But now I recall, on our previous meeting, she made a rather pointed remark: "I know all about the Temple and KCs". I wondered at the time what she meant by it.'

Wright cleared his throat. 'I'm sorry if you thought I— That perhaps you—' He began again. 'When she first saw you, sir, I thought for a moment...' And trailed off, uncertain how to proceed.

'I know what you thought, Constable Wright,' said Gabriel. 'The point is that we have ruled out one of our disappearances. Ivy is not a corpse in the Temple and that is all Sir William and the City of London Police need to know.'

'Yes,' said Wright, more cheerfully. 'But no help with your Miss Tillotson's beau neither, I'm afraid.'

'No,' Gabriel said.

He thought again of that young woman, beaten down by poverty and life and the rigid moral code that did not recognise the injustice of its application nor the casual cruelty it imposed. He tried to push away the memory of Ivy Bunch's obvious unhappiness and, to help him do so, negotiated the cracks in the pavement with even more care than usual. And he wondered very much who George's father was and thought he might know the answer.

Wright's mind was apparently travelling along the same lines. 'Someone ought to be paying Miss Ivy Bunch a bit of money to my mind, even if she did go wrong. She can only be in her twenties now. She must have been very young. How unhappy she looked. I don't like to think of what she has been through, bad though what she did was. I suppose it was one of the Temple nobs; he could at least help with the boy.' He broke off, in some confusion. 'Not that it is my place to say so. I beg your pardon, sir.'

'There is no need to apologise. I happen to agree with you, Constable Wright,' said Gabriel. 'And I am going to do something about it.'

When he returned to his chambers, he asked Chapman to arrange a meeting with General Ivo Rawlings.

Gabriel's first impression of the General, when they met the next morning, was one of rigidity. His tall figure fairly bristled with tension, his square shoulders braced, his arms held stiffly by his sides, his expression set. When he raised his arm to shake his visitor's hand, Gabriel was reminded of the little clockwork soldier he had had as a boy, which had first raised its arm in just such a way, straight-elbowed, when its key was turned, preparatory to its eventual salute.

The meeting had been arranged at the General's club in Pall Mall, only about twenty minutes' walk from the Temple; he happened to be in London, he had informed Chapman, for his monthly visit to the barber. And so, reluctantly, Gabriel had emerged from the Temple gates and made his way down the Strand. It was a little further than he felt comfortable with. He was himself, he seemed to recall, a member of two of the most distinguished of the gentlemen's clubs situated in Pall Mall, membership having been obtained for him as a matter of course by his father as soon as he came of age. But he had never been to either.

The hand that shook Gabriel's was as cold as the General's first words.

'I have half an hour if I am to catch my train, Sir Gabriel, so I would be grateful if you would be brief. How may I help you?'

Gabriel cast his eyes around the room, apparently an anteroom to a rather more convivial one, glimpsed through the door left ajar at the other end. Elaborately draped curtains almost wholly obscured both the light and the view to St James' Park. Sound was muffled by the thick carpet. There were no pictures on the darkly papered walls. A single unlit chandelier hung from the lofty ceiling. There were no chairs. The General stood by a bare circular table in the middle of the room on which was displayed a bell for service and nothing else. There seemed no other course to take but to plunge in, standing facing the taut figure on the opposite side of the table.

'General Rawlings, I wish to ask you about your grandson Simon. I hope,' said Gabriel carefully, 'that you will believe I would not raise with you such a tragic matter had I not very good reason for it. I hope also that you will accept that my concern not to cause you greater unhappiness makes me reticent about those reasons. But I wish to ask you about the precise circumstances of your grandson's death.'

It felt like addressing a statue. There was a pause.

Then the General said, 'Your reputation precedes you, Sir Gabriel. I do not doubt that you do indeed have a very good reason. But I think you should understand that this is a matter of the most extreme sensitivity. No doubt you are aware of the bare facts?'

'Yes. A dreadful tragedy. But young men, as you in your profession will know, take small reversals hard. They do not understand that sexual scandal fades so quickly.'

General Rawlings seemed struck by astonishment.

'Fades quickly? Good God, man, I thought you were a distinguished lawyer!' Suddenly the man seemed to come alive. He gripped the table edge and leaned towards Gabriel. 'Fades quickly? He would have been disbarred! His sister was about to come out; no decent man would have had anything to do with her! I would have had to resign from my club! None of us could have appeared in society again! He would have disgraced his father's memory. He died, already decorated for his bravery, in the second Anglo-Afghan War. Simon was still a baby. My God, that his brave father's son should have come to this degradation!'

Gabriel wondered if he was encountering a religious zealot or a madman.

'My dear sir,' he said, 'surely you overestimate the consequences of an unsuitable dalliance? It was very unfortunate for a young member of the Bar, but it would not be the first time, I fear. The girl and her child could have been provided for. Indeed, if I may say so without impertinence, I really do feel they should have been. I hope you may find it in your heart to remedy that.'

'Girl?' cried the General. 'Girl? Would to God it had been a girl!'

Gabriel gazed for a moment in stunned silence. Even for his lightning intellect this took a moment's processing.

'I fear I have made an erroneous assumption,' he said at last, and he said it very humbly. 'I – a maid left the Inner Temple expecting a child at around the same time as your grandson's disappearance. I met her by chance lately. She has a boy of ten. I had understood – Barton his pupil master told me…' His voice trailed away. Barton, he recalled, had spoken only of a sexual transgression of which he did not know the details.

'Barton? Barton knew nothing about it. He quite rightly told the boy to come to me. And Simon told me the police were on to him. There is no mystery, Sir Gabriel. The boy knew he had one course open to him.'

'You knew he intended suicide and did nothing to prevent it?'

The General suddenly moved from his side of the table and his stiff hand grasped Gabriel's arm.

'Ward,' he said, 'I will trust you, as a senior member of the Inner Temple, with what only Sir William and I know. I *trust you, you understand?* But I want no more investigation into this matter, whatever your reason. Simon is not dead. After he had told me, I sent him back to the Temple and told him to stay there, the safest place from the police thanks to the extraordinary status of your institution. We got him across the Channel that night. Sir William assisted. He did not want matters of *that kind* contaminating the Inner Temple community.'

Across the General's stiff face there was a rictus of some indefinable emotion. 'Simon now lives in Tangier. With a remittance. Provided we never hear from him again.'

Gabriel digested this. 'His grandmother? And his sister?'

'Have no idea. You do not imagine I would tell this to any woman in my household, even if she were able to understand it? His brother was told when he came of age. Simon's sister and grandmother know only that he disappeared. Over the years they have come to believe the rumour that he threw himself into the Thames. Overwork, you know, and some unspecified silly romantic nonsense with a young lady.'

'Is it better they should live all their lives with that uncertainty?' Gabriel recalled what Vernon-Osbert, whose life had been spent trying to heal souls, had said: *There seems to me no greater suffering than that caused by uncertainty.* 'You believe it is better they hope for his return or believe him dead? All their lives? You truly believe that?'

'I know it.'

It was clear to Gabriel that the General's moral code and self-belief were as unbending as his body.

'And the other – er – participant? Did he, too, leave the Bar?'

This time, the rictus across the other man's face was unmistakably disgust. 'One hopes so. I know nothing about him. Sir William dealt with all that, and the least said the better. May I suggest you apply to him?'

He rang the bell decisively and a club servant appeared.

The stiff clockwork arm rose again and he proffered Gabriel his cold hand.

'Show Sir Gabriel out if you please,' he said.

17

Returning to the Temple, deep in thought, Gabriel met Sir Edward Hopkins strolling down Middle Temple Lane. Hopkins greeted him with a bonhomie that put Gabriel at once on his guard.

'Just the man I want,' said Hopkins. 'Going to your chambers? I shall walk with you.'

He thrust his hand into the crook of Gabriel's arm. Gabriel unhooked himself. Undeterred, Hopkins fell into step beside him.

'Now, Ward,' he said. 'Confidentially, are you going to drop this little trollop's case?'

Gabriel stood still. 'If you are referring to my client Miss Tillotson, then confidentially, Hopkins,' he said, 'I am not. I am going to win it.'

'Oh-ho, Miss Tillotson, eh? If you did not lead quite such a sheltered life, my boy, you would have heard tell that our Topsy is quite a little handful. Out for what she can get, like all her sort.'

'Indeed? said Gabriel with the utmost cordiality. 'I will bow to your superior knowledge of the propensities of young ladies in the theatre. But I, too, am out for what I can get, Hopkins, and in this case, it will be massive damages against the *Nation's Voice*. They have defamed Miss Tillotson disgracefully. She does not even know Frederick Sewell.'

'She knows him all right, in every sense including the biblical, and I shall be calling him to tell the jury so; how she was the shameless instigator of the irresistible passion that flared between them like a burning—'

'Really, Hopkins,' said Gabriel, 'save your rhetoric for the jury if you must, but do not subject me to it in the middle of the Temple on a sunny Tuesday morning. I shall see you in court.'

Sir Edward grinned and subsided, quite unabashed. 'Very well, Ward, you take that airy tone if you wish. You will indeed see me in court, and you and your client will live to regret the day.'

They had by now reached Gabriel's chambers and Hopkins swung past jauntily on the way to his own.

'Hopkins!' called Gabriel after him and his colleague instantly turned back as though he'd been awaiting the recall.

'Second thoughts?' Sir Edward said. 'I can probably do a deal on our costs to date if you drop the case?'

Gabriel shook his head. 'Didn't you tell me you were Master of the Inner Temple Silver?'

Hopkins blinked at the apparent irrelevancy and, caught off guard, answered without his usual bluster.

'Why, yes.'

'Do you recall two silver salts going missing? Some ten years or so ago?'

'Yes. Only thing we have ever had stolen. Seventeenth-century. A very valuable pair. Bequeathed to the Inn by some ancient judge. Can't remember who. We got them back eventually. Why do you ask?'

'How did the loss come about? Do you recall?'

Hopkins' curiosity was now aroused. 'I recall that it was a bit of a mystery. They were counted into the silver vault after a dinner by the silver butler. Apparently, Sir William locked the vault himself. Next morning they were gone.'

'Where were the keys?'

'Where they have been for the past two hundred years. The Treasurer has a full set of every key in the Inner Temple, of course, kept in his apartments. I have one on my watch chain for the silver vaults. Neither went missing.'

'What happened over the loss?'

'Nothing happened. The Treasurer told me he had reported it directly to the police.'

'The police?' exclaimed Gabriel. 'Sir William went to the police? He did not ask Simmonds as head porter to deal with it? Why on earth was that?'

By now Sir Edward had lost interest. 'Really, Ward, it was years ago. I have no idea. Anyway, the police retrieved them, and Waring dealt with it all. I never learned how they were removed in the first place. If you want the detail you will have to apply to Waring. No point in worrying about it now. You stick to your trial preparation, my boy. You are going to need it.'

And with that, and a slap on the back that Gabriel was unable to dodge, he departed.

That afternoon Gabriel had attended Vernon-Osbert's funeral. All thoughts of the morning's events were dispelled by the occasion; the sombre beauty of the service officiated over by the Bishop of London, Vernon-Osbert's friend since the days of their ordination; the pure, clear voices of the Temple Choir soaring above the great waves of the organ; the reverence of the packed congregation. Walking back to his chambers after the service, Gabriel thought with anger and disgust of those moments, the last moments, when Vernon-Osbert had opened that parcel and found its ghastly contents. He would find the culprit.

He was beginning, very slowly, to make a number of deductions. He would have to follow them up gradually. Amongst them was the interesting fact he had learned from Hopkins that morning. Sir William, with his marked aversion to permitting the City of London Police anywhere near the Temple, and almost complete reliance instead on the Temple porters, had reported the disappearance of the valuable silver salts to the police and kept the porters in the dark. Why should that be? Gabriel tucked the question away for later consideration. Just for now, with the trial imminent, there was a more pressing one, and that was what strategy Hopkins would opt for in presenting his client's defence.

Gabriel was well used to the tactics employed by members of the Bar towards their opponents in upcoming trials and Sir Edward Hopkins' bluster would normally be water off a duck's back. But this time he thought he had detected a kind of triumphant certainty underlying it, which made him feel a little uneasy. His detecting was all very well, but paramount now was his meticulous preparation for the trial which, he recalled with a squirm of tension, began in only two days.

Settled back at his desk, he thought hard about Topsy Tillotson and her case. He knew of course that Topsy would give evidence denying all knowledge of Frederick Sewell and that Sewell would be called by the newspaper to say that the account they had given was the truth. He knew that in the telling of these two diametrically opposed accounts, the scales were weighed heavily against Topsy whose very career made her veracity open to doubt and her reputation questionable. But Gabriel was too old a hand to think any case hopeless. The jurymen might be charmed by Topsy to such a degree they believed her protestations. Sewell might make some fatal mistake in his evidence or reveal terrible flaws in his personality. Sir Edward Hopkins would, he knew, be making the same assessments and coming to the same conclusions.

He hoped, for the sake of her case, that the girl was as innocent as she insisted.

It was at this exact point in his reflections that there was a knock on his door and Chapman came in.

'Miss Tillotson is here asking to see you. She is alone, sir. And she says she did not tell Mr Brindle that she was coming. She will not tell me what she wants, sir. I have told her you cannot see her without her solicitor, but she tells me the matter she has called about has nothing to do with her case.'

Gabriel sighed and removed his wire-framed spectacles still held together with a paperclip. 'Very well, Chapman. You had better show her in.'

Topsy, slight though she was, somehow filled Gabriel's room and he was reminded once again of Delphinium's similar silent force of personality. The resemblance was strengthened by Topsy's exquisite blue-grey fur wraps and muff. From the latter she withdrew a small hand clutching a piece of paper, which she thrust, without any preamble, under Gabriel's nose.

He peered at the message.

Come at half-past midnight tomorrow to Drury Lane Garden.

It was unsigned.

She announced with a stage tremor in her voice: 'Sir Gabriel, this note must be something to do with George. I am going. And there is nothing that will stop me.'

'Your very vehemence,' he said mildly, 'suggests a lack of conviction. I have often noticed this trait in witnesses. I have not as yet made any attempt to stop you. Would you care to take a seat, Miss Tillotson, and we will discuss the matter calmly?'

A little deflated, as Gabriel had intended, Topsy sat down.

'Miss Tillotson, this note makes no reference to George. And I should tell you that I have, as I promised you, caused enquiries to be made about the young man in the Fleet Street print rooms. The gentleman I asked to assist with them is in fact a policeman. Fleet Street is on his beat. He is a most reliable and thorough young man. He has found six Georges. All have been carefully enquired into. None, I am afraid, is your George.'

Topsy fiddled with her muff. Gabriel hoped she was not going to cry. But instead, she raised her chin and looked at him with a defiant gaze.

'I told you he had disappeared. Sir Gabriel, I wonder if – if he is in some kind of trouble. I'm afraid he must have been kidnapped!'

'Forgive me, but why should anyone kidnap a young man of very modest means living with his mother in Smithfield? And furthermore, there is no report of any George who has disappeared from a printer's post in Fleet Street.'

'I don't know! I just know I must go to that meeting. I could never forgive myself if I did not. But half-past midnight is a very late hour and that little garden is quite isolated at night. I wondered if you would escort me?'

'*Me?*' In his consternation Gabriel's voice rose markedly. 'My dear young lady, you cannot possibly be serious.'

Topsy looked wistful. 'I am sorry,' she murmured. 'You have been very kind. And I do not want anyone else to know about George. You're the only person I have told. I forgot what an important man you are.'

'No, no, I do assure you, it is nothing to do with... not that I am...' Under her steady gaze Gabriel had become uncharacteristically lost for words. Now he looked helplessly at her. How could he explain to this girl why what she asked of him was so impossible? That at exactly half-past midnight he went to bed secure in the Temple? That late-night London was, to him, a distant country? That no ritual he could devise would enable him to negotiate such an outing? Then he remembered Constable Wright and his usual urbanity returned.

'I hardly think that I would be much use as a protector, Miss Tillotson. Nor would it be proper for me to undertake such a duty for a client. Nor, for that matter, do I think you are wise to go. But if you insist upon doing so, I will enlist the help of my policeman friend. You can trust his discretion and I have already told him about George. You will be quite safe with him. He is young and of formidable bulk.'

'But would he mind?'

Gabriel chuckled. 'My prediction is that he will be only too delighted, Miss Tillotson.' And he bowed.

18

The Reverend Master's house was elevated on a mound at the top of a flight of ten stone steps leading from the churchyard up to its gates. It stood, along with its charming garden, as though on a platform, a gentle presence overseeing the Temple.

When Gabriel visited the next morning, Mrs Jenkins was sitting in the kitchen. The room predated by a century the eighteenth-century house above it, and the extreme irregularity of its proportions was in sharp contrast to the rest of the house. The old range dominated the room and Mrs Jenkins' dried spices and herbs, in bunches and muslin bags, stored on hooks on the staggered chimneybreast and warmed by it, filled the air with their scents. Copper pans, cleaned so that it was hard to believe they were ever used, were displayed on the enormous wooden dresser. The dresser itself was wedged into an awkward alcove between range and window. The table occupied most of the floor space and the ceiling was supported by irregular beams. In contrast to the vast pieces of furniture, Mrs Jenkins seemed even more Lilliputian than usual.

'I thought,' Gabriel began, 'that you would care to know that Delphinium is being cared for by Mrs Bugg.'

Mrs Jenkins nodded listlessly. 'I can't hardly see to Mr Rupert, let alone Delphinium. My poor master, I cannot think of anything else, Sir Gabriel. And now the police say he might not have died a natural death, though how that could be they will not tell me. Many is the time Dr Newman said, "Look after him, Mrs Jenkins, his poor old heart is that fragile." And so I did, Sir Gabriel. I devoted my life to him. Anything he wanted to make him happy and comfortable, I would go to the ends of the earth to give it to him.' The tears began to trickle down her sharp little nose.

Gabriel thought, selfishly and protectively, of his pristine handkerchief and hastened into speech.

'I know that, Mrs Jenkins,' he said gently, 'and in so doing, you made his life a longer and happier one. But if you wish to help the police enquiries, the best thing you can do is to give me a little information.' He drew up a Windsor chair and sat down opposite her.

'Forgive me if I tread on sensitive ground, but was one of the things that made your master happy McVitie and Price digestive biscuits?'

It was as though he had pressed a switch. Mrs Jenkins burst into floods of tears.

'Oh! Oh, how do you know? Oh, do not tell anyone!'

Gabriel gave up and handed her his handkerchief, noting wistfully its pristine condition.

'Oh, Sir Gabriel, he loved them so; he even had a little joke about them. "These are the best medicine, Mrs Jenkins," he would say. Ever since they were first sold, ten years ago, 1892 it was… I remember because it was the year I turned fifty… ever since then he craved them. Every day. And their recipe is kept secret. Try as I might, Sir Gabriel, I could not make mine taste the same.'

'So you ordered in bought ones?'

Mrs Jenkins nodded miserably. 'I asked the grocer in Fleet Street not to put them in with the rest of the Inner Temple orders but to send them here in plain boxes, and then I put them in plain tins in the kitchen so that – so that—'

And Gabriel, his own words to Wright echoing in his mind – *I am quite sure that no bought biscuit would ever show its face in the Temple* – completed the sentence.

'So that Mrs Bugg wouldn't know you could not make digestive biscuits?'

Mrs Jenkins rocked back and forth in a seemingly wholly disproportionate paroxysm of grief. But Gabriel knew that it was not. That he was witnessing all that made up Mrs Jenkins' feelings of pride and self-worth and love and loss and fear of redundancy in every deepest sense. And despite himself he felt an ache in the back of his throat.

'Mrs Jenkins,' he said solemnly, 'I promise you that your secret is safe. All I wish to know is where those boxes are.'

'They were such a useful shape,' sniffed the housekeeper. 'And I never like to throw anything away.'

'You gave one to Mr Rupert so that he could pack Reverend Master Vernon-Osbert's Christmas present?'

She nodded. 'I showed him where I kept all my old packing. In the yard storage cupboard.'

'Will you show me?'

She led him through the scullery and adjoining larder behind. An outer door led to a walled yard, also below ground level. There were doors in each wall and Mrs Jenkins opened one. Inside were various piles of packaging – old flour sacks, wooden crates, and a pile of the familiar boxes, now empty. Under the housekeeper's astonished gaze Gabriel fished one out and sniffed it. The smell was unmistakable, the cardboard impregnated by the sugary fat of its previous clandestine contents.

'What is kept in the other cupboards?'

'The fuel in one and some gardening tools in another so Joe Brockley does not have to carry everything across from the main gardens. And one has a water closet.'

Gabriel peered into the first. It contained an organised collection of clean old-fashioned gardening tools hanging on one wall, a pile of wooden stakes and a mallet leaning against the other, a stepladder, a teetering pile of flower pots, and some old fruit-cage nets.

'Is the only way into here through the kitchen?' asked Gabriel.

Mrs Jenkins sniffed dolefully and, opening the last of the doors, indicated a precipitous stair.

'There is a disused wine cellar below this and another store. They are both too damp to use. And there is an archway down there which leads outside, with a little flight of steps to get back on the same level as the rest of the Temple.'

'With a door?'

The housekeeper shook her head. 'Just an open archway.'

'So, anyone can come in?'

She shrugged listlessly. 'No one does. Except the coalman brings the sacks up that way.'

'But is the door through to the kitchen kept locked?'

Mrs Jenkins looked bewildered. 'Oh, no, Sir Gabriel. Why should we lock doors in the Inner Temple? Safe inside with the porters on the gates?'

Walking back to his chambers, Gabriel felt an acute sense of frustration. It seemed to him that whenever he made a step forward, the truth became more elusive. Thanks to Wright, he had learned the relevance of the smell of the boxes; he had found, as a result, their source. But where on earth did it all lead him? Mrs Jenkins had told Rupert Brandish where the boxes were stored; there was nothing odd in Brandish putting Vernon-Osbert's Christmas present in one, nor in his giving a few to John Gibson in which to pack his fern collection. But why had Gibson reacted so oddly to enquiries about them?

And as far as anyone else was concerned, it seemed that the boxes were readily available to anyone in the Inner Temple who walked through the archway into the cellar and up the stone steps to the scullery yard. Admittedly, the little entrance arch tucked below the level of the house was an obscure corner of the Temple; Gabriel himself had not known of its existence. But it was there to be found by anyone from the coalman to the Treasurer. And the boxes were there to be used by anyone who cared to do so.

19

When Constable Wright was asked to accompany Miss Topsy Tillotson to Drury Lane Garden, he had indeed been delighted. As he made his way up Drury Lane at five-past midnight with Topsy's elegant little figure walking beside him, he wondered if anything so exciting had ever happened to him before.

The freeze was now over and it had been pouring with rain relentlessly all day. It had stopped, but the pavements still gleamed wet and the sky was still threatening, dark and heavy with cloud. The tall buildings were black hulks, all lights extinguished, all doorways barred for the night. Down alleys to either side a vast clearance was taking place of the slums that had lined them. In the few that remained amidst the rubble, candles guttered in attic windows, a drunken voice occasionally called out in indistinguishable elation or despair, a baby wailed. Just audible from the nearby Strand was the intermittent mournful clop of horses' hooves.

Topsy shivered and drew her furs closer around her. They had reached the gate to Drury Lane Garden. It was ajar; inside the small park, the darkness was scarcely lightened by the one gas lamp's weak glow that seemed only to emphasise the pitch black around it.

'It was a cemetery, wasn't it?' whispered Topsy, peering in.

'Not for the last twenty or so years,' said Wright firmly. 'There is nothing to be afraid of, miss. It is just a public park now. And I won't let you out of my sight, not for a moment.'

But he felt uneasy. It seemed a rum place to ask a young lady to a night-time meeting. The gate squealed when he pushed it open and Topsy jumped. Wright hoped she had not noticed that he had jumped too. He got out his pocket watch. It was quarter-past midnight.

'Now, miss, I am going to take you to the light and you just stand under it and don't you move a muscle from there. And I will go behind this bush here, see. I'm only six feet away, we can whisper to each other and just wait, miss.'

Topsy's courage was returning. 'And if it is George, then of course I'll call to you to come out. And if it is someone with a message about him, well, I will just take it and when they have gone, we can find a hansom cab to take me home.'

'I'll be seeing you to your door like Sir Gabriel asked me to.'

'Unless it is George. Then he will see me home.'

Wright did not reply. The pure trust in the girl's voice made him even more uneasy.

'Don't you be too sad if this is nothing to do with your George,' he said protectively. 'Remember, we don't yet know who sent the note.'

'I have a strong feeling it will be about—' said Topsy, but the rest of her reply was lost in the squeal of the gate and in the sudden rush of boots.

And then there was the confused flurry of a rough voice shouting and her sharp cry of pain as she fell to the muddy path in a whirl of velvet skirts and fur stole. Just for a second, Wright remained behind the bush, paralysed with shock. Then he leaped out to see Topsy's assailant already running off into the darkness and Topsy herself sprawled across the path, ominously still.

Meanwhile, back in the safety of the Temple, it was Gabriel's bedtime. *Tillotson v The* Nation's Voice was to begin the next day and he had worked long and hard in preparation for it. All was, he told himself, in order for the next morning. Despite the interruptions and the dramas he had endured, he felt on top of the facts and he had researched the law with great care. He now felt the sense of peace that anticipation of the familiar ritual brought with it. Tomorrow he would put on his wig and gown and play his part as he had done for decades. He would put out of his mind parcels of body parts and mysteriously missing bodies; yes, even the tragic death of Vernon-Osbert. He would do the job he loved so much with all the concentration that he could command. Tomorrow, nothing else would matter at all.

Outside the rain had resumed, but in his large square bedroom all was snug. On the white coverlet of the single bed lay his pyjamas and dressing gown. Beside it were his leather slippers. A fire flickered gently in the grate. On all sides, lining the room, were books, random volumes on every subject under the sun, the overspill from his drawing room. And on a shelf above the bed were those that had always been above his bed, for as long as he could remember, ever since the first iron nursery bed. He checked automatically, although he knew that the spines would be in their obligatory order; red, green, blue, red, their gilded titles so faded as to be almost unreadable. But Gabriel did not need to read the titles. *The Fairchild Family*; *Struwwelpeter*; *The Children of the New Forest*; *Andersen's New Fairy Tales* — worlds into which, as a child, he had retreated. He still knew them off by heart. They had been his refuge from a sometimes bleak reality. He turned sharply away from them, slowly prepared for bed and, settling himself against his pillows, opened with some curiosity the book of short stories he had discovered by an unknown lady author, Miss Edith Wharton, *The Greater Inclination*. The first few pages, he thought, showed promise. He read on contentedly.

Directly below his window there was a loud knocking on the outside door of the building, now closed by the porters for the night. In some astonishment he put down the book, threw open the sash to the cold air and peered out. One floor below him, indistinctly illuminated under the dim gas lamp, were two upturned faces each with a pair of beseeching topaz eyes – one face very low down and the other rather higher – and the top of a policeman's helmet. After a confused moment, Gabriel identified them: Delphinium, Topsy Tillotson and Constable Wright were standing on the doorstep.

In consternation, he put on his thick brocaded silk dressing gown, decorously frogged to its high neck, and hurried down to unbolt the front door. Delphinium shot in. Behind her, Topsy clung to Constable Wright's arm and Gabriel saw that her face was muddy and her hair dishevelled.

'Miss Tillotson has had a bit of a shock, sir,' said Wright, 'and the Temple was nearest. I could not take her home to her mother in this state. I explained to the porter I was coming to see you. I am sorry, sir...'

Gabriel ushered them up to his rooms. Having seen the trembling Topsy into a chair, he felt just a little fussed. Dishevelled young women were outside his experience; he was not quite sure what she needed. It was Wright, with long experience of his mother and four sisters and of his Aunty Violet living next door, who rescued him.

'A little bowl of water, sir, and a cloth and a comb.'

Armed with these, and with Gabriel's shaving mirror, anxiously watched by the two men, Topsy wrought miracles in moments, and having done so looked woefully at Gabriel.

'It was nothing to do with George at all, Sir Gabriel.'

He looked queryingly at Wright who hastened into explanation.

'She was attacked, sir. A man just pelted in and grabbed her. He shouted out and attacked her.'

'But where were you?' Gabriel tried and failed not to sound reproachful.

Wright looked abashed. 'I was no more than six feet away, behind a bush. But it was only twelve-twenty, sir, when he rushed out of the dark and shoved and shouted and was away again before I could grab him. And I could not leave Miss Tillotson to follow him.'

Topsy said angrily, 'He hurt me. He punched me in the stomach so hard I fell over and he yelled: "Drop the case!" And as he ran away he shouted "Trol—"' she looked doubtfully at Gabriel '—a bad word about me.'

Gabriel looked horrified. Elusive suitors and midnight meetings were one thing, but interference with the course of justice was quite another. He manoeuvred his way through the piles of books and extracted from the cupboard his brandy and three glasses.

From the top of the encyclopaedia pile Delphinium made an attention-seeking noise halfway between a mew and a snort.

'How does Delphinium come into all this?' asked Gabriel.

'She doesn't, sir. She was sitting on the doorstep when we arrived.'

Gabriel sighed and got out the Spode saucer and the milk. When they were all settled, he turned his attention to the events of the evening.

'You did not recognise the man or his voice?'

Topsy shook her head.

'Neither did I,' said Wright. 'But I will bet it was to do with the newspaper, sir. I don't think he meant to do more than give her a good fright. After all, he did not know I was there, sir, but did not wait to do more harm. He was off in a couple of seconds. And I found this on the path.'

He laid on top of the nearest pile of books, a metal-cased propelling pencil. The case was red and chipped and topped with a small ring that enabled it to be clipped to a man's watchchain.

'Miss Tillotson,' said Gabriel, 'this is a very serious situation. Someone was making a last-ditch attempt to prevent you from seeking justice.' He thought of the august name of The Honourable Frederick Sewell; of the ruthlessness of the newspaper men; of Topsy's songs; and most tellingly of all, of the confidence exhibited by Sir Edward Hopkins KC. Lastly, but far from least, he thought of his own professional reputation. He did not like taking on hopeless cases and losing them.

'I wonder whether this incident may cause you to rethink your position?'

But Topsy raised her chin. The topaz eyes were blazing. 'The word he used, Sir Gabriel, was a word they use about bad women. They have written lies in their newspaper. They have driven George away. He will not come back unless my name is cleared. I will fight my case with your help, if you please. I will not be deterred.'

'And you are not afraid?' said Gabriel curiously. He was unused to young women as determined as this. He wondered if she realised what she was taking on.

'How can I be afraid when I am telling the truth?'

Into Gabriel's mind came all the trials he had appeared in over his long years at the Bar and all the litigants and their protestations and his professional indifference to them. The courage behind Topsy Tillotson's query shone in the dim room, and in spite of himself he felt humbled by it. He must do his utmost for this girl. And the first thing was to get her home to rest before the challenging day ahead.

As they prepared to leave, and whilst Topsy was rewrapping herself in her furs in Gabriel's hall, Wright, pocketing the propelling pencil, said in a lowered voice, 'Shall I go and sniff around that newspaper tomorrow, sir?'

Gabriel nodded thoughtfully. 'Before the trial begins. But do not, for heaven's sake, mention Miss Tillotson's name or we will have yet more sensationalist headlines.' He hesitated; could he find time to meet Wright on the first day of a trial, when his whole being was concentrated on the forensic battle ahead? Such a distraction seemed at first unthinkable. But for the first time in his professional career, he now found the demands of detection crowding in on his precious time almost as compelling as those of the upcoming trial. He drew a deep breath. 'And before you to do so, might you have time to come very early into chambers? Before eight o'clock, say? Court begins at ten-thirty. I have a pretrial consultation with Miss Tillotson and her solicitor at nine o'clock. And we cannot talk freely now.'

The next morning when Constable Wright appeared in Gabriel's chambers, Chapman was in the hallway removing Gabriel's wig tin and robes from a cupboard. Beside him stood the chambers boy packing a huge, wheeled book cage with all the *Law Reports* that might be needed during the trial. The air was thick with the tension that precedes battle. Chapman ushered Wright into Gabriel's room, bristling with disapproval. He did not hold with anything that might distract his guv'nor on the day of a trial and there had already been one little upset, with the arrival of the morning newspapers.

Wright, himself clutching this morning's edition of the *Nation's Voice*, saw another copy already spread out on Gabriel's desk with the headline prominent: *A WORD IN YOUR EAR*, and beneath it, *Shocking Revelation! Temple Reverend receives horrible parcel on day of death!!!*

'You've already seen it, sir.'

'Chapman brought it in. Where the deuce are they getting their information, Constable Wright?'

'Who knew about this, sir?'

'Only those who were there in the aftermath of the death. Mrs Jenkins, of course, Reverend Rupert Brandish, Dr Newman, the Treasurer and myself. And the City of London Police.'

'And the other two recipients of the boxes, sir: Sir Edward Hopkins and Sir Vivian Barton. They were asked by the police to keep it to themselves. Interviewed by us the same day we were called in, sir.'

'I cannot imagine any of those people leaking this information.'

'Well, one of them must have done, sir, or there is someone else in the Temple who knows more than we think and has made it his business to spread the story,' said Wright robustly.

'It reinforces why I wanted to see you this morning. I could not speak freely last night. If you are going to the newspaper to see if you can find out anything about the attack on Miss Tillotson last night, you just might discover something that will assist us as to the reporter's source of information in relation to the body parts. Could you, in particular, check whether from the *Nation's Voice* offices it is possible to see the hydrangea border in the Inner Temple gardens?' Gabriel smiled. 'And thereby you will have an excuse for your visit to offer Inspector Hughes; I am sure he would approve of enquiries relating to the body parts rather more than investigations into Miss Tillotson's private affairs. Although she undoubtedly sustained an assault, it plainly relates to my litigation and Inspector Hughes would not like you wasting time on that.'

Wright looked rather glum. 'I am happy to have a general sniff around the newspaper offices, sir. But I haven't been much help so far, I'm afraid. I could not find George. I did not prevent harm to Miss Tillotson. And as to the mysterious body parts, I can't find the body and I can't discover who is sending them.'

'Well, neither can I,' said Gabriel. 'Cheer up, Constable. We are getting there.' He told Wright of the whereabouts of the cardboard boxes. 'All thanks to you and The Great Digestive Biscuit Mystery.'

Wright looked more cheerful.

'And furthermore,' said Gabriel, 'together we have ruled out Ivy and subsequently I have ruled out another possibility.'

He wondered how Wright would respond to the story of Simon Rawlings and his grandfather. He told it with such delicacy that he wondered if the young policeman had grasped what he was being told. It was soon apparent that he had. His face stiffened with embarrassment.

'Well, sir, you cannot do my job and not know it goes on. And I am not one to try and catch them out by – by pretending to – well, you know, sir. We are sometimes asked to do that. But that I won't do. All the same, I have had to arrest plenty of them, sir. You would be surprised.'

'No,' said Gabriel, 'I wouldn't be particularly surprised.' And was back for a moment at Eton and at Oxford.

'Terrible thing for the families, sir.'

'Yes. I am afraid the world is unforgiving. The boy is probably better off in another country. But at least we know he is not our corpse.'

'Yes, sir. That, I suppose, leaves the young porter, and then we have run out of possibilities.'

Chapman knocked on the door. 'Nine o'clock, sir. Miss Tillotson and Mr Brindle are here.'

Wright went at once to the offices of the *Nation's Voice*. Sullivan was in his eyrie and with him was Frank Holloway. They, too, were readying themselves for court that morning, heads bent in close consultation, and there was the same bellicose tension in the air as Wright had felt in Gabriel's chambers.

They broke off as he appeared in the doorway and Sullivan greeted the sight of a policeman with a combination of relish and aggression.

'Wodja want with us?' he demanded as the constable hovered on the threshold.

This lack of deference to his uniform stiffened Wright's resolve. He took off his helmet to negotiate Sullivan's low attic doorway and spoke authoritatively.

'Just a few questions in private. I won't keep you long.'

'You'd better not. We're in court at ten-thirty. Holloway can hear anything you have to say,' said Sullivan. 'Nothing like a witness, I find, when talking to a copper.'

'I haven't come to cop no one,' said Wright, deliberately mild. 'There was a bit of a to-do in Drury Lane Garden last night and a girl was given a fright. Just wondered if you lot had heard about it?'

'Any girl who was in Drury Lane Garden on her own at night was asking for trouble. Can't see any story in it if she got it,' said Sullivan disagreeably.

Wright fished from his pocket the red propelling pencil and laid it on the editor's desk.

'That's Holloway's,' said Sullivan. And a second later, Holloway echoed him: 'Why, that's mine!'

Wright was so taken aback by this ready confession it was a moment before he collected himself. He wondered if he should issue a caution. Recalling Gabriel's strictures in relation to Topsy's name, he refrained.

'I found it in Drury Lane Garden. How did it find its way there?' he asked.

'I was in there yesterday,' said Holloway. 'Went for a cig and to write up my notes. I'd been in Bow Street Police Court chasing a story. Must have dropped it under the park bench. Thanks. I've had it for years.'

And he pocketed it. He seemed so entirely at ease that it was impossible not to believe he was telling the truth.

It was all a bit of an anticlimax. Wright wondered how on earth he could prolong the interview and so return to Gabriel with at least a snippet of information. He strolled over to Sullivan's window and peered down upon the Temple. From here he had a bird's eye view of that little world laid out below, but only a partial one. From this angle it was impossible to see the hydrangea border tucked away on the east side. He wondered why Sir Gabriel thought it mattered. He could just make out Joe Brockley in the Reverend Master's garden. He was industriously wielding a mallet, driving in props to support the sprawling branches of an ancient mulberry tree. Delphinium, balanced on one of these, was observing with a casual interest that would fool no one what Wright, squinting, could just see was an unsuspecting robin. As he watched, she sprang down, disappearing from view into the shrubbery. Wright lingered to see the robin's fate, but Delphinium did not emerge again.

'You have a good view of the Temple,' he said turning to Sullivan. 'Looks that peaceful in the winter sunshine.'

But Sullivan was no fool. His piggy little eyes narrowed. 'This isn't really about no girl in Drury Lane Garden,' he observed shrewdly. 'This is about them body parts. I heard they'd at last got the police involved. Well, you'll get no information from us, my lad. And it's no crime to report what we find out, eh, Holloway? First rule of journalism.'

'That depends on how you found it out,' said Wright, directing his attention to the nondescript Holloway. 'Were you the finder-outer?'

Holloway shrugged. 'Might have been.'

'Well,' said Wright, irritated, 'this here investigation is now a murder enquiry. You be a bit careful with your finding out.'

Neither man seemed the least intimidated. Deflated, Wright made for the door. He was not consoled to see the smirk of triumph on Holloway's face.

It was not until he was halfway back to Old Jewry police station that he suddenly remembered something. Yesterday, when Holloway said he was sitting on a bench in Drury Lane Garden having a cigarette and writing up his notes, it had been raining torrentially. All day, without ceasing, until late at night when Wright had escorted Miss Topsy there for her disastrous meeting.

20

It was seldom in his distinguished career that Gabriel had attracted so much attention as he did that morning when he made his way across the Strand to the Royal Courts of Justice. On both sides of the crossing, crowds pressed and yelled, and on the steps of the Law Courts phalanxes of newspaper men were jostling for pole position.

Behind Gabriel's slight self-deprecatory figure scuttled the junior barrister who was nominally appointed to assist him and who, thanks to Gabriel's insistence on preparing cases meticulously himself, had in fact done very little. Behind the junior came Mr Brindle, bursting with self-importance. On Mr Brindle's arm was Topsy. The honour of escorting so famous a client would have been claimed for himself by any other barrister who had had the luck to represent her, but Gabriel, holding his precious trial preparation notes under one arm and his copy of Odgers' scholarly *Digest of Libel and Slander* under the other, had delegated the task to Brindle. Bringing up the rear was Chapman, followed by the chambers boy wheeling the book cage.

Topsy was heavily veiled and her costume was of discreet and unembellished dark green. No one seeing her immaculate little figure would ever have known that she had been attacked the night before, nor that her heart was breaking at the disappearance of her beloved George. Topsy knew how to put on the required performance. She was the very model of decorum, her tumbling Titian tresses severely confined in a knot. But nothing could subdue the vivid little face visible through the veil, nor quell the 'oohs' and 'ahs' of her adoring public.

As he walked Gabriel was troubled with a deep sense of foreboding, engendered by the news, conveyed by Chapman, that he was listed in front of Mr Justice Whittington-Allsop. All judges have weaknesses, there to be recognised and exploited by the advocates who appear in front of them. In Mr Justice Whittington-Allsop's case, it was snobbery. It was something of a lottery how this particular characteristic would manifest itself in the circumstances of *Tillotson v The* Nation's Voice. Mr Justice Whittington-Allsop (he had, so the Bar gossip said, added the Allsop himself) would not think much of the *Nation's Voice*; but on the other hand, he would be only too conscious of the nobility of The Honourable Frederick Sewell's family. It was anyone's guess how these prejudices would play out and Gabriel did not like any element of chance, in his life or in his litigation.

As for Topsy, the judge would deplore the vulgarity for which her performances were known, and Gabriel was not sure how he would respond to her obvious allure. The judge was very determinedly married to a fierce woman who excelled on the hunting field and was, as he not infrequently reminded people, the great-niece (once removed) of an earl.

In the packed courtroom, with Topsy's parents in pride of place in the public gallery, Sir Edward Hopkins was already seated in the row especially designated for leading counsel. In front of him, at a lower level but placed for easy conference, was his instructing solicitor; and behind him sat his junior; and behind him, Lionel Sullivan and Frank Holloway.

There was no sign of Frederick Sewell, a circumstance which, when the trial was about to begin, was smoothly explained away by Sir Edward Hopkins.

'The Honourable Frederick Sewell, My Lord, who will be my client's witness, has been unavoidably detained by the postponement of the ferry from Calais to Dover. The *Nation's Voice* is content that we commence the trial and he will be here in time to give his evidence.'

'Calais, Sir Edward?'

'Mr Sewell had an engagement at the Casino last night, My Lord, and the weather has not been advantageous.'

The judge smiled at the jury. 'Well, members of the jury, it is not essential for a witness to be present until he is called into the witness box, and young gentlemen will be young gentlemen, will they not?'

The twelve stolid men on the jury, all members of the respectable middle class, called away from shop and bank counters and offices to perform jury service, were none of them remotely familiar with the legendarily fashionable Casino in Calais. They all looked admiring.

Gabriel, carefully considering their deferential expressions, opened his case. When he had explained to them the facts and the law upon which, subject to the direction of the judge, he relied, he concluded with an understatement in relation to Topsy's career that caused Sir Edward Hopkins to smirk.

'... My Lord will tell you,' he concluded, 'that you should decide this case on the evidence you hear in this court, and not on the basis of anything you may think you know about my client and her career as an actress. I submit to you that no reasonable person, reading this article, would interpret it in any other way than as an imputation against Miss Tillotson's virtue. Miss Tillotson does not know The Honourable Frederick Sewell, let alone has she had intimate relations with him. What the newspaper says is untrue and therefore it is a gross slander upon her character.'

He called his first witness. 'Miss Vera Perkins, please.'

Vera Perkins had made no concessions to the dignity of the law. She wore still the egg-stained tweed jacket and the shapeless old skirt. Regarding her immense bulk and short-cropped hair, the judge looked a little startled but he recovered himself and, when she had taken the oath, enquired if she would like to sit down.

'I would, thanks, ducky,' said Vera Perkins, settling herself down in the witness box, 'with my weight, standing comes hard.'

Gabriel, suppressing an involuntary snuffle of amusement, said hastily, 'It is customary to address the judge as "My Lord", Miss Perkins.'

'Sorry,' said Vera with a cheerful indifference, and addressing herself directly to Mr Justice Whittington-Allsop, 'No offence, dearie.'

But despite this unconventional beginning, her evidence was clear and her throaty voice held the ring of conviction. She had employed Miss Tillotson since the beginning of her stage career. How well she remembered Topsy coming into the theatre that first time – a real little Miss Goody Two Shoes, if her name was Vera Perkins. And she knew girls. Oh, her hat and boots, did she know girls! She had employed dozens of chorus girls. Some had become stars, most had not. Some of them were good girls, some were not. Once they knew the theatre world, it was up to them. Topsy was an exception in every way. The biggest star the variety theatre had had since Miss Marie Lloyd. And she had stayed a good girl, modest and pure as… as… (at this point Vera cast around for inspiration and, that failing her, fell back disappointingly on the conventional) the driven snow.

'Do you know The Honourable Frederick Sewell, Miss Perkins?' asked Gabriel.

Vera Perkins winked. 'I knows all the men who come regular to the stage door to see the girls. The Honourable Freddy is sometimes one of them. And, my word, I'll give him handsome! Nearly enough to turn my tastes!'

The jury looked uncomprehending. There crossed the judge's face, however, a curious expression of embarrassment and incredulity.

'I *beg* your pardon?' he exclaimed almost involuntarily.

Vera Perkins raised her eyebrows. 'He's too young for me, duck— My Lord,' she said smoothly.

Gabriel hastily intervened.

'Are you aware of any relationship or association between Frederick Sewell and Miss Tillotson?'

'Not him nor any of the gents. Out of the stage door of an evening she goes, never lifts her head to look at any of them, pushes away the bouquets – shuns them, she does. No champagne suppers for her but straight home to her mother every night,' said Vera Perkins soulfully.

Gabriel felt a little uneasy. This ongoing eulogy was all very well, but when the jury heard Topsy's vibrant purring little voice in the witness box, and felt her extraordinary presence, would they believe this portrait of saintliness? He would have wished Miss Perkins a little more subtle. He turned, hastily again, to the technicalities of what he was required to prove.

'When you saw the newspaper article containing the words complained of, what did you understand them to mean?'

Vera Perkins seemed overcome with an unexpected prudery, but she rallied, and bending confidentially towards the judge, hissed, 'It meant she had gone wrong.'

The judge bent forward, his manner equally confidential. 'Miss Perkins, I know what you mean when you say that, and so, of course, do the members of the jury, but the law requires that you specify your understanding.'

Rising to the drama of the moment, Vera Perkins addressed the jury directly in something near a shout.

'It meant that The Honourable Frederick Sewell had seduced our Topsy. And it is a wicked lie!'

There seemed little else to say and Gabriel relinquished his witness to his opponent.

Sir Edward rose ponderously to his feet and it seemed to Gabriel that he avoided eye contact with Vera Perkins. His cross-examination was extremely effective, however, and brief.

'Sometimes, Miss Perkins, it is sadly the case that young women are not always as frank as they might be with their elders and betters. Would that be fair?'

'That would be fair, dearie,' said Vera Perkins, walking straight into the snare laid for her. 'Many's the time I've been deceived by some little madam; you need eyes in the back of your head with some of them—'

'Thank you,' interrupted Hopkins firmly, 'I have no further questions.' And casting a meaningful glance at the jury, he sat down.

Gabriel was unsurprised by this economy of effort on Hopkins' part. Both advocates knew that triumph or defeat lay in the evidence of Topsy and of Sewell and how they told their diametrically opposed stories. But Gabriel still had a nasty feeling that Hopkins had something up his sleeve. He was relieved that it was time for the luncheon adjournment.

At two o'clock he called Topsy into the witness box and she took the oath.

The judge looked severely at her, raised an almost imperceptible eyebrow at the jury and then turned to Gabriel.

'Would the lady – no, perhaps I should say, would your *client* like to sit down, Sir Gabriel?'

So that was how it was going to be.

'She would, My Lord,' Gabriel said, and tried to sound utterly neutral.

The judge nodded to Topsy who perched meekly on the high seat in the witness box.

Gabriel led her carefully through her simple story. She lived with her mother and father and younger sister. Her father was a butcher in Hackney. Hers was a very happy family. There had been little money and Topsy had always known she would have to work, in order to help her parents, just as soon as she could. She had always loved to sing and dance. Then she had seen the advertisement for chorus girls and that had been the beginning.

Here the judge intervened. 'And these responsible parents of yours made no objection to such a – er – career?' The gentlemen of the jury, who had seemed to Gabriel to be thawing a little, now looked disapproving. Hopkins smirked. Topsy hesitated.

'My parents did not want me to at first,' she said, rather unwillingly.

From the corner of his eye, Gabriel saw his opponent make a note.

'But, in the end, my mother said I had been brought up proper and she would just have to trust me whatever I chose to do.'

'Will you tell the gentlemen of the jury about your subsequent career?' said Gabriel.

And Topsy recounted with a becoming show of modesty her astonishing rise to fame. She had only remained in the chorus for a few months, she said, before she had been given a star role. People sent her flowers. She soon earned enough money to help her parents. She had thought she was living in a fairy tale.

'And has the fairy tale continued, Miss Tillotson?' said Gabriel

Topsy hesitated. 'I still love to sing and dance,' she said at last. 'And I am happy that audiences like to watch me. I love my audiences. But I do not like to be in the newspapers.'

'Do you read what the newspapers say about you?'

Topsy gave a little smile. 'If I do not read it myself, Sir Gabriel, then someone is bound to tell me about it.'

'You knew they referred to you as The Unconquerable?'

Topsy was well aware how to portray pathos. She looked down at her hands, clasped in her lap, so that the gentlemen of the jury could see nothing but the top of her bonnet. She nodded.

The judge intervened again. 'Miss Tillotson, I must ask you to answer the question so we can hear you. Nods are not sufficient to constitute evidence in a court of law.'

Topsy raised her head and spoke as clearly as though she was addressing the back row of the stalls.

'I knew the newspapers called me that, and why. They called me that because I would not accept attentions from the men who come to the stage door.' She looked earnestly at the jury. 'They are bad men who want girls to – to do what they shouldn't. They are rich and they think that they can buy anything. They make some of the girls go wrong.'

On defence counsel's row, Sir Edward Hopkins shifted suddenly in his seat and in so doing knocked his notebook to the ground with a clatter. Ignoring the interruption, Gabriel continued with his next question, deliberately designed to bring his examination to a finale that would, he hoped, stay with the jury through the ordeal of cross-examination that was to come.

'Could they buy you, Miss Tillotson?'

'No,' said Topsy. 'They could not.'

'Do you know The Honourable Frederick Sewell?'

'No,' said Topsy, and her vibrant voice rang with conviction, 'I do not.' She gazed earnestly and directly at the jury. 'It is a lie. I had never even heard of him until – until the newspaper printed that dreadful story.'

'Has he conquered you?'

'No, Sir Gabriel. He has not.' She looked again, appealingly, at the jury, and like a child, said, 'I promise you.'

Gabriel sat down.

The judge looked at the clock. It showed four o'clock.

'Would that be a convenient moment?' he said, and rose from the bench. The court was adjourned for the day.

Gabriel happened to leave close behind Frank Holloway. From the sheaf of paper the journalist was carrying, a single sheet fell to the floor. Gabriel could almost hear Nanny's voice: *Tidy habits, tidy mind*. He picked it up. Holloway had apparently been composing his copy on it. Amidst the scrawls and crossings out, Gabriel read: '*Topsy as pure as snow,*' *said Miss Vera Perkins, forty-six-year-old theatrical impresario of the Drury Lane Theatre. 'I know girls,' said Miss Perkins. The* Nation's Voice *can certainly endorse the second statement.*' And after this Holloway's trademark three exclamation marks.

He was already disappearing into the distance. Gabriel sighed and shoved the paper into his pocket. He was still in his wig and gown; he could not chase after the wretched man.

Having disrobed and left the Law Courts, he happened to see Holloway again, loitering on a corner in Fleet Street, and crossed over to return the notes. But then he saw that Holloway was in close consultation with another man. His dirty cap was pulled low over his forehead, and his scruffy suit was so baggy with age that it was difficult to discern his body shape. But his cadaverous face betrayed extreme emaciation, and the straight villainous-looking knife scar that ran down the left side of his face, from sandy eyebrow to jaw, was eloquent of crime rather than accident. As Gabriel walked by, something passed from Holloway's hand to the other man's. Holloway, thought Gabriel, was plainly paying off a source. He involuntarily remembered another of Nanny's maxims: *Tell me with whom you associate and I will tell you who you are.* Then with a snuffle of mirth recalled that the maxim was not one of Nanny's after all, but one of Goethe's.

In any event, Holloway was not in company that a gentleman member of the Bar should be seen with in the close environs of the Royal Courts of Justice. Gabriel turned down Middle Temple Lane. Holloway would just have to rewrite the notes for his scurrilous rag.

The next morning, there was an air of barely suppressed excitement in the courtroom. The journalists were packed even tighter into the press box and the public gallery was so full that many were standing. Sir Edward Hopkins was always guaranteed to put on a performance. He got ponderously to his feet, savouring his moment in the spotlight. Thrusting his thumbs under the lapels of his waistcoat, he rocked back on his heels and then launched himself into his first onslaught on Topsy.

'So, you are suing to protect your – ' he paused and smiled at the jury with a nice mixture of incredulity and mirth '– reputation?'

The gentlemen of the jury, flattered by Hopkins' camaraderie as he had intended them to be, grinned back.

'Yes,' said Topsy.

'You are of course quite a famous name, Miss Tillotson,' purred Sir Edward at his most charming. 'Quite a celebrated little lady.'

'Yes,' said Topsy. She did not sound at all charmed.

'Now let me see,' he said, getting into his easy avuncular stride, 'speaking of names... you are such a very young lady that I think I may call you Topsy, may I not?'

'No,' she said. 'I would prefer Miss Tillotson.'

Sir Edward's eyes narrowed but he was too experienced an advocate to respond to impertinence.

'Well, well,' he said, and tried to sound amused. He fumbled among his papers to give himself time to regain his stride and turned to the meat of his cross-examination rather earlier than he had intended. He had lost ground to make up. He rifled through a pile of stage programmes.

'Let me remind the gentlemen of the jury of the songs that have made you famous.' Deadpan, he began to read aloud.

"'Would You Like a Nice Little Tart for your Tea?" "Love Me, Love My Pussy."'

'I was only fifteen years old,' said Topsy, 'when I first sang those songs. I sang what the management told me to sing.'

'Fifteen years old!' rapped out Hopkins. 'And defied your father in order to become a chorus girl, did you not?'

'I did not defy him, Sir Edward. I persuaded him that I should go on the stage.'

'Oh-ho! Persuaded him, eh? You mean, you got round him, miss?'

Gabriel stood up. 'I am not wholly clear, My Lord, what part my client's attitude to parental discipline plays in the trial of this matter?'

The judge nodded to him. 'There is some force in that, Sir Edward,' he mildly addressed the defence counsel. 'I would like you to confine yourself to issues relating directly to justification for the imputation of unchastity, please.'

Sir Edward changed tack smoothly, the damage done. There were a fair few fathers on the jury who would have got the point, he thought.

'And what, pray,' he said, addressing the slight figure in the witness box, 'did you think the audience thought was the meaning of those songs?'

'I thought they meant what they said,' said Topsy simply. 'I do not know what the audience thought.'

'Oh-ho,' said Sir Edward again. 'A spirited little lady, gentlemen of the jury; I must watch my step!'

The jury chuckled. Gabriel's heart was sinking. This mixture of banter and bullying was what Sir Edward Hopkins did best, he thought. He feared the girl was going to be mincemeat. But he had under-rated Topsy.

'Come, miss.' Sir Edward swung easily into schoolmasterly mode. 'That will not do. What do you imagine was the meaning of those words?'

In the silence of the court, Topsy put her reticule on the edge of the witness box and burrowed in it.

'Handkerchiefs will not help you,' said Sir Edward contemptuously.

From the reticule, Topsy produced a very small pair of wire spectacles, which she perched on her nose. They made her look rather different. Next, she extracted a book and proceeded to open it and run her finger down a page.

'"*Tart*",' she read out, '"*…a flat small piece of pastry with no crust on the top, filled with fruit preserves or other sweet confection*".'

'Stop playing games, miss, and answer the question.' There was an ugly note now in Sir Edward's voice.

Gabriel intervened.

'Miss Tillotson has every right to answer the question in whatever way she wishes,' he said. 'You asked her what the word meant. She is entitled to consult a dictionary.'

Topsy turned some pages in the little volume.

'"*Pussy*",' she read out, '"*a nursery or pet name for a cat*".'

She put the book away. 'That is what I thought the words meant, Sir Edward. What do *you* think they mean?'

There was silence while the fascinated courtroom registered a phenomenon they had thought they would never see: Sir Edward Hopkins KC momentarily lost for words. Furiously angry, yet too experienced an advocate to show it, he changed the subject. But his gloves, thought Gabriel, were now off. On and on his cross-examination went, switching from point to point with dizzying speed.

'You are quite an experienced little lady, are you not?' he said, and his tone was as offensive as he had intended it to be.

'Experienced?'

Sir Edward consulted his notes.

'Your schoolfellow Tommy Benson? Kissed him in the bushes, did you not?'

'He kissed me. I pushed him away.' There was a note of defiance in the husky voice.

'Mr Albert Tilby,' Sir Edward rapped out.

Topsy looked confused. 'I don't... he is the man who runs the grocer's shop at the end of our road.'

'Yes, he is indeed, and Mrs Tilby had to speak to you, did she not?'

'Yes, she did, Sir Edward,' said Topsy, still defiant. 'But I hadn't done nothing wrong. I have known him since I was a little girl. I could not help that he – that he – that Mr Tilby asked me to meet him.' Topsy's voice was firm. 'And Mrs Tilby overheard him and came out of the backroom in the shop and said it was my fault for – for smiling at him.'

'And another lady has had to speak to you, I believe. Mrs Thompson? When you let her husband help you into a hansom cab?'

'I-I... How do you know about that? That was not my fault! He – he tried to—'

'Oh, so it was the gentleman's fault once more, was it? What a coincidence!'

The jury grinned collectively.

'Sir Edward,' said Topsy, rather desperately, 'you do not understand. I – my name – they know me because of the theatre, and they like other men to think that I – that I – that they have-have—'

'Yes, miss? Have what?'

Topsy stood silent and Hopkins, in some triumph, turned to his main theme.

'Tell the jury about your pursuit of Mr Sewell.'

'I did not pursue Mr Sewell.' Topsy leaned forward earnestly in the box. 'Truly, I have never met him, Sir Edward. I had never even heard of him until I read his name in the newspaper.'

Hopkins made an indescribable scoffing noise. 'I apologise,' he said with heavy sarcasm, 'I am confused amongst all these names. This is another gentleman whose fault it is that you were intimate, is it?'

'We were not intimate!' cried the angry Topsy. 'We were not!'

On it went, as Hopkins teased and blustered and bullied. At last, at the end of a long day, he brought his cross-examination to a conclusion, and a weary jury, admonitions from His Lordship not to discuss the case over the Saturday and Sunday adjournment ringing in their ears, were sent home.

With thoughts of his own home, Gabriel walked back through the Temple feeling conflicting emotions. He found it hard to evaluate the impression that Topsy had made on the jury. She had undoubtedly scored a point or two with Hopkins; he had thought that he had seen a certain realisation dawning on the judge that here was a very clever young woman. But would the jury see it like that? Or would they dismiss her, as was often the fate of clever young women, as unbecomingly pert?

As he reached Middle Temple Lane, thoughts of the trial were dispersed by the sight of Mrs Bugg, still wearing her apron, puffing up the road from the opposite direction. She looked anxious.

'Oh, Sir Gabriel, thank goodness you are back. Delphinium has disappeared,' she said. 'We have searched everywhere. She did not come in for her turbot last night. I left her an oyster as a treat this morning and it is untouched. She is nowhere to be found.'

21

Enquiries ultimately revealed that the last person known to have seen Delphinium had been Constable Wright from the attic window of the *Nation's Voice* offices in Fleet Street the previous morning. She had been missing for the best part of two days.

'She was bent on massacring a robin,' he told Gabriel. 'And I wouldn't bet much on the robin's chances. Balancing she was, right on the end of the branch, and you know what a whopper she is, sir.'

'How unchivalrous, Constable Wright.'

'Well, all I can say is, the branch was bowed right down to the ground,' said Wright with a grin, 'and then she just did a massive leap – not sure if it was on purpose or by accident – and disappeared into the shrubbery head-first. The funny thing was, she didn't appear again.'

Gabriel sighed. 'I suppose we should look and see if she is somewhere in the Reverend Master's garden.'

They all went to look; Gabriel and Wright and an anxious Mrs Bugg, and Meg whom no one had invited but who had emerged from the kitchen bursting with curiosity and a certain enthusiasm, Gabriel noticed uneasily, for Wright's company.

He asked the constable, dropping behind with him as they walked, 'Did you learn anything from Sullivan in relation to the attack on Miss Tillotson?'

Wright relayed the conversation, and Holloway's easy and open reclaiming of the propelling pencil, with his usual thoroughness.

'Sullivan recognised it at once, sir, and Holloway explained how it must have got there. I realised after, sir, that because Sullivan immediately identified it, he – probably innocently – put Holloway on the spot. So, Holloway lied, and I don't mind admitting that he convinced me proper, sir, at the time. It wasn't until I was walking back to the station, I remembered it was fair pouring with rain all day so he couldn't have been sitting out there writing notes like he said he was.'

Gabriel nodded. 'Well, that confirms our suspicions, Constable Wright, and I am glad you did not follow it up. We will bide our time until the end of the trial. I doubt that Holloway realised Miss Tillotson was quite such a force to be reckoned with when he printed this story, so he made a last attempt to make her drop the litigation.'

'Yes, the bast— sorry, sir. And by the way,' Wright added, 'I had a look out of the window from Sullivan's room and you certainly cannot see the hydrangea border from the *Nation's Voice* offices. Why did you want to know, sir?'

Gabriel briefly related Holloway's conversation at the dinner Sir William Waring had given, and his own careful perambulation around the Temple the morning after it. 'It looks as though Holloway had been inside the Temple although he denied it.'

'We knew his source for all these stories was almost bound to be someone in the Temple,' said Wright. 'Perhaps he was visiting someone there.'

'Yes. The question is, who? Anyway, thank you, Wright. It is another little piece in the jigsaw. And it was a very profitable visit, what with propelling pencils and hydrangea beds, not to mention seeing Delphinium.'

Wright looked pleased.

Gabriel tucked all the information away for later consideration. It occurred to him as it would not immediately to Wright, that Simmonds and his little band of porters would not regard

Frank Holloway as a man who looked as though he had legitimate business in the Temple. Unless he had somehow managed to get in unobserved, he would have been challenged. And he would then have had to come up with a plausible explanation for visiting. Gabriel must, at some convenient moment, make some enquiries.

'At least I had a clear enough view of the Reverend Master's garden and that varmint Delphinium,' said Wright darkly. 'When we find her, I've a good mind to arrest her.'

The winter shrubbery of the garden, awaiting its spring pruning, was tangled and still dense. Gabriel frowned at the disorder. He liked his gardens to mirror the considered control of his own life. It was dark now, on this late-January afternoon; the resourceful Wright was forced to light his hand lantern. Under the mulberry tree he indicated was a tangle of undergrowth, undoubtedly indented. Gabriel pushed aside the shrubs with his umbrella tip and revealed the mangled corpse of a robin, red breast and pathetic starry little feet upturned. Mrs Bugg and Meg tutted in unison.

'The evidence backs up your story so far, Constable Wright,' said Gabriel.

They called for Delphinium and searched, but there was no sign and no response.

Then Meg said, 'I thought I heard something. I'm sure I heard a cry.'

They all listened into the unbroken silence.

'I'm quite sure,' said Meg firmly. And then they all heard it: plaintive, distant, impossible to trace. And once their ears were attuned, they heard it again and again, very faintly. Yet there was nowhere left to search for her.

Gabriel's trust in the quirky little connections made by his own mind was infinite. It was, he supposed, what other people called intuition though he knew it to be nothing so nebulous and romantic, but rather the subconscious summoning up of all the data he had accumulated over his years of learning and experience. Standing in the Reverend Master's garden, just such a connection was made and he thought quite suddenly of Sir Edward Hopkins. But what did that oily individual have to do with this bleak austere place? He grappled for the link and after a minute or two heard again Sir Edward Hopkins' mellifluous voice recounting the Treasurer's directions as to the planting of the garden: *He instructed Brockley to plant a vine. It died, so he told the gardener to put in a climbing rose. That died too. And then, last year, all the rhubarb died...*

Out loud, he exclaimed, 'Vines and climbing roses and rhubarb!'

The others, diverted from their search, regarded him in some bewilderment.

'Very nice, Sir Gabriel,' said Mrs Bugg soothingly, 'but not at this time of the year you won't find them, sir.'

'No, no,' he said, 'what a fool I am! What do they have in common?'

They looked blank.

'They all have very deep roots. Why won't they grow here?' His audience remained blank-faced. 'Why, because the soil must be too shallow!' said Gabriel triumphantly.

'Well, yes, sir,' said Wright at last, doubtfully. 'But I don't quite see—'

'If the soil is shallow, yet the garden is elevated above the rest of the Temple, there must be a cavity beneath it. And Delphinium must be in that cavity.'

Wright looked around him. 'Beneath the garden, sir? How could she get there?'

'I cannot imagine how she got there. More to the point is, how do we get her out?' Gabriel looked carefully at the Reverend Master's house. The kitchen window, slightly recessed, looked out onto the retaining wall, which was otherwise butted up against the width of the garden.

'Maybe we should see if we can hear her from inside the house,' said Wright.

The party knocked at the front door and were admitted by Mrs Jenkins.

As they clustered into the hall, the drawing-room door opened and John Gibson emerged and stood there staring at the motley group in obvious consternation.

'How do you do, Mr Gibson,' said Gabriel politely.

The young man's face flushed deeply. 'B-b-b, oh, I B-b-b-b.'

Rupert Brandish emerged from the drawing room, put a reassuring hand on Gibson's arm and surveyed the deputation in the hall.

'What is all this about?' He said it very sharply indeed. And it occurred fleetingly to Gabriel that he looked and sounded very much like the head of the household.

'Delphinium has disappeared,' said Mrs Bugg, too preoccupied with the drama to heed this unwelcoming reception. But Gabriel, watching, saw both men relax and on each of their faces an unmistakable relief. Catching Wright's eye, he knew he had seen it too. The reaction seemed very curious and Gabriel wondered what could possibly have engendered it. What was more natural than that Gibson should be visiting a friend?

'We are going out,' said Brandish firmly, handing Gibson his hat and coat from the hallstand and putting on his own. And then, more politely, 'May we leave Mrs Jenkins to help you?'

Down in the ancient kitchen, they stood listening intently. Very faintly, a cry could be heard. Now it seemed to be coming from behind the huge pine dresser.

'We'll need help to move that,' said Wright.

Meg piped up eagerly, 'Joe Brockley is sweeping Church Court.'

Joe, when fetched, did not look particularly obliging. 'That dresser hasn't been moved in my lifetime,' he said, on hearing the story. 'I never saw that dratted cat in the garden anyways and there isn't nowhere for her to go except out through the gate.'

'We think she may be underneath the garden, Joe,' said Gabriel.

'Underneath it? How could she be? There's just earth, sir. Unless you mean someone's buried her.' He grinned at the assembled group, received disapproving glares, and turned his ear to the dresser.

'I can't hear nothing,' he said. 'Maybe she's hid somewhere in here.' He began to peer around the kitchen.

Meg was dancing with impatience. 'No, no,' she cried. 'I'm certain it is coming from behind the dresser.'

'It certainly seems to be,' said Gabriel. 'Perhaps we had better check, Joe.'

Joe acquiesced with a surly shrug. Between them, he and Wright pushed and rocked and at last one end of the vast piece of furniture was slowly shifted away from the wall.

From the small gap that had been revealed, Delphinium shooting out like an enormous blue fur cannonball, landed with outraged dignity at their feet and glared round at her rescuers.

Seeing Gabriel, she flung herself piteously against his knees.

'I have no sympathy with you whatsoever, Delphinium,' said Gabriel severely. 'You fell whilst engaged in a murderous impulse and like all murderers you faced just punishment. You have no one but yourself to blame.'

And bending over, he scratched the top of her head with one finger, just where she most liked it.

Wright, catching Meg's eye, winked at her, and the girl giggled.

Gabriel meanwhile was peering behind the dresser. 'She could not conceivably have been in that space when the dresser was against the wall. Pull it out further.'

Single-handed this time, exerting his considerable strength, Joe Brockley did so, revealing the bare kitchen wall with, in the centre of the space usually covered by the dresser, a dark aperture.

Mrs Jenkins squeaked in alarm. Mrs Bugg and Meg stared round-eyed.

'Poor, poor Delphinium,' cooed Mrs Bugg. 'All alone in there in the dark with nothing to drink or eat.'

'It's plenty damp in there,' said Joe.

'And she'd recently had half a robin,' said Gabriel drily.

The men pressed forward, and Wright held up his lantern. Through the opening its beam revealed a stone-walled space, its proportions impossible to discern in the encroaching shadow. Gabriel stepped towards it, Wright following, but Joe stood back.

'I ain't going in there.' Apprehension was clear in his voice and the two other men looked at him, Gabriel with amusement, Wright with some contempt.

'My dear Joe, it is only an old cellar,' said Gabriel mildly. Reluctantly, the gardener slid through the aperture after them and Wright played his light around once again. They were in a small angled passageway, pitch dark, deeply cold, only a few feet long. The walls were rough and blackened with filth, and the uneven paving stones underfoot gleamed from the small puddles that had collected there. They felt their way along the wall and in a minute found themselves, not in the rough cellar that Gabriel had predicted, but in a far more formal inner chamber with walls of dressed stone.

A partition wall divided it into two halves, each entered through its own archway. Two sets of roughly carved stone steps, one for each half, led up, redundantly, to blank stone walls. Carved in the arch on the left side was the Lamb and Flag, the emblem of the Middle Temple, and on the right side the prancing Pegasus of the Inner Temple.

Gabriel turned instinctively to the latter side. Edging through the archway, he saw rows of stone shelves, arranged in narrow columns, open to view revealing ranks of lead coffins. As Wright raked his lantern across the shelves, Gabriel could discern on each a name. He read some aloud:

'*Sir Roger Blackley Knight d. 21 May 1689 aged 62. Mourned.*

'*Sir Thomas Wreath gone to eternity on 22 March 1690 in the 81st year of his age.*

'*John May Corbell Esq. d. 7 January 1691 of olde age.*'

On the names went, down the long columns of shelved coffins, a roll call of once-distinguished judges and barristers, many bearing the names of great families of England.

And then, on lower shelves, the servants of the Inner Temple:

Mary Bligh, washpot, died of the fever 1700

Joshua Roberts, butler, faithful servant b. 1650–d. 1702

And gardeners, porters and laundresses, periwig-makers and turnebroches… the occupants of the shelves that lined the space from stone floor to stone ceiling were kept as hierarchical in death as in life. Each name was illuminated briefly and each then darkened back into obscurity as Wright's lamp played over them, a metaphor for each life, its illumination so clear, ultimately so brief.

The columns ended in a deeply recessed decorative arch at the top. It was empty. Peering at the topmost coffin, Gabriel saw that it was dated 1740.

Oblivious of Wright and Brockley, he stood gazing at the solemn spectacle and felt the familiar little ache in the back of his throat. Decades of Inner Temple barristers and the men and women who had served them, lying together, according to status it was true, but nonetheless still united and protected as one community. Here they had all lain, long-forgotten, underneath the Reverend Master's garden.

'The earliest burial here is 1689,' he said. 'And the last interments made in the Church were in 1684. We had always assumed that was the end of burials within the Temple gates. But these vaults must have been built then to house bodies into the next century, until they, too, became full and were then sealed and forgotten.'

Wright's deep voice broke into Gabriel's thoughts as he pointed upwards. In the roof above them was a small grille covering a long ventilation shaft through which fading light and a pattern of broken branches were just discernible. The bars across the grille were corroded with rust and a couple were broken.

'That's how she fell through, sir. Lucky she didn't hurt herself. What a place, sir!' Wright shone his lantern over the floor. The remains of two mice suggested that Delphinium had had a second course after the robin.

But Delphinium was now far from Gabriel's mind. He murmured, half to himself, 'The steps lead straight up on either side, right out of the garden and under the Church. They must originally have come out on either side of the altar. One on the Middle Templars' side, the left side, one on our side, to the right.' He chuckled. 'They did not have to meet even in death; brought down straight from their funerals to lie on their own side of the Church, facing one another, as they had done when they worshipped there in life. And the doorway we have come through must have been made so that the Reverend Master could come here to pray for them from his own home. What a fascinating piece of our history. We must certainly commission a learned paper on...'

Joe Brockley broke in. 'There's nothing else to be seen here. I don't want to explore no further in.' His voice was rough with revulsion and Wright looked at him disapprovingly. Funny, he thought, how some men reacted to death; what a girl Brockley was! Anyone'd think he was Miss Topsy in the Drury Lane Garden what had once been a cemetery. Joe Brockley certainly wouldn't make a policeman, not for one moment he wouldn't...

Into these complacent thoughts Gabriel said soothingly, 'We'll be off then, Joe. It is certainly an extraordinary place. We will linger only a moment longer while I look into the Middle Temple side.' Without waiting for a response, he ducked under the other archway into an identical space. Here again were the shelves lining one wall, and the lead coffins stacked in columns mounting to the stone-vaulted ceiling, with a decorative arch deeply recessed above the top shelf.

But the arch on this side was not empty.

For a moment, all Gabriel could think of was the great painting by Wallis depicting the death of the eighteenth-century poet Thomas Chatterton. This corpse lay on its back in an identical graceful pose to that of Chatterton in the painting, slightly twisted towards its right side. The left arm lay on its chest. The right hung over the edge of the topmost lead coffin on which it lay.

But there the resemblance to the painting ceased. The right arm ended, not in the long pale fingers of the young poet, but in a handless ragged stump. The right leg had no foot. The face was turned towards them, leathery brown, the skin stretched over the bones, the eyes sunken deep in their sockets, the lips drawn back from the exposed teeth. There was a hole on one side where the upturned ear should have been.

There was a short silence. Into it, Gabriel spoke drily. 'Well,' he said, 'it seems we have found our body.'

They peered cautiously into the aperture. The torso was covered in the remnants of a wool suit, ravaged by mice and moths. A nondescript leather boot remained on one foot, the other lying empty nearby.

'How did it get like this?'

'It is very much warmer and drier here than in the Inner Temple vault,' observed Gabriel. 'Why should that be?'

'Do you mind giving me a leg up, sir?'

Gabriel locked his hands together and Wright hoisted himself gingerly up level with the arch.

'The wall is warm too, sir,' he said, 'but not warm enough to…' He pulled himself a little higher and felt deep inside the alcove that closed in on three sides around the body. 'Blimey,' he exclaimed, 'it's hot as – as an oven practically. What the devil…?'

'That must be the Reverend Master's kitchen chimney wall,' said Gabriel. 'I think there is our answer. The body was left here and it has become desiccated – whether by design or accident, who knows, though the latter seems more likely. Anyway, it was deposited here, wedged next to a hot wall, and this is the consequence.'

Wright lowered himself down and brushed his uniform conscientiously. 'Do you know who it is, sir?'

Gabriel shook his head. In the drama of the discovery, both men had forgotten Joe Brockley. He stood motionless behind them and, turning to him, Gabriel saw by the lantern light that he looked greenish-white.

'Sorry, Joe,' he said. 'We must get you out of here. But are you by any chance able to assist with identification?'

Joe wiped his sweaty brow and shook his head. 'I dunno who he is. Shouldn't think anyone would,' he said gruffly. 'With him all dried up like. Horrible.'

'No,' agreed Gabriel. 'Horrible indeed and nothing much to identify him.'

'There's a bit of a kerchief, sir,' pointed out Wright, 'poking out of one pocket.' And with Gabriel's assistance, he climbed back up and retrieved it. Of the type worn knotted around men's necks as well as used as handkerchiefs, the cotton from which it was made, like the leather of the boots, had survived largely intact. A blue fabric with a lighter pattern that had once been white was still just discernible.

He handed it to Gabriel, and then, recollecting his duty, said, 'I will let Detective Inspector Hughes know what is here, sir.'

'Yes,' said Gabriel, sounding very sober. 'And I will inform Sir William Waring.'

Back in the warm brightly lit kitchen all three men heaved a sigh of relief. Mrs Jenkins and Mrs Bugg and Meg stood by expectantly, peering into the gap. Delphinium was lapping rather desperately at a bowl of milk.

'Can we go and look?' said Meg, eager with curiosity.

'No call for that, Miss Meg,' said Wright. "Cos there's nothing to see. Just a bit of an old cellar. And me and Joe is going to put that there dresser back and no one won't be able to look then.'

He grinned at the girl who tossed her head.

The dresser was shifted back to its proper position. Away from the horrors of the vaults, the gardener seemed recovered. 'Thank you, Joe, for your assistance,' said Gabriel. He hesitated, aware of the female listeners. 'I need hardly ask for your silence with regard to this matter, for the time being.'

Joe understood. 'You can rely on that, sir,' he said, with a surprising degree of deference, and then backed thankfully towards the back door, grabbing his broom as he did so. Gabriel accompanied him. When he was about to leave, Joe said, 'Will it be all right to tell my father? If anyone knows anything about those vaults, it will be him. He might be able to tell us if anyone else knew about them. And,' he hesitated, conscious of nearby listeners, 'he might help with – with what is in there.'

'Indeed yes.'

Joe lowered his voice still further. 'It would fair upset him to see – to see *that*, sir. Shall I just show him the kerchief? Just in case it jogs his memory? I will bring it back to you later this evening, sir.'

'Yes. That is a kind thought, Joe,' said Gabriel with not a little relief. 'Let us spare your father if we can.'

When the gardener had gone and Mrs Bugg and Meg had scurried back to their own kitchen, Gabriel picked up his top hat with a curious sense of anticlimax.

'Will you accompany me, Mr Wright?' Across the kitchen, his eyes met those of Delphinium, raised from her saucer as she observed his departure. 'Well done, Delphinium,' he said.

Detective Inspector Hughes and Sir William Waring were informed of the discovery of the lost vaults and of the extra body concealed within them. Each reacted characteristically. Sir William greeted the news with a petulance that suggested more personal affront than any deeper emotion, accompanied by panicky speculation as to how long both discoveries could be kept from the press. Detective Inspector Hughes took immediate action. The kitchen in the Reverend Master's house was closed later that evening under the pretext that builders would attend to close off a structurally dangerous cellar. Mrs Bugg, bursting with importance, meanwhile undertook the cooking for Rupert Brandish, Mrs Jenkins and the two maids. A message was sent requesting the urgent attendance of Professor Humphries, but the professor, Hughes was informed, had left the hospital for his home in Herne Hill.

First thing next morning, accompanied by genial grumbles at being called out on a Saturday and much squeezing and puffing, Humphries negotiated the aperture in the kitchen and the narrow passageway to the vaults. He was accompanied by Gabriel, Detective Inspector Hughes and Sir William Waring.

Behind them came four police constables, including Wright. The latter brought with them stronger lights and ladders and the stomping of boots and a sense of normality that somehow dispelled some of the romance of that long-hidden place. But nothing, thought Gabriel, could detract from the strange grace and the horror of the mutilated body with its wizened ageless face that lay gazing at them from the top of the uppermost coffin.

With the foot of the ladder held firmly by two police officers, Humphries mounted gingerly and rolled the body over gently.

'Light as a feather,' his cheerful matter-of-fact voice announced, resounding in the stone surroundings, 'and dry, you might say, as a bone.' He chuckled. 'Dead as a dodo. With bits missing. What else can I tell you?'

'Can we be told how he died, Humphers?' said Gabriel.

'No mystery about that. Biffed on the head from behind, with a blunt instrument. Depressed fracture of the skull.' He peered more carefully, gently rolling the head forward so that the grinning face seemed to be bowing to the party standing below. 'God knows what was used. Something with a big surface area. Bigger than a hammer, say. Jolly hard, too.'

'And you said you might be able to tell if the body parts were removed from a dead or live person if we found the body?' chipped in Wright hopefully.

Humphries gave his little bark of laughter. 'That certainly doesn't need an expert! They have been removed years after the body became desiccated; recently, in fact. Hacked off quite easily and there are little fragments lying around the severed stumps. Not a job that needed an expert either,' he added cheerfully. 'Less skill than butchers employ every day.'

He descended from the ladder, brushed down his jacket and retrieved his leather bag, ominously bulging with the instruments of his profession. 'Otherwise, it's as I told you. A man, young, desiccated by the heat, been there some years.'

'And his identity?' asked Hughes.

'No identifying feature of any kind that I can see. Just a young man.'

After the departure of Humphries, Simmonds, the head porter and Sugden, the signwriter and carpenter, were both summoned by Sir William, with Detective Inspector Hughes' assent, sworn to secrecy, and asked if they could identify the body.

Neither of them was able to do so.

Gabriel, intervening, and with the fact in mind that the only remaining disappearance of anyone from the Temple seemed to be that of Durrant the young porter, asked the question directly.

'Do you remember Durrant? Could this possibly be him?'

Beside him, Sir William made a sudden impatient movement and scowled meaningfully. Before he could speak, however, Simmonds had answered.

'It could be, sir. He was dark and of slight build. But I couldn't say more than that, not with the face in that state, I couldn't. Impossible to tell.'

For the time being at least, there was little else they could do. As they left, the corpse seemed to grin at them through its bared teeth, still tantalisingly anonymous.

Back in Sir William's room a conference took place.

'In summary,' said Gabriel, 'we have an as yet unidentified body in our vaults. The evidence suggests he was murdered. Either the murderer or someone else has discovered the vaults and deposited the corpse in that strange point of concentrated heat. It has been there for some years. Someone, the same someone or perhaps a different one, has recently cut from it the foot, toe, hand and ear, as packed in those gruesome parcels, and delivered them to the Treasurer, Hopkins and Barton. As well as, most tragically, Reverend Master Vernon-Osbert.'

As he spoke, those in the room involuntarily imagined that Gothic scene, in the darkness of the vaults, witnessed by those ranks of silent coffins. There was a collective shudder.

'Well,' said Detective Inspector Hughes briskly, 'we'll have that body moved for you. I agree, a bash on the back of the head looks almost certain to be murder.'

Waring addressed Gabriel. 'Is there nothing which would help with the identification of the remains?'

Wright opened his mouth, caught Gabriel's eye and the slight shake of his head, and subsided. No mention was made of the blue neckerchief, removed from the pocket of the corpse earlier in the day, borrowed and faithfully returned an hour or so later by Joe Brockley, with the information that his father had not recognised it; it was now lying on Gabriel's table in 4 King's Bench Walk.

Nothing disturbs for very long the rhythms and rituals of the Temple, not violent death nor turbulent emotion. On Sundays there was a service in the Temple Church, which all residents were expected to attend. That Sunday was the first for the best part of half a century for which Vernon-Osbert was not standing at the door, welcoming in his congregation. It was a large one. Thanks to a children's book, *Millie the Temple Church Mouse*, published a few years previously and now very famous, families with no connection to the Temple came to worship there alongside Bench and Bar.

Instead of Vernon-Osbert's familiar stooped figure, Rupert Brandish stood alone in his scarlet clerical robes, deputed by the Treasurer to take Vernon-Osbert's place whilst a suitable new incumbent was decided. He looked, thought Gabriel, older from the responsibility, deeply sober, somehow gaining in presence. No longer a lanky boy but a figure of authority.

He took the service and gave the sermon, a tribute to Vernon-Osbert's life dedicated to the Temple, with an impressive and warm gravitas. Beside Gabriel, Sir William Waring grunted approvingly.

'I am minded to suggest that the boy is given the post permanently,' he said to Gabriel under cover of the organ's closing voluntary. 'I have discussed it with Hopkins. He feels Brandish is too young, but that was an impressive performance.'

'I agree,' said Gabriel, glad for once to be able to share an opinion with Sir William.

The two men made their way outside into Church Court where Sir William's customary self-absorption reasserted itself.

'I will be glad to get the matter settled. Amelia's marriage will be taking place here. As the church is a Royal Peculiar, I have had to obtain a special licence from the Archbishop of Canterbury.' He looked smug. 'One he was delighted to grant, given – as he was good enough to say – the distinction of the two families concerned. It will be the biggest event for decades in the Temple Church and it should of course be conducted by our own Reverend Master. We need to appoint a permanent incumbent as soon as possible.'

The topic inspired in Sir William an unexpected geniality. Rather to Gabriel's surprise, an offer of sherry was made. He felt unable to refuse.

'Perhaps just a brief interlude, thank you, Sir William. I am in the midst of a trial and tomorrow is a most important day.'

'Oh, nonsense, nonsense,' said Sir William, still genial. 'All work and no play, you know.'

'I have never myself recognised any distinction between the two.'

('That of course is the man's trouble,' observed Sir William later to his cronies at the Garrick Club, when recounting this conversation. 'Ward needs taking out of himself.' Gabriel, had he been present in that convivial group, would have pointed out the fatuity of this particular expression; but Waring's companions all agreed heartily.)

'Well,' Waring said now, when the two of them were settled either side of his fireplace, 'business first. We seem to be no further forward in relation to the identification of the body?'

'I fear we are not, Sir William.'

The Treasurer grunted. 'The sooner the police have finished sniffing around, the better I shall like it. It is probably some vagrant from Fleet Street who trespassed.'

'Even vagrants have identities,' said Gabriel mildly. 'I would like to think that we, as an institution, had done our best for this man. Whatever the circumstances of his death.'

But Sir William looked unconvinced. 'He may count himself lucky he has spent the years being cooked in our vaults,' he observed callously, 'when the alternative was a pauper's grave or the anatomist's slab. Well, I rely on you to ascertain the truth, at least with regard to the disgusting use of this ancient body to spread horror throughout the Temple. And if, on the way, you discover the member of this institution who spread the story to those damned ferrets in Fleet Street, I shall be even more pleased. But kindly remember—'

I know what you are going to say, Gabriel thought. And hoped he had not inadvertently said it aloud.

'—discretion is what matters most. By the by, do you see much of your new neighbour?' he said casually.

Gabriel was immediately on the alert. Waring was never casual.

'Now and again,' he volunteered cautiously.

Waring fiddled with his paper knife. 'Does he seem to you to be progressing satisfactorily in his pupillage?'

'Goodness, Sir William, I would have no opinion on that. We have exchanged the merest neighbourly chit-chat.'

'A most distinguished family.' Sir William seemed to have forgotten that he had already told Gabriel this. 'Simply born for success; at the Bar, in Parliament.'

In Gabriel's lack of response Sir William seemed to discern reservations. Rather defensively, he said, 'Of course the boy will have to pull himself together and amend that little – hesitancy in his speech. But when he gets into court, as his father says, a bit of ragging from his opponents will soon knock that out of him.'

Gabriel, impassive externally, shrank inwardly. With his finger, unseen, he traced one of the familiar little patterns on the underside of his chair. He thought of that so plainly unhappy boy. Although he had not very often been the recipient, he had seen the damage ragging could do. He must say something, without giving away a confidence.

'His botanical knowledge and skills are very impressive,' he offered at last.

Sir William frowned. 'The ferns? Not a very *manly* interest, is it? However, he will have no time for such things when he is established in practice. And the cases are very decorative, I suppose, for Amelia's drawing room.'

Gabriel made movements preparatory to leaving, and as he stood up, Waring said, 'Keep an eye on the boy, will you, Ward? You are his neighbour and a good example of hard work, even if you do take it to extremes. Sometimes his father and I think John is a little – *lackadaisical*. Needs to keep his nose to the grindstone a bit more. He is in a competitive world now.'

Before Gabriel could respond, Waring seemed to regret the confidence and had hastened into another topic.

'And how is the case of the century proceeding?' he said jovially. 'I imagine you are relying on the susceptibilities of the gentlemen of the jury to get your client her verdict. Well, good luck to the little lady. She certainly has a nerve.'

'No, I am not relying on that,' said Gabriel. 'I am relying on the fact that Miss Tillotson's reputation has been grossly besmirched.'

Waring snorted. 'Oh, come, come, Ward. We all know the *Nation's Voice* is a disgrace, but really – reputation? That little corker? By Jove, I'd like to...' His voice trailed off at Gabriel's involuntary expression of distaste.

This last remark was not the only reason that Gabriel left the interview with a deep sense of discomfort. Nor was the fact that he had been reminded of the case, hanging in the air, so to speak, and of what tomorrow might hold. He was also aware that there seemed to be a mystery which eluded him but in which Gibson played some undefined part. A young man whose background was so conventionally suited to the Bar. Yet who was so unhappy. That stammer which must make public speaking a torture to him. That passion for those delicate ferns, trembling in their perfect environments. That yearning in him for travel; the boy exuded some kind of deep frustration with himself. What was it he had said? *Neither my heart nor my inclinations nor my aptitudes in any single respect have led me to my present circumstances.* That was pretty comprehensive. And even Sir William, not renowned for his sensitivity, had seemed to feel some *lack* in his future son-in-law.

Gabriel thought again of the furtive arrangements with Brandish. He thought of the boxes stored under the house in which Brandish was lodging; and of the nameless body. Was it really possible that these two young men, oddly defensive when they had been encountered at the Reverend Master's house on the evening the vaults were discovered, were in some way linked to the grinning desiccated corpse that awaited a name?

22

After the turmoil of the weekend, Gabriel could scarcely believe that he was back in court that Monday, bewigged and gowned, calmly seated in counsel's row, client, junior barrister and solicitor at hand, Hopkins and his team alongside, all arranged in their designated places like counters at the beginning of an elaborate board game.

His papers were in a neat pile in front of him, his notebook was aligned so that the middle stitch of the spine was level with his gold pencil lying beside it, and the handle of his jug of water pointed towards the left-hand corner of the inkstand. All was in order. Was it really only two and a half days ago that he had found the mutilated body of an unknown man, mummified in a secret vault under the Reverend Master's garden? The whole episode seemed, in this formalised setting, to be preposterously unlikely.

The reassuring morning ritual of court proceedings in these familiar surroundings began with Hopkins calling The Honourable Frederick Sewell as his first witness. There seemed to be a collective indrawing of breath from the entire court and all eyes turned to watch Sewell's elegant figure proceed nonchalantly towards the witness box.

Gabriel studied the young man with interest and a sinking heart. He was undoubtedly good-looking, with dark hair swept back from a broad forehead and fine dark eyes under beautifully modelled eyebrows. He wore his stylish clothes with a distinct air. He was in fact the embodiment of the aristocratic young man about town. The judge nodded approvingly. The gentlemen of the jury looked admiring and respectful. Sewell climbed the steps to the witness stand, made a little bow towards the judge, and smiled at the jury. It was a smile of great charm and the jury all smiled back at him. The court clerk stood to administer the oath.

At that very moment, Gabriel felt a sudden violent clutching at the back of his robe and then, as suddenly, it was released and there was a hard thud accompanied by a rustle and clatter. He spun round in astonishment and alarm in time to see Topsy fall to the ground and with her the bundles of court papers that had been ranged on the shelf behind him. She lay on her side on the stone floor, her face as white as the papers settling, like a snowstorm, around her.

For an instant, the court remained frozen. Then, as the ushers rushed forward to her aid, the judge said, 'I will rise for a few minutes and the jury bailiff will escort the gentlemen of the jury to their room.'

And with studied judicial dignity he retreated into his room behind the bench. Hopkins leaned across to Gabriel.

'Is this a stunt?' he said disagreeably. 'Quite the little scene-stealer, isn't she?'

'She is unwell,' said Gabriel, 'as anyone can see. And you will have to delay your case until she recovers.'

The ushers carried Topsy out into the lofty corridor and then to one of the small side rooms provided in the Law Courts for private consultation during trials. As they did so, her eyes opened. Once deposited in a chair, she looked dazedly at Gabriel and Brindle, hovering anxiously over her.

'You fainted, Miss Tillotson,' said Brindle.

'It-It was the shock,' said Topsy feebly. 'Th-The shock of-of seeing The Honourable Frederick Sewell. He-He was not what

I thought he was going to be…' And her voice wobbled and faded.

'Not what you thought he was going to be?' repeated Brindle. 'What do you mean? He is a typical handsome, charming, rich and titled young member of the aristocracy.'

'Yes,' said Topsy sadly.

'Did you know him after all?' demanded her solicitor. 'Is that what this fainting fit is really about? Did he beat you? Or abuse you? Or bully you?'

'No,' said Topsy. 'I do not know him at all.' And she looked helplessly past her solicitor to Gabriel.

The dreadful truth was beginning to dawn upon him.

'Miss Tillotson,' he said very gently, 'tell us everything, from the beginning, in your own way and words – and then we will see where we are.'

And so Topsy, in stops and starts, told the rest of her story.

What with her silences and tears, it took some time. A message to the judge secured an adjournment for two hours. In the consultation room, when she had finished, stolid unflappable Mr Brindle buried his head in his hands.

'Dear God in heaven, Sir Gabriel, what an unutterable disaster! We must abandon the case! The astronomic costs we have incurred! Our professional reputations!'

Gabriel shifted his pen, lying on the table before him, very carefully half an inch to the left. It had become misaligned with the corner of the pile of papers next to it. He thought for some moments, the silence broken only by Topsy's sobbing.

Then he said, 'Don't you think we had better see what the jury thinks of it?'

'The jury? Tell the jury?' said Brindle incredulously. 'You cannot be serious. We have no case left to put to them! No, no, we must withdraw. There is no hope for us!'

Ignoring this nihilistic approach, Gabriel turned back to Topsy and sacrificed, not without a pang, another beautifully pressed and folded handkerchief.

'Miss Tillotson,' he said, 'will you be a very brave young woman and tell to the jury the story you have just told us?'

Topsy gulped and twisted the immaculate white linen into a tight ball. Gabriel averted his eyes.

'I am not sure I can. I would not know where to start. They would never understand.'

Gabriel hesitated. Should he take this gamble? What was the best way through this tangled mess, so far from the dry realities of the law he loved?

Then at last he said, 'I recall two striking things that you have said to me Miss Tillotson, over the course of our acquaintance. One was when we first met. It was: *I thought the law was about justice.*'

'But I cannot tell them this! They would condemn me for it.' Topsy's voice was now ominously high and tremulous.

'Ah, that brings me to the second thing you said, after the attack in Drury Lane Garden. Do you recall? I asked you if you were afraid and you said: *How can I be afraid when I am telling the truth?*'

The tears trickled down Topsy's face. 'But I do not know what the truth is, Sir Gabriel.'

'It is your truth,' he said calmly. 'And together we will tell it to the jury. Perhaps it will be their truth too, if you are brave enough to tell it.' He hesitated and then said, 'You know, Miss Tillotson, I am aware the witness box can sometimes feel like a vast and lonely wasteland, but you must recall that in your barrister you have a guide who will, as long as you follow him, lead you out of the wilderness.'

Mr Brindle groaned. But Topsy took a deep breath and blew her nose hard. Her face set with resolution and she stood up without a word and put her hand on Gabriel's proffered arm.

'Well done,' he said, and remembered using the same words to Delphinium after she had led them to the body in the vault. They had felt, on both occasions, like a salute to a comrade.

Emerging from the consultation room, Mr Brindle following gloomily behind them, they pressed through the crowd of reporters clustering outside the door of the court. Inside, the rustling and whispering died down as Gabriel took his place and a message was sent to the judge that the case would resume.

Gabriel rose to his feet. 'My Lord, we are grateful for the adjournment and my client is now recovered. But a matter has arisen that the court should know about. Mr Sewell has not yet been sworn and his evidence has not begun. I would like Your Lordship's leave to recall my client into the witness box.'

Beside him, Hopkins harrumphed histrionically, but the judge, after a moment's hesitation, waved a hand in resigned acquiescence. Even judges, Gabriel reflected, have human curiosity. It was an emotion he had been relying upon.

This time Topsy refused the offer of a seat. Standing very straight in the witness box, she was reminded she was still under oath, and then in her husky voice, prompted by Gabriel's gentle questions, she told her story, just as she had told it to him when he had visited her in her dressing room. About the young man in the shabby coat standing out in the rain, and how, over the next few weeks, she had fallen in love with him.

Sir Edward Hopkins rolled his eyes expressively at the jury and got to his feet.

'Is my learned friend going to share with us the relevance of this touching little tale?'

Gabriel ignored the interruption.

'What was your young man's name, Miss Tillotson?'

'His name was George.'

'Tell the court what happened next.'

And Topsy resumed her story. They had had such a short time together. Three or four meetings, that was all. Then, over a simple supper, George said he had fallen in love with her and that very soon, when he had saved a bit, he would like to marry her. Topsy had said she would like that. He had never so much as tried to steal a kiss. He put the band of a cigar, left on the table by a previous occupant, on her finger. Then he said he would take her home in a cab. And there, in the dark of the hansom cab, with the driver's shield down and the leather curtains drawn, in the warm darkness... She trailed into silence.

'Miss Tillotson,' said Gabriel, 'forgive me asking you this, but the jury must understand. Are you saying that you had intimate relations with George?'

Topsy lifted her chin and looked directly into the shocked and disapproving faces of the jury. She spoke very clearly indeed, all hesitancy gone.

'Yes. I loved him. I trusted him. And I had promised to marry him. The next day I did not regret it one little bit.'

In the press box, the newspaper men began to whisper and then to scribble frantically. In the public gallery, there was a gasp. Sir Edward Hopkins' chest swelled with self-righteous triumph and he leaped to his feet.

'May we beg for some elucidation, My Lord? Just what is being alleged? Is my learned friend now trying to suggest that Mr Sewell seduced Miss Tillotson away from this "George"?'

The judge put down his pen and glared at Gabriel.

'Really, Sir Gabriel, what *is* this all about? Is your client now acknowledging that she is unchaste? Because if so...'

'Would Your Lordship please bear with us? All will become clear.'

Gabriel turned, without waiting for a response, to the still little figure in the witness box, but his tranquil tones had restored some calm to the scene. A silence fell and it seemed that the court was now holding its collective breath.

'My Lord has referred to you being unchaste, Miss Tillotson. Were you unchaste?'

'No,' she said. 'You see, I had never been in love before. And I truly believed he would marry me.'

Out of the corner of his eye, Gabriel thought he saw the flash of a handkerchief being extracted from a pocket in the jury box. It was the reaction he had been hoping for.

'What happened after that night?'

'Th-The next day we were to meet,' said Topsy sadly, 'but he did not come.'

'Is your George in court today, Miss Tillotson?'

'Yes, he is,' she said.

Around the court, necks were craned towards the crowds in the public gallery. But Gabriel's timing was immaculate and with his next question all heads swivelled back to face him.

'Yesterday, before Mr Sewell had arrived, you told the court that you had not had intimate relations with him. Did you believe that to be true?'

'Yes.'

'I am going to ask you the same question now. Did you have intimate relations with Mr Sewell?'

Topsy looked across the courtroom at Sewell, lounging on a bench behind Sir Edward Hopkins, one arm draped along its back and one silk-socked ankle crossed over the other. The young man smiled knowingly at her.

A silence, palpable in its intensity, fell.

And then, just when it became unbearable, Topsy looked at the puzzled judge and jury and said, very clearly, 'I was deceived. You see, now I know he *was* George all along.'

23

Trials, like life, always go on to some sort of ultimate conclusion, however shockingly they unfold along the way.

Stan the cabman, waiting outside the court expectantly, was no longer needed, since the incident he had described, Topsy now admitted, had occurred. He returned reluctantly to his cab rank, his moment in the spotlight denied him.

Sewell, called once more into the witness box, apparently unashamed, gave his evidence. His full name was Frederick George Bramley Sewell. Yes, he had told Frank Holloway that he had had intimate relations with Topsy in a hansom cab. Well, it was absolutely true, wasn't it? She had just told the jury so. He *had* conquered The Unconquerable. He was a bit of a gambling man. Never could resist a wager. It had been a bet with a friend. To conquer The Unconquerable. After all, she was no innocent, singing those songs, was she? In fact, in his view, she had been asking for it. It was obvious she had liked him. Well, he couldn't help that, could he? If he had used the name George in order to achieve his ends, it was one of his names – and anyway, a rose by any other name, eh? And there were plenty of men besides him who had to say something about marriage in order to do a little persuading, weren't there? A lot of men in England would be in the dock if that were against the law.

Frank Holloway gave evidence too, in a mixture of self-righteousness and defensiveness. A member of the aristocracy had told him that he had had intimate relations with a chorus girl turned star in a hansom cab. The chorus girl in question had made quite a stunt out of her chastity. It was not the newspaper who had called her The Unconquerable. It was the public. All they, the *Nation's Voice*, had done was to say 'unconquerable' was a bit of an exaggeration and they knew as much from a very reliable source. The horse's mouth, you might say; well, the horse's driver anyway. Here he grinned at the jury. And no one could say that what he had written was untrue.

Sir Edward's closing speech followed. Of course, he told the jury, no one should approve of Mr Sewell's conduct. But in the end, he pointed out, Mr Sewell was not on trial. Young men will be young men. And, whatever Mr Sewell might have done, Sir Edward was bound to say that Topsy Tillotson's self confessed behaviour in the hansom cab with a young man who, by her own admission, she had known for just weeks, was so utterly reprehensible that he was rendered speechless!

Gabriel, listening with a sinking heart, wished his opponent *had* been rendered speechless.

But on Hopkins went. What had the *Nation's Voice* done, except tell a story true in all its essentials? Even if the jury were to conclude it was not wholly true, was this young woman really entitled to say her reputation had been damaged? What did the jury, men of the world, think her reputation had been prior to this case? Sir Edward warmed to his theme. An actress! And furthermore, the jury might think there was ample evidence that she was not averse to receiving attention from men.

By the time Gabriel got to his feet, the mood of the court had swung from sympathy for Topsy's heartbreak to a far more judgemental attitude. Hopkins' speech had made the jurors remember the stern moral values inculcated in them.

Gabriel waited, as he always waited, until concentration centred on his still figure, in a rather shabby gown and a wig that was a little too large for him. He waited while the silence lengthened and the expectation of hearing something interesting heightened. And then he plunged in, in his dry precise voice. But what he said was neither dry nor precise.

'Gentlemen of the jury, you have witnessed Miss Tillotson's grief. Was that grief heartfelt? She is, as Sir Edward Hopkins has repeatedly pointed out, an actress. But you know more about her than that, do you not? She is not just the embodiment of fame. She is a young girl, fifteen years old when she first began in the theatre. Only nineteen years old now. She comes from a humble family. You heard what Miss Vera Perkins thought of her; Miss Tillotson could have had a life of roses and lilies and top hats and suppers at the Café Royal. She could have dreamed of glass slippers. But instead, she wanted to go home every night to her own humble, loving family. Then she met a young man who she believed was, like her, a humble person, not a prince to anyone except, perhaps, to her. Who, over their few meetings, asked for no physical affection from her, who gave her a worthless little symbol of love and who said he wanted to marry her. She agreed. And she has told you what happened next. It may seem to you, gentlemen of the jury, the final irony that when he did not come to meet her, she thought it was because the *Nation's Voice*'s scurrilous story about her had led him to reject her. Well, you now know the sorry end for this particular little Cinderella.'

The judge raised his eyebrows. He did not expect this kind of histrionics from Sir Gabriel Ward KC. Beside Gabriel, Hopkins shifted a little uneasily and looked sideways at the jury to see how they were reacting. This, he thought, was *his* kind of advocacy, and Ward seemed to be doing it rather well. The jurymen were now all leaning forward, gazes intent as they listened.

'Encapsulated in the Magna Carta, gentlemen of the jury, we have entrusted our justice system, in all serious cases, criminal and civil trials alike, into the hands of jurors. Whatever we lawyers tell you, whatever a judge may say, it is your right and duty to act in accordance with your consciences. Where do your consciences lead you now? Are you content to say, as has been said to you by Sir Edward and will be summed up to you by My Lord, that the *Nation's Voice* has proved the truth of what they published? That Miss Tillotson had intimate relations with a man named George in a hansom cab and so they are entitled to drag her reputation in the dust and tell the world that she is unchaste? Is even the first half of that proposition true? In these circumstances, is it really and truly true *in its essence*? Even if you come to the conclusion that those bald facts are true, can the second half lead on from that when Miss Tillotson was so grievously deceived?'

One or two of the jurymen shifted in their seats. One closed his eyes in fierce concentration. The one who earlier had extracted his handkerchief did so again. The remainder just looked puzzled.

'Miss Tillotson has had her heart broken. But far, far worse than that, she has lost her trust. In love and in life and in decent behaviour. You, gentlemen of the jury, are in a position to restore at least a little of that trust by the verdict you come to. I ask you to do so.'

And Gabriel sat down, more drained than he had ever before felt at the end of a closing speech.

The jury were out for four hours. In two separate conference rooms, the teams of litigants waited.

In the judge's room, Mr Justice Whittington-Allsop, apparently so confident in his summing up against Topsy, sat uneasily. In part because deep in his heart there was a feeling of some disgust at the behaviour of The Honourable Frederick Sewell, a young man whose father was a member of the same club as he was and whose mother was invited to the same tea parties as the judge's wife. And in part because, looming over his shoulder, were the judges of the Court of Appeal who might, if further proceedings should take place, say publicly that he had erred in his exposition of the law.

The press, dispersed among the uncomfortable wooden benches that lined the grim stone corridors of the Law Courts, waited too, as tense as litigants and judge even though indifferent to the result, since either way the newspapers the next morning would be breaking a story of unparalleled sensation.

And then, just as everyone began to speculate as to whether the jury had fallen out or could not make up their minds or were all twelve in dead faints in the jury room, the jury bailiff emerged for what was his own moment in the spotlight.

'The jury has a verdict,' he announced over and again, to the judge in his room, to the two consultation rooms, to the corridor at large.

24

And the verdict, pronounced by the foreman of the jury into the tensest of silences, was for the Plaintiff, Miss Topsy Tillotson, with damages set at an astronomical £3,000.

Then there was nothing but noise. Lionel Sullivan gave a furious exclamation and, leaning forward, seized Hopkins' arm. There was crashing of the press seats as their occupants shot for the door. Then there were cheers from the public gallery. The judge's sonorous pronouncement, his eyebrows raised, that judgment was for the Plaintiff Miss Tillotson in the sum determined by the jury, Defendant the *Nation's Voice* to pay all costs, followed on.

At last, the tumult died down.

A pale-faced Topsy was escorted from court by Brindle. In the corridor outside, released from the public gallery, Vera Perkins and the Tillotsons awaited her. Topsy's mother hugged her. So, too, did Vera, flaming with indignation.

'Those cads!' she hissed. 'That Sewell is a wicked, wicked man. Never again will my girls be allowed near him. And that journalist... I'd like to wring the little rat's neck for him! And as for Sir Edward Hopkins – liar not lawyer, I say!'

Topsy extricated herself from this fierce embrace. Behind Vera stood Gabriel. Topsy held out her hand to him, and he took it.

'Thank you,' she said. 'You were wonderful.'

'No,' said Gabriel, and heard in his head an echo of their conversation in her dressing room. He gave his little bow. 'You were the wonderful one, Miss Tillotson.'

When Topsy had left, Gabriel received the astonished admiration of his junior, and the pompously expressed gratitude of Mr Brindle. Escaping at last, he made his way to the robing room.

Standing a few yards from the door, locked in quiet and plainly vicious conversation, stood Lionel Sullivan and Frank Holloway. As Gabriel approached, Sullivan, with a last hissed word, stormed off down the corridor, leaving Holloway alone. He, with studied insolence, stuck his foot in Gabriel's path, forcing him to stop.

'Oh, you think you have been very clever, don't you, *Sir* Gabriel?' he said with a sneer. 'You think you have won the race and ruined the *Nation's Voice*.' He leaned forward, his voice bitter with venom. 'Maybe you will discover that I have another horse yet to run.'

Gabriel stepped around the foot without comment. He could not, in any event, imagine what Holloway meant. Was he thinking of mounting an appeal? Surely not. His very lack of reaction seemed to goad the journalist to further bitter rage. He called after Gabriel, 'Maybe you lot will soon find yourselves down in the mud where we lesser mortals have to live.'

Stepping into the robing room, Gabriel, already shaken from this exchange, was confronted by a furiously angry Hopkins, plainly lying in wait, who burst into speech at the sight of him.

'This was a perverse verdict, Ward. It was contrary to the evidence and the law, won by an over-sentimental plea to the emotions of the jury. We shall appeal.'

Gabriel raised his eyebrows. 'That, if I may say so, is a little rich coming from you.

'And you will do nothing of the sort. Firstly, the *Nation's Voice* cannot afford to launch an appeal. Your fees in this action will have seen to that. Secondly, you will not take the risk. As you know, the result would be highly unpredictable, and if you lost on appeal also the costs would be enormous. The *Nation's Voice* is a scurrilous rag. If it is now ruined there are many who will be glad to see it so. Thirdly, Sewell behaved like a cad and you cannot deny it. I think he will lie low for a while, not invite yet more opprobrium.'

'Oh, it was reprehensible of him, of course, but these young men must sow their wild oats, eh? And if it had not been him, it would have been someone else. The young lady was ripe for it, was she not? And I daresay she will be rather less gullible the next time a good-looking fellow spins her a yarn.'

'How dare you, Hopkins?' said Gabriel, and was surprised to hear that his voice shook a little.

His opponent looked at him with aggrieved charm. 'Well, don't blame me for it; I was only conducting a case, like you were. I knew nothing about the bet or the subterfuge until Topsy Tillotson made her revelation.'

'I did not suppose that you did. Had I thought that, I would have reported you for professional misconduct.'

Gabriel hesitated. But now, he thought, was as good a time as any. Since the trial was over, there was the body lying unidentified in the Temple to think of, and certain loose ends still trailing. Tie them up, he thought to himself, and at least I can see what is left more clearly.

'Whilst we are here, Hopkins, I may as well raise with you another matter. Just after Christmas, in a quest to find Miss Tillotson's George, a quest which we now know was doomed to fail, I found by sheer chance another George. A little boy, ten years old, living in circumstances of extreme poverty in an alleyway off Smithfield Market.'

Hopkins, in the act of removing his wig and brushing his hair into its usual immaculate style, shrugged. 'A lot of it about, I am afraid. Those alleyways are an insanitary disgrace. The responsible authorities really should do something about the Poor Laws, don't you think?'

'I do. But in some instances, the responsibility may lie elsewhere.' Gabriel paused and then said deliberately, 'The child's mother's name is Ivy Bunch. She was formerly one of the Temple servants, dismissed in disgrace when her condition was discovered.'

Hopkins continued to look at himself in the mirror as he removed his court bands and put on a fresh stiff collar. But Gabriel, looking at the reflection, saw that his eyes had narrowed suddenly and dangerously.

'Why should you think this unfortunate occurrence has anything to do with me?'

'You are rather more transparent than you believe, Hopkins, to those who have known you as long as I have. Your discomfort when I called Miss Vera Perkins was obvious, as it was when Miss Tillotson was telling the jury about the behaviour of the men at the stage door.'

'Being a little detective has gone to your head, Ward,' said Hopkins, and his voice held a darker edge.

'I did not have to be much of a detective. When I first met Miss Perkins, she told me, in extolling your virtues as a great advocate, that you were one of those who sometimes wait at the backstage door of the Drury Lane Theatre. When, on the same occasion, I met Miss Rosie Bunch, I wondered why she said to me, "I know all about the Temple and KCs", with a bitterness that varied markedly from her normal sunny manner. I wondered then if it might be an allusion to some grubby behaviour by you towards her. Then I discovered Miss Ivy Bunch is her sister and it all fell into place. This was not about misbehaviour at the theatre, but in the Temple. Rosie's bitterness arose as a result of what you had done to Ivy when she was working there.'

There was a brief silence. Gabriel added for good measure, 'I suspect you have never laid eyes on the child. Neither, as yet, have I. A very good-looking little boy, I am told, dark hair, blue eyes, would charm the birds off the trees. I rather suspect he may seem familiar to me.'

'If I were you, old boy, I would mind my own damn' business,' said Hopkins, now with undisguised venom.

'That,' Gabriel said with the greatest cordiality, 'is exactly what I intend to do. And furthermore, I will tell you why. It is because I intend in a month's time to revisit Miss Ivy Bunch. And I have the greatest possible confidence that when I do so, I will find her circumstances relieved by a modest allowance, from a mysterious source unknown to her, that allows her to live decently without sending a ten-year-old boy out to sweep floors. Such a situation should not be allowed in 1902, whatever the precise laws as to child labour may be, and well you know it, Hopkins.'

'And what makes you feel such confidence?'

Gabriel realised, to his own surprise, that the emotion he was feeling in the face of this unshakeable complacency was an uncharacteristic and glorious anger. He drew a deep breath. 'I derive it,' he said very deliberately, 'from the knowledge that if I do not find the situation remedied, I will make your name mud in the Temple. Oh, do not tell me these things happen, I am aware they do. I also know that not everyone will condemn you for what they may describe as a dalliance. Waring must know of your role in all this; he dismissed the girl. Hence his reluctance for me to investigate her apparent disappearance. But barristers are gentlemen, Hopkins, and gentlemen should acknowledge their responsibilities. And there are those, as you well know, who will think very much the less of you for choosing a Temple servant for your "dalliance". The Temple is, I thank God, a small world. It exacts its own punishments.'

Without another word, Hopkins flung on his overcoat, grabbed his wig tin, strode to the door and left, slamming it behind him hard enough to shake the windowpanes.

That evening Gabriel sat exhausted by his fire, his mind still swirling with the events of the last few days, and with none of that sense of peace and release from tension that usually came over him at the end of a trial. This one had been so tumultuous, so unlike his usual passionless cerebral gymnastics, and so punctuated by the discovery of the body in the vault, that he could scarcely process all that had happened.

Gabriel was confident that his prediction was correct. There would be no appeal. But there remained to be seen, the next morning, how the huge assembly of gentlemen of the press would decide to report the trial; and with that decision, he knew, Topsy Tillotson's reputation really stood or fell. He thought that he had seldom had a trial end in such a triumphant victory and yet with such a sad client.

The mystery of the body was far less conclusive. It had lain secure in the vaults for years; but the fact was that now it was discovered, it had an imperative presence that demanded answers. And he had none to give.

All these thoughts and impressions whirled through Gabriel's tired mind. He was brought back to his present by a furry thud on his door, its perpetrator instantly recognisable. Resignedly he opened it.

'I am too exhausted to argue with you, Delphinium.'

He resumed his place by the fire. But Delphinium did not take her customary flying leap onto the *Encyclopaedia Britannica*. Instead, she padded over to him and leaned against his knees.

'Thank you,' said Gabriel. 'I appreciate the sentiment. Just so long as you recall, Delphinium, that there is a thin line between acceptable gestures of support and quite unacceptable ingratiation.'

Delphinium closed her eyes, leaned more heavily, and made her traction-engine noise.

25

Lionel Sullivan was a very early riser. *Early birds catch worms* had been inculcated into him from his earliest days as a journalist, and the habit had never left him. At five o'clock in the morning on the day after the trial of *Tillotson v The* Nation's Voice, he was already fully dressed, standing at his shaving stand, manoeuvring his cut-throat razor around his dimpled chin and glowering into the mirror at his own cherubic reflection. He was thinking very hard indeed about Frank Holloway's fate.

Malign and devious though Sullivan was, he was not a stupid man and, like many of those who had attended the trial, he readily saw the curious logical dilemma posed by Sewell's deception and Holloway's reporting of it. The verdict of the jury had reflected their condemnation of that deception rather than any real analysis of the facts. Helped, thought Sullivan with a certain sour admiration, by Sir Gabriel Ward KC. 'Little Cinderella'… that's what had won them over.

On the face of it, Hollway had told the truth in his article. But the fact remained that as a result of his actions, the already tottering finances of the *Nation's Voice* had suffered what might be a death blow. Only some very hard work would bring them round. Should he sack the journalist as a sacrificial lamb to public opinion? Or should he rely on Holloway's undoubted snooping skills to assist in restoring the newspaper's fortunes? Holloway had hinted last night he had something up his sleeve; could it be valuable enough to save the *Nation's Voice*?

Sullivan was still mulling all this over at half-past five when he began the morning tramp from his rooms near King's Cross to Fleet Street. As he turned into the alley that led to the newspaper's offices, he saw that Holloway had already arrived and was sitting on the doorstep. Sullivan grunted to himself with some approval. There was no doubting the man's industry, nor his effrontery. Back at work as though nothing had happened. What would he have to say for himself? He hastened his step. Griffiths the doorman was late as usual. Only Griffiths and Sullivan himself held keys to the offices.

Sullivan's eyesight was not as good as it had been. It took until he reached the front door before he saw that Holloway was not so much sitting as propped. That the eyes that seemed to look straight at him did not hold Holloway's usual insolent, challenging stare but were blank and bloodshot. And that one of the deplorable ties, so disapproved of by Sullivan, was not hanging in its usual loose careless knot around Holloway's neck but was instead drawn so cruelly tight across his windpipe that it was almost invisible, buried in the contused flesh around it.

As Sullivan stood transfixed in the alley, Griffiths arrived, late and puffing, and at the sight that met his eyes gave a horrified yelp.

Sullivan came to life. 'Well,' he observed to his doorman, 'he's today's scoop now all right.'

An hour or so later, Gabriel was eating his breakfast boiled egg and reading with great relief the reactions of the more respectable gentlemen of the press to the outcome of the trial. With the notable exception of the *Nation's Voice*, unpublished today for reasons unknown, it seemed the press were unanimous, their stance determined equally by the knowledge that Topsy Tillotson was the nation's darling and their delight in the downfall of the *Nation's Voice*.

OUR TOPSY DECEIVED BY WICKED SUBTERFUGE! screamed a halfpenny paper. With underneath: *Sewell a cad – how's that for libel!!*

MISS TILLOTSON VINDICATED BY BRAVE JURY declared the *Daily Chronicle*. And their leader observed: *Here is a jury who for the first time in decades voted with their consciences, and d–n the law. Hats off to you, gentlemen!*

HISTORIC PERVERSE VERDICT thundered *The Times*. And the body of the article it headed concluded magisterially: '*The* Nation's Voice *has a great deal to answer for. And it is irresistible to observe that "The Honourable" Frederick Sewell is something of a misnomer.*'

Gabriel was still basking in this general approval when Constable Wright arrived unexpectedly at his door.

'Detective Inspector Hughes has requested that you come at once to Sir William Waring's office. I don't know why, sir, but I understand it is very urgent.'

Gabriel felt a slight sense of panic. It was five to seven. He always left for chambers at two minutes to seven. But Wright had by now become sensitive to these routines and waited patiently while Gabriel, carefully timing it, put on his overcoat, closed his door and pressed it three times. As they proceeded towards the Treasurer's office, Wright burst into pent-up speech.

'I see you won the case, sir! The newspapers are full of it. I felt so angry when I read what happened, I thought – I thought I would *burst*. That *bastard*. Sorry, sir,' he added automatically, 'but I would like to – to— I cannot think of anything bad enough. No decent man does that, sir. That lovely little Miss Tillotson. Faithful, loyal, loving. Like what any man would dream of. When I think of her standing in the Drury Lane Garden full of hope... well, I can hardly bear it. What will happen to that devil?'

Gabriel felt warmed by the straightforward vehemence of this, though a little unnerved by the enthusiasm for Topsy. He thought for a fleeting moment of Meg.

'I entirely share your outrage, Constable Wright, but Sewell was not on trial, you know. He was merely the witness. And he did not perjure himself in court.'

Wright stopped dead in his tracks. 'You mean no one will do anything to him?' he said incredulously.

'No, not quite that. I suspect he will be expelled from his clubs and I think he will find he is not welcome in society for a while.'

Wright made a noise of extreme disgust, and so deep was his outrage that he expressed himself in terms he did not usually use to Gabriel.

'Expelled from his clubs! Is that all? What kind of punishment is that? My father would say he needs a bloody good leathering he won't forget for a long time to come, that's what he needs. Never mind not being welcome in society. I'd like to make sure he wouldn't want to show his pretty face there, welcome or not!'

Gabriel was silent. His respect for Wright was boundless but a social chasm yawned between them. Gabriel understood that expulsion from the highest echelons of London society was an unimaginable humiliation for a young man from Sewell's entitled background; less bloody, certainly, than Wright's concept of punishment, but nonetheless very real. But there was no language in which to convey that to Wright. Equally, although Gabriel did not avail himself of the privileges open to him as a result of the clubs to which he nominally belonged, he had nonetheless been born into a world in which they mattered. He had no words in which to explain to Wright that membership of a gentlemen's club was not just about having a convivial place to go and read the newspaper. That it was a label signifying far more than a leather armchair and a glass of port with old school and university friends. That it signified acceptance into a tribe. And that exclusion from it was severe punishment.

They had reached Sir William Waring's office. The Treasurer sat at his desk. On chairs in front of it sat Hughes and, to Gabriel's surprise, Hopkins. Waring looked irritable, Hughes sombre. Hopkins avoided Gabriel's eye. The atmosphere prickled with tension. Mystified, Gabriel took the seat he was offered.

'Detective Inspector Hughes wished us to wait for you,' said Waring briefly, then turned to address the police officer. 'Now what the devil is all this about?'

'Yes,' echoed Hopkins. 'At this hour! Duty called me to the Temple very early this morning and I was using the opportunity to get a long day in my chambers. I am inundated with work, Detective Inspector!'

Ignoring this, Hughes broke the news of Holloway's death with brutal directness.

'The police surgeon has seen him. Garrotted with his own tie, he said. Severe bruising to his neck and back. The doctor reckons he was seized by the tie and held against the wall until he was dead. Identified by his boss, who found him and called us. And do you know what the man said when we arrived?'

Sir William seemed devoid of speech. Hopkins looked shocked.

'Nothing would surprise me,' said Gabriel.

'He said: "I told him not to wear that scruffy old tie no more."'

Gabriel sighed. 'And the time of death?'

'The police surgeon says probably about an hour before he was found. No sign of rigor mortis, not even around the face, and the body not completely cold. Our preliminary view is that it was a planned attack. Holloway arrives at work very early, usually around five in the morning. Anyone who knew his habits could lie in wait. Of course, we all know Fleet Street never sleeps, but they are all down in the printing presses at that time. The doorway is tucked away at an angle down the passage. Anyone who was around, glancing down the alley, would just have seen him where they were used to seeing him. He often sat on the doorstep, apparently. Sort of undisciplined scruffy thing he would do, from all I have heard.'

'Well,' said Sir William, at last finding his voice, 'thank you for informing us. It happened outside the Inner Temple, thank God, and therefore has nothing to do with us.'

Hughes raised his eyebrows. It might have been surmised that he was enjoying himself.

'Nothing to do with the Inner Temple, Sir William? I could take the view that every member of the Inner Temple is a suspect. Very plain you lot did not like your business with the body parts splashed all over the newspapers. I'd say that was a motive for finishing Holloway off, wouldn't you?'

This was so patently true that Sir William was utterly nonplussed. Gabriel intervened.

'I should have thought there were many candidates for his murder with motives stronger than that, Detective Inspector Hughes.'

The detective nodded. No fool, Sir Gabriel Ward, funny cove though he was.

'That is why I am here. We think the crime is probably connected with the trial that concluded yesterday,' he said. 'There was a clear finding from the jury that the *Nation's Voice* had deliberately humiliated Topsy Tillotson. After that, Holloway did not live to see daylight. Miss Tillotson has a huge public following. Could be any of her admirers settling the score for her. We have told Sullivan never mind no scoops, to shut the newspaper and lie low for a while, or he might be the next one. We have likewise suggested to Mr Sewell that he goes down to his country place for a week or two, out of harm's away. There are plenty of suspects: them theatre people, for instance. Topsy Tillotson is staying off work, we understand, on account of all the upset. That cannot be good for their business.'

Gabriel thought of Vera Perkins; he had rather warmed to her, but it was clear from the scrawled draft he had picked up off the courtroom floor that Holloway had not. Was there any way Miss Perkins could have known about his plan to write a piece full of scurrilous innuendo? he wondered. And recalled with sudden alarm what she had said in her fury at the end of the trial.

Hopkins' contribution to the conversation was typical of him.

'What about me? Am I in danger?'

'Well, sir, as part of a legal team that is less likely, but you may wish to be a little more vigilant for a few days.'

Sir William glowered at Gabriel.

'Well, Ward,' he barked, 'can you throw any light on this sordid business?'

Gabriel shook his head. 'Feelings were certainly running high by the end of the trial. There had been a lot at stake on both sides. Some of the jury, I noticed, looked quite unusually upset and there was a lot of noise in the public gallery.'

'That was your fault,' said Hopkins. 'That closing speech of yours had whipped them all up. And now this happens!'

'Really, Hopkins,' said Gabriel mildly, 'I do not think you can hold the emotional power of my advocacy, great though it may be, to blame for the murder of a journalist who had been involved in a fraud as notorious as this one has become.'

Hopkins had not forgiven Gabriel's twofold triumph of the day before, both in court and in their subsequent exchange in the robing room.

He said snidely, 'And what about your client? Plenty of motive there. Sewell may have humiliated her, but it is thanks to Holloway that the whole world knows it.'

'Really, Hopkins,' said Gabriel again, a little less mildly since he was uncomfortably aware that this observation was not without force, 'I cannot see a slight girl of nineteen, alone in Fleet Street at five o'clock in the morning, garrotting anyone.'

Detective Inspector Hughes intervened. 'I agree with you there, sir. But she might have commissioned someone else to do it for her.'

Hopkins looked smug. 'Didn't she inform the court her father was a butcher?'

Hughes concluded, 'I am not ruling out Sullivan altogether either. We always look carefully at the finder of the body. He may not have been feeling too fond of Holloway after the result of the trial. Could have bumped him off, gone home, and then come back and "found" him, so to speak.'

Sir William's terror for the reputation of his beloved institution made him assert his authority.

'All this conjecture is purely a matter for you, Detective Inspector, not for us. You have had your answer. These two barristers conducted a case. It is now concluded. The Inner Temple cannot help you. Will that be all for this morning?'

Detective Inspector Hughes stood up, unruffled by his dismissal. He regarded the three men, immaculate despite the earliness of the hour, secure in their beautiful surroundings, confident in the impregnability of their world both literally and metaphorically. And he thought of the teeming masses of the City of London, the dark poky alleyways, the greed and ambition of the City men, the pimps, the drunkenness, the fallen women, the child beggars. He sighed. Oh, yes, men like these, by nature of their profession, encountered crime and greed and unhappiness, of course, but it was all one step removed, sanitised by legal ritual. They never saw it at the coal face like he did. Didn't really know they were born, this lot.

'That will be all for now, Sir William. But if I were you, I should go carefully until we have this strangler under lock and key. We may return to you as our enquiries advance.' He picked up his hat. 'Oh, yes,' he concluded meaningfully, 'more motives around here than cherries on a cherry tree.'

And he made for the door, his feeling that he had had the last word shared by those he'd left behind.

26

Constable Wright was feeling a strong sense of anticlimax. 'Get back to your normal duties,' the Inspector had told him rather curtly when they had returned to Old Jewry police station. Then, perhaps seeing Wright's crestfallen expression, he had added, 'Keep your eyes specially skinned, lad, in case you spot anything that might help with Holloway's murder.' Well, that was something, Wright supposed; but here he was, just a policeman on his beat again, plodding along as usual, even though there had been a strangling on his patch that very morning.

Fleet Street seemed its usual self, the only sign of earlier drama the roped off alleyway that led to the offices of the *Nation's Voice*. Constable Wright thought wistfully of the Detective Division. He almost wished Holloway had died in the Temple. Then, given his collaboration with Sir Gabriel, he knew he would have been asked to help. But given his lack of involvement in the new and sensational murder, there was something else he planned to do once he had finished his morning duties here.

It was, though still freezing cold, a glorious day with a bright blue sky. Spring, if not close, seemed at least imaginable. Hesitating between the half-hour walk or an omnibus ride, Wright chose to walk. He made his way down the Strand and through St James' Park, with its skeletal trees and half-frozen lake, his rhythmic tread punctuated by the steamy clouds of his breath on the icy air.

Wright had a very strong sense of justice. Or perhaps that was the wrong word; of proper consequences, that was it. 'Work hard,' his mother had always said to him, 'and you will get on.' And: 'Be kind to others and they will be kind to you.' And: 'If you do bad things, bad things will happen to you.' On the whole, Wright had discovered all these maxims to be true. 'Pull Susan's hair again, Maurice, and there will be no dinner.' He had, and there wasn't. And though hungry, he had felt a sense of rightness. It was this upbringing that had taken him into the police force and on the whole he had found satisfaction in a world in which there were always consequences. That way you knew where you were.

But now, suddenly, Wright felt something had happened that had upset the whole balance of his personal code. That Frederick Sewell should behave in the way he had to Topsy Tillotson, and yet face no punishment save a bit of bad publicity and social ostracism, seemed to Wright outrageous.

He had reached Grosvenor Square, Mayfair. Wright thought that the very air here felt different; plusher, sweeter, *richer*. He peered through the wrought iron of the locked gates at the frozen beauty of the vast expanse of green in the middle of the square, in which he could see two large perambulators and two small children playing, watched by what he thought were nursemaids. Sir Gabriel often talked about Nanny. Wright supposed that he meant someone like these women. Imagine a few children having all that garden to play in. He thought of the teeming street and the crowded home he had been brought up in, never any space except on the filthy pavement outside.

One of these two children was riding a hobby horse round and round in a tight circle. Wright could see that it was a beautiful thing, painted and saddled, with a flying mane. He had never even dreamed of owning a toy like that. Then he remembered that he had had his mother and father, and Aunty Violet next door, the three most important people in his life. He thought suddenly that he had never heard Sir Gabriel mention his own mother and father.

South Rising House, town house of Lord and Lady Somerton and their son, The Honourable Frederick Sewell, was situated just off the square in detached grandeur. Wright cast a professional eye over the arrogant stone façade. The blinds were drawn in the imposing windows overlooking the street. Only in the basement did there seem to be signs of life.

He turned his back on the house and made his way down the nearest street in search of a public house. He was a great believer in the information potential of public houses. He found one, on an elegant Georgian corner, bow-fronted, rather superior, with velvet-covered benches. And the publican was also superior, with sleek hair and an embroidered waistcoat. Despite the superiority, he looked with some alarm at Wright's uniform.

'Nothing to worry about, sir,' Wright said soothingly and added unblushingly, 'I had a bit of business with one of the servants at South Rising House, but I can't raise anyone. Family away, do you know?'

The publican relaxed. Nothing to do with opening hours then.

'Someone should be there. The family went down to the country last night, that I did hear. Getting away from all this stuff in the papers, I suppose. Lot of nonsense. The young lady was asking for it, if you want my opinion.'

Wright clenched his fist in his pocket. 'I don't.' He said it sufficiently shortly for the other man to look at him in mild surprise.

'No offence. The Honourable Freddy's father used to come in here occasionally. Always very gracious to me. As for The Honourable himself... My word, he's a looker! She was a lucky girl if you ask...' He subsided hastily when Wright glowered at him, and shrugged. 'Well anyway, the family has been decent enough to me and young Freddy is a good customer.'

'Does he come in on his own?'

'Usually with the same bloke. Dunno who he is. Some business they have together, maybe. Not in The Honourable's class. Nondescript. Not that I'm very good at looking at people. My missus now, altogether different. We met the greengrocer's niece once, when we was in the shop. For five minutes if that. And a year later, we was at the greyhounds and suddenly she's waving away at a woman. "Who's that?" I says. "The greengrocer's niece," she says. "Fancy you not remembering."' Belatedly he seemed to recall the start of the conversation. 'Anyways, you go and knock again. The cook should be there and a few of the servants.'

'When will the family be back?'

'No idea. They'll be comfortable in the country. Twenty bedrooms, I'm told.'

Wright's fury rose a notch higher at the dizzy heights of luxury in which Sewell would spend his exile from society.

'Where is this country mansion?'

The publican wiped his hands and looked at the clock. 'One minute to opening time,' he said with ostentatious precision. 'The London house is named after their village. South Rising. East Anglia. Somewhere godforsaken near King's Lynn?'

Back at Old Jewry, Wright looked it up in the station's *Bradshaw's Railway Timetable*. Three hours from Liverpool Street station to King's Lynn. He found a map. Then another three miles by road. Wright had never lived in the country. He supposed vaguely that there were carts and horses. Or perhaps you could hire bicycles. He would need some back-up of course. He ran through a list of likely companions in his head. There was good old Tufty who'd been at school with him and who was now in the Metropolitan Police. He would help, if he had some leave due. Or if he couldn't, Wright did not think he would be short of volunteers. They'd be lining up, most of the decent men he knew. He'd have to use his own days off what he'd been saving up of course, but he reckoned it was in a good cause. And after all, he told himself defiantly, it was up to him what he did in his free time and Detective Inspector Hughes showed no sign of involving him in the investigation into Holloway's death. All the same, he tried not to think what Hughes would say about a police constable taking matters into his own hands. Or Sir Gabriel. Especially Sir Gabriel.

27

Despite the ongoing investigations by the City of London Police, Wright had not been seen in the Temple for two days. Detective Inspector Hughes, however, had, on three occasions over that period; civil when spoken to, unobtrusive, persistent in these frequent visits. No one knew why. The porters, instructed to do so by Sir William Waring through gritted teeth, permitted him to enter. Once inside the cloistered precincts, he simply walked about. 'No purpose in alienating them altogether by forbidding entry, I suppose,' Sir William observed begrudgingly, 'with this business in Fleet Street going on. No harm in having a bit of a presence here, just so long as he knows it is by consent.' It was the nearest he got to admitting his increasing unease at a death so violent and so close to the Temple, and, as the news spread, the sense of panic within its gates.

'On leave,' Detective Inspector Hughes had said briefly when Gabriel, encountering him, had enquired after Wright. 'These young men don't know the meaning of work like I did. Still, he's entitled to it. Off on some jaunt, I suppose. No idea where he has gone. I'm too busy with the Holloway investigation to worry about it.'

'How is it going?' Gabriel could not resist asking.

The policeman looked cagey.

'Detective Inspector Hughes, we are very aware that there has been a shocking death on our very doorstep. Holloway was not a very savoury character, perhaps—'

'You can say that again,' interrupted Hughes. 'The whole of Fleet Street seems to have hated the man for one reason or another.'

'Nonetheless, it is a life lost and whoever did it is still at large,' Gabriel concluded. 'I would be sorry to see any lack of co-operation between the City of London Police and the Temple.'

Hughes looked immediately alert. 'Do you have information you wish to share with us, Sir Gabriel?'

'No,' said Gabriel. 'May I ask if you are any further on with your enquiries?'

Hughes shrugged. 'Early days.' As he turned away he delivered a parting shot. 'I reckon Sir William Waring is right to be worried, what with an unidentified body discovered in his vaults and a strangler on the loose a hundred yards outside his precious Great Gate. Your porters are not professionals like us. You may yet have reason to be grateful to us.'

Gabriel had a nasty feeling Hughes might be right. But the one thing he thought he did know was where Wright had gone, and his suspicions seemed to be realised when, two days later, the young constable turned up on his doorstep with a large bandage around his knuckles.

'I am sorry to see you have sustained an injury,' said Gabriel politely.

Wright grinned, a little sheepishly. 'It was worth it, sir.'

'Detective Inspector Hughes informed me you were off on a jaunt.' Gabriel looked at him quizzically. 'I was surprised you had not mentioned it.'

'I thought you would try and stop me, sir.'

'I rather imagined that might be the case.' Gabriel retrieved the sherry glasses and the decanter. He was too old a hand at eliciting information to ask any further questions. The silence between them lengthened.

'Has anything been discovered about Holloway?' asked Wright.

'Not that Detective Inspector Hughes has chosen to share with me,' said Gabriel drily. And waited.

Wright fidgeted for a moment and then succumbed to the urge to confide, as Gabriel had known he would.

'You remember my friend Tufty?'

'He of the Metropolitan Police?'

'Well, yes, sir, but all the same he is a nice chap,' said Wright fair-mindedly.

Gabriel suppressed a chuckle. Wright, he knew, had absorbed the age-old rivalry that existed between the City of London and Metropolitan Police forces.

'Well, me and Tufty, we've been to Norfolk. And we have taught Frederick Sewell a lesson he will not forget for a long time.'

Gabriel looked cautious. 'Really, Constable Wright I am a senior member of the Bar. And indeed, you are a police officer. I am not sure I wish to know.'

Wright's grin grew broader. 'I told Tufty you would say that. But I also said to him, "Sir Gabriel Ward is a regular diamond. He won't say so, but he'll think the same as us."'

Gabriel looked inscrutable.

'Well, anyways, sir, we went to this South Rising place. It's a little village, built all round a green with a nice old inn and a shop and a post office, all called the Somerton something or other, with coats-of-arms and all the cottage doors painted the same colour. The family own the whole village, with their own house down a long drive behind grand gates. You've never seen anything like it, sir.'

Gabriel did not say, as he could have done, that he had seen something very like it, in Somerset, with the Ward family coat-of-arms on every building. That as a small boy, with Nanny, he had emerged through just such impressive gates to pay visits to the villagers who doffed their caps to him, to be allowed to watch the blacksmith at work, to be given sweets by the deferential shop owners.

That rolling park and huge house could have been his. 'The house needs a custodian who will live here and who will care for the land, not moulder among books in London,' his father had said. And had then added meaningfully, 'And raise sons on it. Can you promise me that?' 'No,' Gabriel had said.

And when his father died, although Gabriel had been provided for with a hefty private income, he had been disinherited from the estate in favour of a stolid likeable cousin. He remembered now the last time he had been there, standing on the steps of the portico before the vast house. 'Come back whenever you like,' his cousin had said awkwardly. 'It is still your home.' 'Thank you,' said Gabriel and they shook hands. He had never gone back. He had another life.

He came to with a start to find Wright looking rather anxiously at him.

'Are you all right, sir?'

'Yes,' said Gabriel. 'Forgive me. I was in a reverie. Do please continue. I trust you have not murdered the heir to this feudal kingdom?'

Wright snorted. 'You know me better than that, sir. Of course we haven't. We waited 'til dark, jumped on him when he was going out the gates to meet some friend, ducked him in the village pond and then gave him a good punching. And we told him we were watching out for him from now on. He snivelled throughout, of course. Not so much the fine young man about town when we had finished with him, I can tell you. But we dumped him safely back on his grand doorstep.'

'I shall refrain from comment.'

'Anyway, that's all really, sir. We got back to London yesterday. I went to see the Tillotson family and told her father what we had done. He thanked me. Said if he'd been twenty years younger and didn't have a bad back, he would have done it himself.'

'How is Miss Tillotson?'

'She is having two weeks away from the theatre and her mother seems a very good sensible woman. Miss Tillotson was looking sad. Very pale and quiet. But my, she is a brave lady, sir. As soon as she has had a rest, she is going back to the theatre. And she has had a lot of very kind messages, and some of the newspapers have sent her flowers. She is still afraid people will think she is, well, *fallen*, sir. Of course I did not speak to her of that, but her mother told me, and I told mine. No fear of that, my mother says. Our Topsy isn't fallen, she was wickedly deceived and everyone knows it. Time goes on, my mother said, and people will forgive.'

'Very sensible,' said Gabriel, politely. He felt this conversation was becoming a little out of his experience.

Wright looked self-conscious. 'I am going to introduce Miss Tillotson's father to Tufty. He wants to shake Tufty's hand, he said. And I have told Miss Tillotson, Tufty and me, we are going to look after her with some of our friends. Whenever she comes out of that theatre door, I said, whichever of us is off duty will be there to see her safely into a cab. And,' he concluded with a certain defiance, 'when she is feeling a little better, I have asked her to tea with my mother.'

As he had before, Gabriel thought of Meg, and firmly rejected the thought. All these young people must find their own way. And what did he know about it all?

'That is very kind, Constable Wright.'

'Well,' said Wright gruffly, 'she needs to know there are decent men in the world, sir, what'll look after her.' He got up to go.

'Oh, I forgot. One funny thing: Tufty and me went into the little inn for a beer when we arrived in South Rising and got chatting to the publican. Pat he was called. Nice chap. That's how we found out when Sewell would be going out. But before that, he asked me where in London I worked. Of course, I did not tell him who I was or what I did, not likely, but I mentioned the City, and he asked me if I knew the Temple. Apparently, Brockley comes from that village. He and the publican's family lived in next-door cottages when Pat and Joe and Benny Brockley were children. The Brockleys moved away after Mrs Brockley died. Pat took over the village pub, eventually, from his father. He had heard Benny went to sea, and sent his regards to Old Brockley and Joe. A coincidence, wasn't it?'

'Yes,' said Gabriel, thoughtfully. 'Quite a coincidence.'

Another thought came to him. 'Before you go, there is a little bit of enquiring that would be very helpful, Constable. It is in relation to the missing silver salt cellars. It seems that Sir William did report their loss. I imagine there are records relating to thefts and arrests held by the City of London Police. Could you find out if anyone was ever charged with the theft?'

'Oh, that will be easy, sir,' said Wright with confidence. 'Very carefully kept our records are.'

He retrieved his helmet, hesitated and said rather awkwardly, 'You won't tell Detective Inspector Hughes about – about where we went, will you, sir?'

'Good heavens, no. He would have to arrest you for assault.'

'Oh, no, I don't want him to know I was out with Tufty. That would be worse. He wouldn't like me to have anything to do with the Metropolitan Police. He says they are all wasters.'

Left alone, Gabriel yet again turned over in his mind the events since Christmas Eve, the mysteries that seemed to deepen rather than lessen. He was afraid that he was missing something. Since Holloway's death, outside the Temple though it had been, he, like Sir William, was aware of a greater sense of danger everywhere; yes, even inside this protected place. Applying the same techniques that enabled him to solve intractable legal problems, he wondered if a walk around the gardens would help. Wrapped in his cashmere overcoat and muffler, his breath visible in the frosty air, he made his slow progression (clockwise, as always) around the perimeter.

As he passed the dormant hydrangea border, Delphinium emerged, looking mildly triumphant, and tagged along at his heels. 'I begin to think you lie in wait for me,' said Gabriel severely.

On the South Terrace, old Brockley was standing, leaning on a broom and gazing reflectively across the Embankment at the threatening winter swell of the brown River Thames.

Gabriel stopped beside him. 'Ah, Brockley. I wanted a quick word.' Delphinium stopped too and sat on Gabriel's feet.

'She has taken to you, sir.'

Gabriel was infuriated to find he felt vaguely flattered. He rejected the feeling, moved his feet, and changed the subject. Casting around for a way to get the conversation going, and noticing the cast iron frost everywhere, he said, 'Not too much for a gardener to do in the present weather, eh, Brockley?'

But this was the wrong thing to say. Not for a moment was Brockley having that.

'Always things to do in a garden, sir,' he said morosely. 'And that there Embankment makes life difficult.' He spoke as though it had been built especially to annoy him.

'What has the Embankment done to incur your wrath?' asked Gabriel straight-faced.

'The Corporation have been on at Sir William something terrible about our trees and shrubs hanging over their pavement. All had to be cut back. "Oh," says Sir William, "and the Corporation says not when the traffic is around. Can't have the horses shying." Me and Joe and two porters up before light, out on the Embankment with wheelbarrows. And then Sir

Vivian Barton and Sir Edward Hopkins there to check the work. And then Meg and that new girl Pearl, in early to make us all tea. And then a man what works for the Corporation. The fuss! Drat the horses, I say, no call to be there. And if they hadn't built that dratted road what no one wanted—'

An icy wind was funnelling down the South Terrace. Gabriel shivered and Brockley, noticing, broke off his tedious discourse.

'You wanted a word, sir? Would it be a liberty to ask if you would like a cup of tea?' He gestured to the Gardener's Cottage tucked away at the end of King's Bench Walk.

'No, indeed. It would be very welcome.' They made their way to the cottage.

'Come you in, sir,' Brockley said. He hesitated. 'Is Delphinium to come in too?'

'She appears to think she is,' said Gabriel drily.

The little front room was unsuitably low-ceilinged for a man as tall as Brockley. Perhaps it was not just the gardening that had led to the bad back. With its heavy beams it could have been as picturesque as the exterior had it not been so chaotically untidy. But the windowsills redeemed the chaos. Even in winter they were a riot of pelargoniums, bursting from their cracked pots, some spilling down the wall, others climbing up it.

Brockley looked doubtfully at Gabriel. 'I beg your pardon for the mess, sir. I'm not much of a homemaker.'

'You live with your passion, Brockley, as I do. In my case it is books. Not a spare inch anywhere, I do assure you. Your green fingers work indoors as well, I see. The plants make it a home.'

Gabriel sat on one of the two old Windsor chairs by the fire, placed his top hat on the floor beside him, and removing his kid gloves, held his hands out to the warmth.

'Joe will have told you about the burial vaults we have discovered?'

'He did. I can scarcely believe it. All those years we have tended the Reverend Master's garden without any idea. I just thought it was built on a pile of earth, to put it above the rest of the Temple, like a castle so to speak.'

'I think we all did. But since then, I have looked back in the archives of the Temple, and lo and behold, I found that in 1684 we paid sixty pounds to a bricklayer named Horne for making a burying vault. And they are all there, Brockley, my predecessors and yours. All buried with gratitude and dignity. It warms the heart, does it not?'

'It does, sir,' said Brockley respectfully. Sir Gabriel, he knew, set a fair store by the history of the Temple. For himself, he knew the gentlemen of the Inn would see him all right eventually with a little pension but he would not want his burial place to be there, not even under the garden he had tended all these years; no, for him it would be under a grey Norfolk sky like the one he was born under. Perhaps one day he would go back and leave Joe here with the hydrangeas. And who knew? Maybe one day Benny would tire of the sea. His eyes strayed to the cluttered chimneypiece where he had propped a display of postcards, each a picture of a foreign port, Marseilles and Cadiz, Nantes and Stockholm, Constantinople and St Petersburg, Beirut and Tripoli. Brockley did not know where they were. Only abroad, that exotic place that was not the Inner Temple or Norfolk.

'I believe Joe has also told you that a body was found, unburied and more recent than those properly interred in the vaults?' Gabriel wondered if Joe had told his father about the mutilations. He decided not to mention them unless Brockley did.

The gardener nodded. 'Yes, Joe told me, Sir Gabriel, and I'm only sorry I don't know nothing which might help to tell you who he is. A young man, Joe tells me, there for many years?'

'Yes. Joe and Simmonds and Sugden have all seen the body and could not identify it. So it remains a mystery.'

Brockley shook his head again. His voice trembled a little and he looked suddenly older. 'It grieves me to think of it, sir, in that happy garden.' And then the gardener in him emerged. 'I suppose it explains why some of the plants did not thrive. The earth was too shallow for the deep-rooted ones.'

'Exactly my view, Brockley. In fact, that was how we determined where the vault lay. Delphinium had got herself lost down there. And I suddenly remembered the problems you had with the climbing rose and the vine and the rhubarb.'

Brockley nodded approvingly. Knew his gardening did Sir Gabriel. 'Well, I hope – respectfully, sir – someone points out to the Treasurer it was not down to me or Joe the rhubarb would not thrive.'

Gabriel changed the subject. 'I must leave you to your rest, but before I go, you may care to know a friend of mine had occasion to visit South Rising in Norfolk. The publican asked to send his regards to you and Joe.'

Brockley's habitually gloomy expression lightened into what was nearly a smile.

'At the Somerton Arms? Why, that will be Pat. I heard he took over from his father. A decent boy.'

He looked into the distance and seemed almost to have forgotten Gabriel. The green at South Rising, where you could hear nothing but the blacksmith and the birds and the children playing and the clock on the church chiming away those uneventful unchanging hours.

'A beautiful place that was.'

And Gabriel heard the Norfolk accent grow stronger in his voice as he remembered: 'bootiful'.

'Joe and Benny were out there all the time with young Pat and the other children of the village; the son of the Somerton Estate land agent and the son of the cook at the big house, and the vicar's two little daughters, and the blacksmith's twins. Young

Frederick Sewell at the big house used to give his old governess the slip, never mind what trouble he got her into, so he could join them. He got beat for it, too, by his father, but he didn't care. A difficult boy.'

'Difficult?'

'Aye, and deceitful. Frederick was the oldest. Tell any lie, he would, and one of the others always got blamed. He would side up with the agent's son, both of them always wanting to be top. Top of the group, top climbing the wall, fastest on their bicycles, and Joe tagging along behind, trying to keep up. Young Sewell and the agent's son used to chase the little 'uns on those bicycles, Joe running behind, to give them a fright. Not in play; over and over, to make them fall and hurt themselves. Mind you, they were the ones who got into trouble. Both lads fell off their bicycles, Sewell cut his head open and the other boy broke his ankle and it never healed straight. My Joe just tripped over and cut his knee bad. I couldn't afford a bicycle for him. "Let that be a lesson, Joe," I said, "that is what happens if you chase your little brother."'

He broke off from these rambling reminiscences and came back to the present.

'I heard from Mrs Bugg that you had a big case that has been in the newspapers about young Frederick Sewell and that Miss Tillotson the actress. A bad business. My old father would have said he needed a good hiding.'

Gabriel wished he could tell Brockley that Sewell had had one. Instead, he took his leave, with food for thought.

28

It was with an air of triumph that later that day Wright told Gabriel of another discovery.

'Well, sir,' he announced, 'I had a breakthrough!'

'You have discovered Holloway's murderer right under Detective Inspector Hughes' nose!' said Gabriel.

Wright grimaced and looked a little huffy. 'Nothing to do with me, sir. That is the Detective Division. The word in the station is that no progress has been made. Cast-iron alibis everywhere, they say. No, it is not to do with Holloway. I have found out what happened about the silver salt cellars. It *was* Durrant who stole them. Well, at first I couldn't find a record nowhere, sir. Now that is not like the City of London Police. Detective Inspector Hughes always says if it isn't there, it didn't happen and that is that. So I thought to myself, there is only one other answer and that is that the theft happened in the jurisdiction of another police force. And in London that can only be the Metropolitan. And then I thought of Tufty!'

'I must meet this Tufty,' murmured Gabriel. 'He seems to be becoming a frequent presence in my life.'

'He is a good sort, sir. I told him what you wanted to know.'

Wright had settled into his account and was now glowing with achievement.

'So, he looked it up in the Metropolitan Police files. And there it was! And of course it gives information on the crime; arrested on the information of a gentleman. Two silver salt cellars, the property of a gentleman, engraved with a flying horse, worth, if you can believe it, two thousand pounds! Blimey, sir, I wouldn't mind seeing what two thousand looks like! I could buy my mother a palace with that!'

He came to a gleeful halt and looked expectantly at Gabriel like a gundog who has just dropped a dead duck at his master's feet, confident of acknowledgement and praise. He was surprised to see a look of uncharacteristic anger cross Gabriel's face. But he only said, 'Well done, Constable Wright,' as Wright had hoped, before asking thoughtfully, 'why the Metropolitan Police?'

'As far as I could work out, Durrant was picked up on information received at the British Museum station on the Central London Railway. So, in the Metropolitan force's district, not City's. When they opened his bag, there was the swag.'

Gabriel winced. He disliked slang.

'Sorry, sir,' said Wright with a grin, 'it's just what we all say.'

Gabriel said drily, 'Well, don't say it here, please.'

'Anyway, he pleaded guilty; didn't have much choice when he had been caught with the sw— stolen goods on him. He got five years because of the value of the property. He served four of them and then he died of influenza in prison.'

'And why just "the property of a gentleman"?'

'Oh, I can answer that too, sir,' said Wright, his confidence soaring. 'The records will sometimes say that, if it is a nob who for some reason doesn't want his name to appear. Maybe he doesn't want people to know he owns something so valuable, or maybe it is a lady's jewellery, that sort of thing.'

'Hmm,' said Gabriel, and he said it very meaningfully indeed.

'Anyway, it all ties in, doesn't it, sir? And it rules him out as our body.'

'It certainly seems to do that. Thank you, Constable Wright.'

Gabriel wasted no time in going to see Sir William, nor in plunging in with the matter uppermost in his mind.

'Master Treasurer, you will recall Durrant, the young porter who disappeared some years ago?'

The Treasurer, bent at his desk over a pile of papers, looked up sharply and dropped his fountain pen. For a split second something crossed his face that might have been shame. But it was transient; he then regained his usual expression of implacable smugness and answered briskly.

'I do indeed. He was the thief who stole our silver salt cellars.'

'No, Sir William,' said Gabriel, quite calmly. 'He was no thief.'

Waring's eyes narrowed. 'He was found with the stolen property on him and he pleaded guilty.'

'I think that you made sure of that for your own purposes.'

'Really, Ward, are you seriously suggesting that I, the Treasurer of the Inner Temple, a retired judge, a knight of the realm — are you suggesting *I* was in some way implicated in the theft of the silver salts?'

'I am suggesting, Sir William, that you removed the salts and ensured that they were found on Durrant's person. He was a potential embarrassment to you. You wanted him out of the way. And you wanted the Inner Temple protected at all costs from what you regarded as a particularly unsavoury scandal. Did you know that Durrant died in prison before he had served his sentence? A young man died, wrongly accused, Sir William.'

The Treasurer, caught off guard, began to bluster.

'Really, Ward, I warned you not to meddle in things which are none of your business.'

'Before you say anything else, I should tell you that recently I had an interview with General Ivo Rawlings who told me the story behind young Simon's disappearance. That young man lost career and home and family. But who was the other man involved? It was Durrant, was it not? A servant who paid an even greater price? He left that night because he was mortally afraid of the exposure you threatened him with and the shame that came with it. And you put the silver salts in his bag. Your information that he was on his way home on the underground then led to his arrest, and I think, Sir William, you ensured that Durrant was arrested at his destination outside the jurisdiction of the City of London Police and that the Inner Temple's name was kept out of it. And Durrant was put away for a good long time. You made sure of that, too. You, as a lawyer, were aware that the sentence for theft is determined by the value of the property.'

'Quite the detective,' said Waring with a sneer.

'You may recall that you asked me to become one. It was not particularly difficult. Why else would you go to the police rather than asking our porters to investigate? Why else should the silver salts, engraved with the Inner Temple Pegasus, be entered on the record merely as "the property of a gentleman"?'

'If you have spoken with General Rawlings, you will know that young Rawlings had not even had the decency to stay within his own class. And as to Durrant, he had committed degraded acts with a young member of this establishment which were much worse than theft. Prison was the best place for him, whatever the crime that was written on the record.'

Gabriel's face stiffened. One finger carefully traced the little pattern on the underside of his chair, and he drew in his breath resolutely as he stood up to go.

'That last observation is unworthy of you, Sir William. As a lawyer and as a man.'

And before the astonished Treasurer had time to reply, the door had closed.

Gabriel returned to his chambers and turned his mind to what he had just heard. The Treasurer of the Inner Temple, to protect the institution from scandal, had ensured a man's wrongful conviction for theft. That was a criminal offence. The man was dead. No exoneration was now possible. Yet surely, he thought, I have a moral duty to set the record straight?

And thinking of things being straight, he wove his way through piles of books to the window and meticulously adjusted the folds of the curtains. He felt a little clearer.

What record would I be straightening by substituting a stain on a young man's memory with a far more scandalous one? But on the other hand, that is how Sir William justified his own conduct. Am I beginning to think like Sir William? But he knew that he was not. That he would stay quiet not for the reputation of his institution, but for the unknown young porter himself.

With his customary self-discipline, he tried to turn his thoughts to the implications of what he had now learned. But at the back of his mind the ethical dilemma lingered. He knew it would haunt his sleep.

He felt he was getting somewhere, if only by a process of elimination. The disappearance of Simon Rawlings and Durrant the porter had been explained; one was in exile, and one had died in prison. He realised with sadness that neither young man would have known of the fate of the other. Ivy Bunch was alive and living with her young son, and hopefully her circumstances would soon improve a little. None of them, at any rate, was the mysterious corpse from which the body parts had been removed. The Treasurer's reluctance to have all the disappearances investigated was also explained. A scandal such as that of Rawlings and Durrant would have rocked the Temple and done irretrievable damage to its reputation. And as for Ivy, the identity of her little boy's father, a close friend of Sir William, and his dismissal of her, explained his anger at Gabriel's interference. Now, surely, the investigation was down to psychology. And putting his head together with Wright.

29

The blue silk curtains drawn against the inhospitable dark afternoon, cups of tea beside them, with Delphinium, an uninvited earlier arrival, sprawled blissfully across the *Encyclopaedia Britannica*, Gabriel and Wright were in close consultation.

'Sir Vivian Barton asked me some days ago whether I had received one of the parcels,' said Gabriel. 'And after I had said I had not, I wondered why that should be. Since then, I have pondered on it a good deal. Why? Or rather, why not?'

Wright, wedged into his usual chair between Delphinium's pile of *Encyclopaedia Britannica* and a positive mountain of Sir Walter Scott's *Waverley* novels, looked a little confused.

'I mean, I wondered what was different about me in comparison to Sir William Waring and Sir Edward Hopkins and Sir Vivian Barton and Reverend Master Vernon-Osbert?'

'I bet there are a whole lot of things,' said Wright, stoutly and loyally.

'Well, so there are,' said Gabriel. 'But I do not mean characteristics of personality; I mean things to do with our respective roles in our little world. And it seems to me there is one thing that distinguishes me from them. All four of them have been closely involved in the running of the Inner Temple. Waring as Treasurer, of course, with Hopkins as his closest associate – Waring's lieutenant he calls himself, Master of the Silver and of the Wine. Barton is Master of the Garden. Vernon-Osbert was responsible for the care of the souls of all us Inner Templars.

All are or were charged with heading the little committees that report to Waring and ensure the servants are doing their jobs. I fear I do nothing whatsoever to ensure the smooth running of the Inn. I am not a man who likes organising anything but my own work. I do not wish to be responsible for others, nor am I comfortable with administering reprimands and discipline, however well deserved.'

Wright looked respectful. He himself rather liked reprimands and discipline. When they were deserved, of course. That was one of the reasons he was a good policeman.

'Constable Wright, now I have thought of that common characteristic, I have a little theory. It is really no more than that. I would not wish to share it with Detective Inspector Hughes until I have tested it out. May I ask you to carry out a small experiment with me?'

Very carefully, he explained what he wanted Wright to do.

Wright looked doubtful. 'I will do my best, sir. I am just not sure I will do it very well. I've never done – acting like. You just sees what you gets with me. And – I won't know exactly what to say.'

'You will do it splendidly,' said Gabriel firmly.

'And I am not sure why, or what you think will happen,' said Wright, still more doubtfully.

'I would prefer not to tell you why. You will do it so much more convincingly if you do not know *why* you are doing it. And perhaps nothing will happen. And that will mean my little theory was wrong. But if something does, why, one of the biggest mysteries is a good way to being solved, and if it is, I promise to tell you at once.'

That evening, when he was least expecting it, walking back through the Temple late from a meeting with a colleague, Gabriel stumbled quite unexpectedly on a tragic little scene that simultaneously answered and posed questions more intractable than any that had so far faced him.

It was late and the Temple was deserted. Gabriel's meandering path took him back through the perfectly proportioned arches of Sir Christopher Wren's cloisters that bordered one side of Church Yard.

At the end under the last arch stood two young men, their dark silhouettes clear against the gaslight, heads bent together. Two young barristers, thought Gabriel nostalgically, standing in the spot he recalled that he had once stood with Barton, nearly thirty years earlier, after a lecture, discussing the implications of the new Supreme Court of Judicature Act. How serious he and Barton had been, and industrious, at the threshold of their careers. It seemed to Gabriel that memory walked beside him through this loved world, not past, but ever-present, not frozen but dynamic, the experiences of the young of today simply a part of the centuries-old revolving wheel of young men who were living the life he had led. It will never change, he thought contentedly. When I am gone there will be many to follow on, to live the same lives in these same buildings, to debate in scholarly quiet, as we did, as these two are this evening. But on drawing nearer to the figures, he became aware, all at once, of three things flooding all together into his consciousness and dispelling this elegiac construction of what he was looking at.

The first was that the two young men were Rupert Brandish and John Gibson. The second was that they were engaged in a quiet, angry argument conducted with such passion and intensity that its subject could not possibly be the latest piece of legislation. And the third was that, despite the anger, they were holding hands, clinging together with a desperation that held one clear message.

He had nearly reached them, his footsteps quiet on the paving; he could not turn back; they started and saw him and sprang apart. Gabriel did the only thing that a gentleman in these terrible circumstances could do. He lifted his top hat and bowed.

'Good evening,' he said.

And passed straight on, steadily, past them and out of the cloisters in the direction of home in King's Bench Walk.

He wondered if he would be halted or hailed. Despite the silence, he felt as strongly as though he could see and feel it, the tumult of consternation and unhappiness he had left behind him.

In his rooms, he pulled down his blind (right hand only, thumb folded into the palm), drew his blue silk curtains, and stirred up his slumbering fire. Settled beside it in his wing chair, he thought about the implications of what he profoundly wished he had not discovered.

Analyse the unknown based on the known. He should have known. The surreptitious meeting outside the library late at night and the furtiveness that had accompanied it. Brandish's tapping of his watch and Gibson's acknowledgement of it at the press dinner. Gibson's extraordinary reaction to Gabriel's queries about the boxes. It had not been because of the boxes themselves, of course; Gabriel saw that now. It had been the link with Brandish, whose very name Gibson had been quite unable to utter. He recalled Brandish helping Gibson to move in; his uncharacteristic abruptness and defensiveness when they had descended on the Reverend Master's house, searching for Delphinium, and found the two young men together.

And then he thought of Brandish's position in the Church and of Gibson's father, once Home Secretary, responsible for the maintenance of the laws of the country, and of Gibson's strangled tortured stammer and of his engagement to Miss Amelia Waring. And he thought of Simon Rawlings and what had happened to him some years before; disgrace and exile.

A great deal now seemed to have an explanation that had never occurred to him. But did it mean the two young men could be dismissed from his investigations? Or could it possibly provide some kind of answer?

It was half-past midnight. Gabriel was conscious of that ache at the back of his throat that he experienced when confronted with the emotional entanglements of others, when suffering came too close and tugged at his heart strings. Very slowly, he put the guard on the dying fire and went into his bedroom. He would read for exactly half an hour, and then he would go to bed and not think about it all any more until the morning. On a whim, he reached up to the shelf above his bed and took down *Andersen's New Fairy Tales*.

Leaving his rooms on Monday morning and turning to check that his door was closed, he saw to his horror a butcher's knife sunk deep into the wooden door frame, impaling to it a small oblong card.

Looking closer, he found it was a cigarette card bearing the image of a tall-stemmed blue flower. He did not have to read the printed script identifying the species. It said, as he knew in that sickening instant it would, *Garden Flowers Series No. 6 Delphinium*.

Afterwards, Gabriel was amazed by the speed of his own reaction. He was breathless by the time he had crossed the Terrace and reached the kitchen door. He flung it open.

Mrs Bugg was rolling pastry at the large kitchen table. Beside her, Meg was whisking eggs.

'Mrs Bugg,' he gasped, 'where is Delphinium?'

Mrs Bugg looked at him in some astonishment and gestured to the fireplace. There was the cat, a half-consumed oyster on a plate bearing the Pegasus emblem in front of her.

Without a word, Gabriel crossed the kitchen and snatched her up. Delphinium struggled in his arms. Devotion was all very well, but she had not finished her oyster.

Mrs Bugg and Meg surveyed the ensuing tussle with open mouths.

'Is – are you quite all right, Sir Gabriel?' said Mrs Bugg at last.

By now, he had recovered his equilibrium and Delphinium, having succumbed to the softness of his cashmere overcoat, was still.

'Yes, I thank you, Mrs Bugg,' he said with as much dignity as he could muster. 'There is a purpose for which I need Delphinium this morning.'

'Bless you, Sir Gabriel,' said Mrs Bugg, still bemused. But it was not her place to question the eccentricities of senior barristers.

When the two had departed, she and Meg looked at each other round-eyed.

'Bless him,' said Mrs Bugg, finally and soulfully. 'Perhaps he gets a little bit lonely.'

But Meg knew Sir Gabriel better than that. 'More likely he's got mice,' she said, and giggled.

Back at King's Bench Walk, Gabriel deposited Delphinium on the hearth rug and filled her Spode saucer with milk. He ensured that all the windows of his rooms were secure. He turned the key in his drawing-room door and pocketed it. He locked the door to his set and secured the outer huge oak door in front of that. Then he proceeded to his chambers in 1 Crown Office Row. Here he found a hovering Chapman anxious at his unprecedentedly late arrival. Gabriel requested him to send a message asking Constable Wright to call at his convenience.

Half an hour later, a disapproving Chapman showed him in. Sir Gabriel Ward should, in Chapman's opinion, be left alone to concentrate on his work. There was a new and lucrative case coming up.

'Has anything happened?' said Wright eagerly.

'I think it has, Constable Wright. Now which of us shall go first? Let us approach the matter in chronological order; always best, I find, when preparing a trial. You first.'

'Well, sir, I haven't much to tell. I did just what you told me. I went Saturday afternoon to the garden and then I sees Joe Brockley in the shed, so I goes over and I says good afternoon. Not very friendly, he wasn't, but civil enough. So, I thought I would start by saying the garden was going to look nice in the spring. I don't know nothing about gardens but it seemed as though it was a polite beginning, so to speak...'

'Indeed yes.' Gabriel moved his desk calendar which was misaligned with his blotter. 'A very nice touch. And then?'

'Well, then, when I had worked up to it a bit, I mentioned you, sir, and I said what you asked me to, as though I was gossiping like: that you knew someone looking for a gardening job who you thought was a lot more skilled than Joe would ever be. You were going to ask Sir William to consider this chap to be put in above him.'

'How did Joe react?'

'Well, as you would expect, sir,' said Wright rather reproachfully. 'He got angry and swore a bit. "Don't blame me," I said, "just letting you know. We working men have to stick together against the nobs."'

Gabriel chuckled. 'Good heavens,' he said. 'I never asked you to say it in quite those terms.'

Wright looked a little sheepish. 'It did the trick anyhow. We had a bit of a chat and then I bid him good day. And that was that. What was it all for, sir?'

'This,' said Gabriel, and he placed on his desk the butcher's knife and the cigarette card. 'This knife was stuck through the card and impaled on my door frame.'

'Blimey!' said Wright, when he had digested this. He sprang to his feet. 'Where is she, sir?'

'Safely locked up in my rooms.'

Wright subsided back into his chair and mopped his brow.

'You think Joe Brockley did it?'

'Well, it is not conclusive evidence, of course, but if it is a coincidence, it is a very remarkable one that the day after you tell Joe Brockley I am planning to do something to his detriment, this arrives.' Gabriel hesitated, and then added a little self-consciously, 'Joe was aware that when Delphinium went missing in the vaults, I was – was – concerned for her safety. I think he sent this to distress me. After all, he did not know that I had set up his conversation with you; there was no reason he knew of for me to associate the gesture with him; cigarette cards are ubiquitous. In the absence of a body part, it was the only gesture of anonymous spite he could think of.'

'You made the plan because you think he sent the body parts too?'

'Yes. I wondered how he would react to the conversation you had with him. Well, this is perhaps a cruder, more immediate, threat than sending human remains, but it seems to have been issued in retaliation, just as the others were. Joe had been reprimanded by both Waring and Hopkins for insolence. Barton had Joe told off for not keeping the paths properly swept after he had a fall in the snow. Vernon-Osbert had spoken to him about his non-attendance at church. All of them received parcels. And now, when he hears that I might threaten his position here, and the body of course is no longer available to him, we have this clear evidence of his capacity for spite and revenge. I would be surprised if there were two people in the Temple who fit the same bill; and I can think of no motive that fits so well either.'

'But someone cut the parts off the body. And Joe discovered the body along of us.'

'I don't think so, Constable Wright. I think he well knew about that body. As you may have noticed, he is a young man of considerable strength. Although you helped him at first, he was later able to move the dresser masking the entrance without your assistance. Before we went in, he reassured us as to the damp inside when we were concerned about Delphinium being able to find water. Do you recall how he tried to hurry us out before we went into the Middle Temple vault where the body lay? And Joe is usually the gardener who tends the Reverend Master's garden, not old Brockley. If I, an amateur gardener, deduced that the soil was shallow, I think perhaps Joe did too, and explored and found the grating Delphinium fell through. Once he had done that, it was not hard to deduce, as we did, that the entrance must lie within the house, and to investigate. And then he discovered the vault and the body that lay there in that strange condition. And, I am afraid, used it for his own horrible purposes. I fear his contempt for his masters here runs very deep.'

'Do you think he meant to kill the vicar?'

'I think,' said Gabriel sadly, 'that he did not care one way or the other. He just wanted to get his own back and settle a score, so to speak. He did not see a well-loved, good man but only someone who sought to exert an authority over him.'

'What about how all the parcels got reported in the newspaper?'

'I don't know,' said Gabriel. 'It is plain Holloway had been in the Temple despite his protestations to me; he could not otherwise have seen the hydrangea border. But we no longer have him to ask whether Joe was his source for the stories. It could have been anyone. Nor, if Joe was the culprit, was it in his interests to make the matter public and risk exposure. I think he was motivated purely by spite against the individuals who had offended him. And have you noticed, by the way, that though the body-parts parcels have been reported in the paper, the finding of the body from which they came has not? I really don't know how this all fits together. It will need a great deal of further thought.'

He hesitated. Here came the difficult part. Wright, he knew, would expect Joe Brockley to be instantly interrogated.

'Constable Wright, I am aware of your professional responsibilities and I greatly respect them. But I have a feeling that this is only the beginning. Would you feel able to say nothing just for a few days? There is more to this.'

'More, sir?'

'The notes that accompanied the body parts, for instance. They are not the kind of thing Joe Brockley would compose and write. They are – they are the kind of thing a lawyer likes. They are jokes of a macabre kind. Plays on words. Lawyers are good at word games and crosswords and double meanings. I am convinced there is someone other than Joe involved in this. And there is the identity of this years-old body that he had abused and mutilated. We still need time to investigate the background. I feel we, you and I, should tread very carefully.'

Wright hesitated, torn between gratification and duty. The former won. 'Detective Inspector Hughes is very busy investigating Holloway's murder while the trail is hot. He says a body as old as the one from the vaults can wait a bit longer. I reckon a couple of days would be all right. Would that be long enough? Though I don't know what Inspector Hughes would say if he could hear me.'

'And I do not know what Chapman will say. I have a case to prepare. But it is a bargain. Two days to put our heads together, Constable Wright.'

Wright glowed. 'Where shall we start?'

'Why not with the open entrance that leads into the basement of the Reverend Master's house?'

And so they went together, across the Temple side by side, with a companionable familiarity, back to the Reverend Master's house and Garden, and as they walked, Gabriel explained the position of the entrance identified by Mrs Jenkins, through an open arch, leading to the precipitous stairs and so to the yard outside the kitchen.

The house stood proudly silhouetted against the blue sky at the top of its ten steps, as it always had. It had not occurred to Gabriel until recently that there had been any reason other than the spiritual for its elevated position. Now its true purpose had been revealed: to form a conventional burial place. And in addition one less orthodox interment had taken place, that of the unknown young man who had met his end violently and been left there for years before his remains were mutilated. Gabriel felt, to his surprise, along with a sense of fellowship with his Temple predecessors, a sharper feeling; one of protectiveness towards that unknown man. And with that protectiveness came a strong determination to find for him – what? Not justice precisely; no justice could ever be achieved for the loss of a young life. Not reparation. Not vengeance. I want an answer for him, thought Gabriel. I want it both as a lawyer and as a detective. He thought of Simon Rawlings' grandmother and sister, living with uncertainty. He wondered whether this other unknown young man had had a family. Of all things, Gabriel thought, we must have certainty. Then he thought involuntarily of Holloway. He had had a family, Gabriel supposed, who would know of his death by now. Not much uncertainty about strangulation. He shuddered. Too many deaths.

They walked along the retaining wall of the garden and round the back of the house, separated by a narrow space from another wall that ran behind. It was suddenly darker and danker, but feeling their way along, they came to the flight of steps leading down to a little stone archway in the wall of the house, the way in described by Mrs Jenkins as used only by the coalman. And indeed, in front of them, were two disused store cupboards, their rotten doors hanging open and evidence, in the old racks inside, that one had once been used as a wine cellar. The other was empty and beside it was another flight of stone steps that led up this time to the yard store cupboards. The variation in levels owing to the elevation of the house was quite dizzying; it was unsurprising, thought Gabriel, that no one had previously analysed it, and realised that the vaults lay beneath the garden.

They peered into the store cupboard in which Mrs Jenkins had stored the cardboard boxes and then turned their attention to the one containing the gardening tools. Had the mutilator of the body used anything from there? The stepladder would certainly have enabled him to reach the body. How had he cut the body parts? There was no sharp cutting implement that they could see; but, as Wright pointed out, a pocket knife was not hard to come by.

Gabriel ran his eye along the tools. 'A very old-fashioned collection,' he observed.

'Sound enough though, sir,' said Wright. 'All in working order, I'd say.' He picked up the mallet leaning beside the stack of wooden stakes. 'I saw Joe propping up a tree using this when I was looking down from the *Nation's Voice* offices.' He thumped the head of it into the palm of his hand. 'Good old tool,' he observed idly.

He and Gabriel looked at each other. The thought came to them both at once.

'Humphries...' said Gabriel.

'Yes, sir! Biffed hard on the head, he said, by something with a big surface area! Bigger than a hammer. Could this possibly be the murder weapon from all those years back? Anyone who bothered to do a bit of exploring could find their way down here through that open archway and there is no lock on this door either. Anyone could have had access to the tools in here and borrowed this so to speak. But no – surely once he had used it, the murderer would have got rid of it?'

'I think we must take this and consult Humphries first,' said Gabriel slowly, 'as to whether the mallet might have been the murder weapon. Before we consider the other implications if it was.'

They went at once to St Bartholomew's Hospital and made their request. Humphries retreated to his hospital mortuary where the body of the unknown man now lay. Gabriel and Constable Wright waited in his singular room, sitting in armchairs beside his fire, one on either side of the lounging skeleton who still occupied the third, and under the malevolent eye of the stuffed parrot. Their macabre companions seemed to be waiting with them, as eager as they for news.

On his return with the mallet, Humphries confirmed what they had suspected. The depression in the skull of the young man was wholly consistent with a blow on the head from the large surface area of the head of the garden tool. The blow could easily have been inflicted by an assailant standing at close quarters.

'Actually, "consistent with" is Law Courts speech,' Humphries said cheerfully. 'The truth is, this mallet would perfectly explain the depression in the skull. They fit like a glove. I'd put money on it being the murder weapon.'

They walked back, digesting this development, down Fleet Street. Gabriel reflected that their route was becoming familiar.

'I feel as though your beat is becoming mine,' he said to Wright with some amusement.

'Well, sir,' said Wright, entering into the spirit of the thing, 'you should walk at exactly two and a half miles per hour and keep an eye out for lost children, runaway horses and persons showing signs of criminal intent. Like them,' he added as they approached Ye Olde Cock Tavern.

Outside it stood a small group of men, heads close together, huddled around one central figure who seemed to be taking something from them and pocketing it. Gabriel would have passed them without a glance, an apparently innocuous group, but as they approached, at the sight of Wright, the men scattered like a small flock of pheasants put up by a beater. The central figure ran across the street and, dodging Wright and Gabriel and cabs and delivery vans, disappeared down an adjacent alleyway. As he dashed past them, in a flash Gabriel saw the baggy suit, the dirty cap, the cadaverous face and villainous scar. The remainder of the group dispersed with an elaborate casualness and sauntered off singly, bound in different directions.

Gabriel looked at Wright questioningly. 'I have seen that man before, Constable. I recognise that scarred face. I saw him with Holloway during the Tillotson trial, and I thought I saw money changing hands. I suspected he was one of Holloway's sources for his muck-raking journalism.'

Wright shook his head. 'Street bookie,' he said. 'Doing a bunk when he sees me.'

'But what is he doing here?'

'They gets everywhere, taking bets for the horse races. Betting is only legal at the racecourses, so they come and walk about the streets, taking bets for them as cannot get to the courses. That was money, wrapped up in screws of paper, changing hands. The bet is written on the paper with a nickname for the better. All kept anonymous. The bookie, he knows his customers and pays up after the race.'

Gabriel recalled now that Holloway had told him he liked betting on the horses.

'I nab them like I am told to whenever I can catch them,' Wright was saying. 'But there is no denying a lot of men like betting. The nobs can gamble whenever they like in those private clubs they join, while working men are restricted. Doesn't seem fair really, does it, sir?'

Gabriel was used by now to Wright's socialist tendencies, many of which he was obliged to admit carried some weight. He nodded absently. It did not, now he came to think of it, seem very fair. It was true that different laws often applied to rich and poor. He thought of the likes of young Frederick Sewell whose money and privilege opened the doors to private gambling clubs and for excursions across the Channel to the casinos of France—

Gabriel came to a grinding halt, teetering on the edge of the pavement he and Wright were about to step off. A passing hansom cab driver yelled at him and reined in his horse. Behind him a flower seller dropped her posies as she cannoned into him. But Gabriel was oblivious to the small tumult he had caused.

'Wright,' he said, 'I have thought of something! The key to it all is the question I never asked!'

30

'Not here! Not in the street where we may be heard!' He would say no more but urged Wright on through the Temple gates.

Safely in Gabriel's set in King's Bench Walk, while he got out the sherry glasses, Wright picked up the still incarcerated Delphinium as he would his mother's cat at home.

'My, you really are a weight,' he observed cheerfully.

Delphinium glared with outraged dignity, struggled out of his arms and sprang onto her encyclopaedias with an affronted thump.

'She only likes gestures of affection on her own terms,' said Gabriel mildly. 'And she takes exception to personal remarks.'

Wright took his customary seat and tried to avoid Delphinium's baleful eye.

'What had you thought of, sir? What is the question we have not asked?'

'Wright, the bet that The Honourable Frederick Sewell had in relation to conquering the unconquerable Topsy Tillotson – who was that bet with?'

Wright felt rather disappointed. He had hoped that Sir Gabriel had had a breakthrough in relation to the conspiracy around the sending of the body parts; or even to the identity of the body in the vaults. But it seemed that he was still thinking about the Topsy Tillotson case. As far as Wright was concerned, he felt he had done all he could on that matter; when he had given Frederick Sewell a hiding the man would never forget.

'I didn't ever ask, sir. We didn't have a conversation, so to speak.' He added simply, 'We just jumped on him and gave him a leathering. And afterwards, he wasn't doing much talking.'

'No one asked him during the trial either. He just said a bet "with a friend". It is one of the basic rules of advocacy, Constable Wright: never ask a question in cross-examination to which you do not know the answer! It was inculcated in me throughout my pupillage. And so I followed the habit of decades and simply left it; it did not seem to me of any relevance.'

'Well, I don't see that it was. I expect it was with one of the other rich nobs what men like him spend their time with when they have all that money and do not have to work.' Wright did not sound very interested. 'The devil makes work for idle hands, that is what my mother always said.'

'So did Nanny. *Proverbs* 16:27, said Gabriel knowledgeably. 'I confess, insofar as I gave it any thought, I assumed the same; some other vicious young aristocrat in the Calais Casino or at his club or at the stage door.' He paused impressively. 'But, Constable Wright, what if the bet was with Holloway himself?'

'Well, what if it was, sir? We all know he was a nasty piece of work.'

'Psychology, Constable Wright! That is the key here. We both thought Holloway was a nasty, nosy journalist, ruthless in his pursuit of the next bit of grubby gossip he could turn into a headline. But was he worse than an intrusive journalist? He was a gambler; he liked to bet. I realise now it was a way of life to him. What if he was not just the *disseminator* of that news but its *creator*?

'Both Sewell and Holloway knew Miss Tillotson would resist an approach from yet another young aristocrat at the stage door. I think Holloway needled Sewell into attempting the seduction by betting him he could not pull off the deception of pretending to be a humble working man. He knew Sewell was, like him, unable to resist a bet. And Sewell then seduced Miss Tillotson with that wicked story. I had wondered why Sewell had chosen for his alter ego George, the occupation of printer in Fleet Street. How did he have the knowledge to give his story verisimilitude? Holloway provided that background, I am sure. Well, he lost his bet but I doubt he cared much about that since what he got out of Sewell's conquest was what he was really after, a sensational news story. And then he was relying on Miss Tillotson not to sue; he underestimated her courage. Then he realised, if the matter came to court, when she discovered the deception actually *in* the courtroom with Sewell's arrival, the result would be utterly unpredictable. That is why he made a last-ditch attempt to frighten her off in Drury Lane Garden.'

'Then he was as wicked as Sewell,' said Wright stoutly. 'Not much we can do about it now, unfortunately.'

'Well,' said Gabriel slowly, 'it is true that Holloway has gone where no man can reach him. But what do we already know?' He turned, instinctively, as he always did, to his bookshelves and ran his eyes along them. There was a silence, long enough for Wright to relax, as he always did, into the curious sense of peace that prevailed in Gabriel's rooms.

'Dostoevsky,' said Gabriel thoughtfully into the peace.

'What's that, sir? Is that like psychology?'

'He is a who, Wright, not a what. A Russian writer. He died about twenty years ago. He was a gambler. He wrote about it as no one else has, about the kind of person who gambles. Risk-takers, Constable Wright, who believe that they are immune from the workings of chance; driven to try and control where no real control is possible.'

Wright looked bewildered. Russians! There was no telling where Sir Gabriel was going in this sort of mood.

'And outside court, after the trial, Holloway accosted me. I had forgotten the incident, followed on as it was by a difference of opinion with Sir Edward Hopkins. But now I recall what Holloway said to me: "You think you have won the race. Maybe you will discover that I have another horse to run."'

'What did he mean?'

'I have no idea, Constable Wright, but I wonder if his editor and the newspaper's proprietor, Mr Lionel Sullivan, will.'

'You're not even to think of going near that place. On no account! We don't know who killed Holloway. It might have been Sullivan himself. We only have his say so that he found Holloway already dead.' Wright's voice was sharp with anxiety.

Gabriel raised his eyebrows just a little. 'Really, Wright, I appreciate your concern, but you are not my keeper.' He said it gently, but the sting was nonetheless there and Wright felt it.

The young policeman flushed. 'No, sir. But I— Respectfully, sir, we—' He trailed to a halt.

Looking at him, Gabriel felt a sudden strong pang of remorse. Too easy, after a lifetime of doing it, to assume that patrician tone, however gentle. He tried hastily to make amends.

'I beg your pardon. I am at fault. You were speaking as a friend.'

Wright nodded, inarticulate.

And so, in the end, they agreed to go together, when Wright had finished his beat, the next morning.

Wright had only just left when there was a knock at Gabriel's door. Keeping a very firm hold on Delphinium, he opened it.

Outside stood Rupert Brandish. He seemed to be hovering nervously and, on seeing Gabriel, looked confused; as though he had had second thoughts about his visit.

Gabriel greeted the young man with his usual courtesy. 'Were you hoping to see me? Please do come in.'

Brandish seemed to relax visibly. Gabriel realised he had been uncertain of his reception. In light of their previous encounter in the cloisters, it was scarcely surprising. As he led the young man into his rooms, Gabriel maintained an amiable flow of conversation.

'I think you have not been here before? I have occupied them for many years. Built by Sir Christopher Wren; I pride myself on the proportions of my drawing room. They are, in their own way, as pure as those of the Reverend Master's house.'

But Brandish, prowling insofar as it was possible to do so in a room that was full of books, was plainly desperate to unburden himself.

He tripped over a dictionary of legal words and phrases, sat on the only visible edge of a chair otherwise occupied by a world atlas, and burst into abrupt speech.

'You saw us, didn't you?'

Subterfuge seemed pointless. 'Yes,' said Gabriel.

Brandish wrung his hands. 'What shall we do? It is a sin.'

'It is against the law, if that is what you mean.'

'What is the difference?' Brandish's voice shook with despair.

Gabriel was reminded of his conversation with Wright when they had first visited St Bartholomew's Hospital and Wright had learned of the legalities and questionable moralities of dissection of the dead. It was curious, he reflected, how young people found obscure the distinction between legality and morality. But even as he thought this, he remembered Durrant the porter's wrongful conviction and his own dilemma about the matter. That, too, had been a conflict between law and morals and it had troubled him. But nonetheless his articulation of the problem to Brandish was clear.

'My dear Brandish, they may or may not be the same thing at all. One is imposed by the state. One is personal to you, whatever society may say, though your views may of course be shaped by society's.' He thought that this dry analysis offered little comfort and offered: 'The law is quite frequently well behind what society generally believes to be right. If it is any comfort to you, my observation is that the law in the end catches up.'

Brandish shook his head. 'Not in our lifetimes, Sir Gabriel.'

Gabriel thought back to Oscar Wilde's case, only six years earlier, and of the long shadows it had cast. The increasingly harsh condemnation and savage punishment of men convicted of the same crime. The ensuing blackmails and humiliating exposures and very public arrests, and long prison sentences. He thought of Simon Rawlings and of Durrant the porter. It seemed foolish to offer false comfort now. 'No,' he said, as gently as he could. 'Probably not.'

'John's father was Home Secretary. The maintenance of law and order is his god. John has been told from an early age that he was going to be a barrister and a politician and a dutiful husband to a suitable girl. He feels trapped by expectations and family duty and – and by chivalry. Why is it that women can break their engagement but society will not allow a man to do so? Why should John pursue a career he does not want? How can he get out of any of it? And now it has become more complicated even than that.'

Brandish leaped from his chair, found his desire to prowl thwarted by the complete works of Dickens and sat down again abruptly.

'Sir Gabriel, I have been invited by Sir William Waring to be Reverend Master of the Temple Church. The church, of course, is a Royal Peculiar. The appointment is therefore made by His Majesty the King. And I am told he has just approved it. I am very conscious of the great honour conferred upon me.'

'My congratulations. I was aware of the many accolades you have received whilst standing in since poor Vernon-Osbert died. It is, if I may say so, a very great achievement for a young man.

I hope and believe you will become as loved as Reverend Master of the Temple as he was.'

'It is my dream. More than that, it is my calling. From the moment I walked into that wonderful church built as London's Jerusalem, I knew I would remain so long as I could, in whatever role God wanted me to fill there. I cannot lose the opportunity, Sir Gabriel.'

Gabriel struggled in this unfamiliar territory to find an answer. 'I am sure that you are not the only clergyman who has had to reconcile your faith and conscience over this matter,' he began, rather hesitantly. 'Perhaps you should consult—'

But Brandish interrupted him. 'Oh, it is far, far worse than that. Don't you see? Gibson is to be married here with great pomp and a special licence from the Archbishop of Canterbury and the most distinguished people in London present. And who must conduct the service? The Reverend Master of the Temple Church.'

'Ah,' said Gabriel. 'I had not thought of that. That, I see, makes things very difficult.'

'It makes them impossible. I have told J— Gibson I will not do it. I *will not*. My very being cries out against it. It would be wrong on every single level. It would be a crime against the sanctity of the marriage vow. It feels to me that it would be a sin far greater than any other I might be deemed to have committed. It seems almost incidental that it would also break my heart. But so would giving up the Church.'

It seemed to Gabriel that here was a problem so intractable that he could find no helpful comment to make. A problem so far outside his own experience, as a barrister, as an amateur detective, as a man. He wanted to turn away from the suffering so apparent in front of him. He was not sure if broken hearts were in his vocabulary. He traced on the underside of his chair one of the familiar little patterns and remained silent, deep in thought.

Then, at last, he remembered Miss Amelia Waring; the eyes bright with intelligence and humour under her pretty hat. He said, 'This is none of my business, Brandish. But there is one person whom you have not mentioned whose business it undoubtedly is. And that is Miss Amelia Waring.'

Brandish flushed. 'We know that,' he said shortly, and stood up.

'Think about it. How would she feel if she knew of Gibson's turmoil and yours? It is all the help I can offer. I am afraid you will say it is not very much.'

'You haven't judged us,' said Brandish and he held out his hand. 'That is a help. Thank you.'

When he had gone, Gabriel thought of the impossible road that lay ahead for these young men. He felt nothing but the deepest sadness for them. What, then, was that niggle of doubt that remained in his mind? He refused, even to himself, to acknowledge that it arose from a thought he could not quite suppress: that Vernon-Osbert's death seemed to have resulted in the fulfilment of all Brandish's dreams of a life in the Temple Church – and in the Reverend Master's house.

The police barrier blocking off the alley leading to the offices of the *Nation's Voice* had now been removed. All appeared normal. The door was closed. Gabriel was well aware that in the aftermath of the trial he would be a highly unorthodox, not to mention unwelcome, visitor here. The whiskery, incurious doorman who responded to their knock, however, once he saw Wright in a policeman's uniform, seemed at once to assume the visit concerned the ongoing murder investigation and motioned Wright and Gabriel up the stairs to the editor's office.

It was Sullivan himself who reacted with a combination of anger and astonishment. He was sitting at his paper-laden desk, a pen between his fat inky fingers. He dropped it as he jumped up. The ink trail it rolled out across his work made him swear fruitily, pink cherubic face crumpled with rage like that of an angry child.

'What the hell do you two think you want?'

Gabriel removed his top hat, and Wright, following suit, his helmet.

'May we sit down?' Gabriel said politely and did so before Sullivan could respond. Wright sat next to him.

'We have come to ask you for some assistance, Mr Sullivan, in relation to a matter which may be of mutual interest.'

Sullivan, the wind taken from his sails by this mild approach, subsided back into his own chair. Observing him, it seemed to Gabriel that the newspaper man was looking – what? Not quite his usual portly confident self; a little – *haunted* somehow. He wondered whether, despite Hughes' account of the man's flippant reaction to Holloway's death, it had hit Sullivan rather harder than the Inspector had realised. A vulnerability was laid bare. Gabriel hated vulnerability. But nonetheless it was a good place to start with any witness.

'We have recently been engaged in a fiercely fought piece of litigation, Mr Sullivan, but I do not forget the human side. I only met Mr Holloway in circumstances when, I confess, he did not commend himself to me; but you have lost a colleague you knew well. My condolences.'

As Gabriel intended, Sullivan was disarmed. He nodded and said brusquely, 'Been here nearly ten years. A damned good reporter. Did us proud whatever you may think. And a horrible death he had. Have you ever seen a man strangled?'

'I am pleased to say I have not,' said Gabriel. 'But I have read enough to imagine it. May I ask you a few questions, Mr Sullivan? You need answer nothing you do not wish to.'

'Why should I want to answer anything?'

'Because,' said Gabriel deliberately, 'it was a horrible death.'

Sullivan digested this and then nodded at Wright.

'What's he doing here?'

Gabriel and Wright had already agreed the line they were to take, carefully composed by Gabriel in oblique language that did not offend Wright's sense of professional propriety.

'I am here, sir, because we are aware that Detective Inspector Hughes had concerns with regard to your safety. We' (left carefully unspecified) 'thought my presence might be reassuring to your doorman; and indeed to you, sir.'

'What do you want to know?'

'Did you know that Holloway was a very confirmed gambler?' said Gabriel.

Sullivan snorted. 'Is that all? Yes, I did, and so are half the Fleet Street men; goes with the type. Born risk-takers. He could do what he liked with his money so long as he did his job.'

'In view of the outcome of the trial, was he to lose that job?'

It was immediately apparent to Gabriel that he had hit a nerve. Sullivan shifted restlessly in his seat and his confident expression faded into a kind of perplexity. It seemed to his listeners that he was on the brink of a confidence. Wright held his breath.

Sullivan said, at last, 'I dunno. I had a rule, you see. Write what you like, dirty as you like, as long as it is the truth. I don't want no lawyers and such. I don't want Fleet Street to say we peddle lies.'

'And had Holloway hitherto adhered to that rule?'

Sullivan looked shifty. 'So far as I know. Never ask, that's my rule. They get told it has to be the truth. Then I leaves them alone. But if they gets caught out, they pays the price and they knows it.'

'Did you regard him as being caught out with the Sewell story?'

'Well,' said Sullivan, and he sounded bewildered, 'that is what I just dunno. Did he lie? He wrote that Topsy was seduced by Frederick Sewell. And she was.'

'Properly speaking, she was deceived, by Sewell, for a bet. He knew she would not succumb to the advances of any of the rich young men she met at the stage door. They had all tried. So he pretended to be something different.'

'Yes,' said Sullivan, stubborn now, his position clarified by articulating it. 'But what Frank said was still true.'

'If I were to tell you that I strongly suspect Sewell's bet that he could pull off the deception and seduction of Miss Tillotson was made with Frank Holloway himself, who knew just how Sewell was going to try and do it, what would you say to that?'

Sullivan's eyes narrowed. 'I'd say you are a clever guesser, Sir Gabriel. I'd say that I did not know that until Holloway blurted it out to me himself after the trial. You saw us rowing, if you remember? And I'd say that I still don't know if his newspaper report of the seduction counts as the truth.'

In the ensuing silence, Gabriel thought hastily. He had got what he came for; Holloway had set up the bet as he had suspected. One more matter and he would leave while he was winning.

'I did indeed see you in an angry exchange outside court, Mr Sullivan. After you had hastened off, Holloway made an offensive remark to me about how clever I thought I was, to ruin the *Nation's Voice*. And then he said: "Maybe you will discover that I have another horse to run." Do you know what he meant by that?'

'He said that to me as well. Blurted out he'd set up the bet and insisted it did not affect the truth of his report. "I'll have a think about it, my lad," I said. I was that taken aback, I did not know what I thought. "This little gamble of yours may have ruined us," I said. And he said, "Keep me on and I will save us yet. I have another horse to run," he said. And I said, "I don't want to hear no more of your horses. I have had enough of them for one day. Tomorrow is another day. I've had enough of you for this one." And I left him.'

Into the ensuing pause, Sullivan added bleakly, 'Only he didn't have another day, did he?'

When they had taken their leave and were walking back, Wright said, 'You didn't ask him about Holloway's stories about the body parts, sir.'

'No,' said Gabriel. 'I did not feel I needed to. I believe the pieces of this puzzle are now all there, Constable Wright. And together we must construct the jigsaw.'

31

The choreography of the afternoon was challenging, requiring all the planning that was normally expended by Gabriel in preparation for a trial, but with an added element with which he was very uncomfortable. He felt he was being all the things he least wanted to be. Judge (God forbid), impresario (Vera Perkins floated through his imagination), puppet master, manipulator. What was happening to him? He wanted only to be back in chambers with the next brief on his desk and the beautiful clear horizon of learning shimmering ahead. He dreaded the terrible emotional tangles that he had to untwine, tangles that did not affect him.

But even as he thought this, he knew it was no longer correct. Despite himself, it had crept up on him, this feeling that he had rejected all those years ago while standing as a little boy on Hunstanton beach with the gulls overhead. Perhaps Donne had been right after all; he was not quite the island he had always believed himself to be. The lives of those around him seemed increasingly of some relevance to his own. With Chapman, Brockley, Mrs Bugg, Mrs Jenkins, Meg, Wright, those whom he had been brought up to think his social inferiors, he had discovered common ground. The terrible betrayal suffered by Topsy troubled him, as did the fundamental rottenness of Frederick Sewell. The secrets of those he had inadvertently stumbled upon in his investigations, the unhappiness of Ivy Bunch, the tragedy of Rawlings and Durrant, the terrible dilemma faced now, this very moment, by Brandish and Gibson and Amelia Waring. They mattered to him.

Above all, there was the need to investigate these different deaths: the unknown body; Vernon-Osbert; Holloway. '*Any man's death diminishes me,*' Donne again, '*because I am involved in mankind.*' Involvement. That was it. And he shrank from it. What routine or ritual could hold involvement at bay?

He pushed this introspection away. There were arrangements to be made; the placement of people and objects to be carefully planned.

He had conferred with Wright first of all. When he had heard the request, Wright was doubtful.

'I am not sure Detective inspector Hughes will be happy about the use of his men without knowing why they are needed,' he said. 'He is sore enough now about the lack of progress.'

'Tell him that it is a matter of life and death. It is our last chance to get to the bottom of this.'

After that Gabriel went to see Chapman in the clerks' room and gave him instructions. The timings of the afternoon's visits were very important. The callers were not to encounter each other before entering Gabriel's room. And not a word of this was to reach the ears of any other member of the Inner Temple. Although Chapman would, Gabriel knew, carry out these directions to the letter, his face conveyed extreme disapproval. There had, in Chapman's view, been a bit too much of this detecting nonsense and it was about time Sir Gabriel applied all his concentration to the next lucrative brief.

It was three-thirty in the afternoon. Gabriel sat behind his immaculate desk. His inkwell, his perpetual calendar and his tortoiseshell pencil case were all in their accustomed positions.

With him stood Detective Inspector Hughes and Constable Wright. There was an air of almost unbearable tension that reminded Gabriel of those moments before the beginning of a big trial, and the police officers of those breath-taking seconds before the door was smashed down and the criminal nabbed.

Wright, uniformed, looked trusting and expectant. Hughes, in the anonymous plain clothes of the detective, also expectant but grumpy. He did not like all this secrecy and theatrics that Wright was so taken in by. He was a straightforward detective and he liked to investigate in his own way. But he was a fair man and he could not discount Sir Gabriel's memorable role in a previous investigation into the death of the Lord Chief Justice; and then, the Temple was, in Detective Inspector Hughes' view, a rum old place. What with its secrecy and ritual and all nobs so far as he could see – and all of them too clever by half. To him this was a foreign country, that's what it was, and he had begun to realise that Wright, who seemed to have found acceptance there, was a useful guide to help him navigate it.

His thoughts were interrupted by Chapman's usual deferential knock on the door and old Brockley was ushered in, cap in one earth-soiled hand and in the other a bulging envelope. The latter he put on the edge of Gabriel's desk. Gabriel straightened it so that it aligned with the top of his calendar. Brockley looked in some confusion at the soil left by his boots on the worn Turkish rug inadequately covering the wide oak floorboards.

'I beg pardon, Sir Gabriel, for – for the earth. I was in the garden when Chapman said you wanted to see me and to bring these with me. So I came here quick as I could.'

'Thank you, Brockley,' said Gabriel. 'I wanted to ask you a couple of things which just might help the present police enquiries in the Temple.'

He took from behind his desk the wooden mallet he and Wright had found. 'Do you recognise this?'

Brockley smiled. 'I should think so, Sir Gabriel. It is one of an old set of garden tools I give to Joe when he began in the garden.

A lovely bit of oak. They were all my own so I brought them with me when I left the Somerton Estate in Norfolk. The Inner Temple bought me new ones. "You have these," I said to Joe, "they done me well for years, they'll see you out."'

Gabriel put the mallet away and, opening his desk drawer, produced from it the blue neckerchief with its distinctive pattern found on the body in the vaults.

'And this?'

Brockley picked up the handkerchief with a gentle hand. He looked wistful rather than disturbed.

'Why, yes, sir, that is my Benny's. I'd have known it anywhere. I give it him when he was a little 'un. It was his grandfather's before him. You have found it, have you? And after all this time! Where did he leave it?'

Ignoring the question, Gabriel enquired, 'Have you yourself seen it recently?'

Brockley shook his head. 'Not since my boy went to sea, sir. He always was a lad for mislaying things.'

'Brockley, Mrs Bugg is outside with Chapman. She has invited you to the Inner Temple kitchen for tea. Would you be good enough to accompany her? I will join you in a while, I promise, and explain things to you then.'

Brockley looked bewildered. 'We are in the middle of the winter pruning, sir. Wh-What has happened?'

Gabriel rang for Chapman and urged Brockley to the door with a gentle hand and a murmur of 'shortly'. And Brockley, used to obeying his masters, made no further demur.

Left alone, the two policemen looked enquiringly at Gabriel, both plainly bursting to speak, both somehow paralysed by Gabriel's calm.

Chapman's characteristic little knock came again. Joe Brockley was ushered in. He stood awkwardly by the door and then tensed as he saw the neckerchief lying on Gabriel's desk.

'Good afternoon, Joe.' Gabriel gestured to a chair. 'We have just been speaking with your father. He tells us that this neckerchief belonged to your brother Benny.'

'I asks you if I could borrow it to show Father.' Joe sounded defiant. 'And he did not recognise it. So I brought it back.'

'You did indeed, Joe. And the reason you did that was so I would think it unnecessary to show him myself. Foolishly, I trusted you. Had I not done so and had I shown it to your father myself, I would have learned sooner what I learned only a few moments ago. The handkerchief was Benny's. But when I showed it to him today, your father told me he had last seen it years ago, before Benny left to go to sea.'

Joe scowled. 'He is getting old, Father. And muddled like.'

'No, Joe. You will have to do better than that. That handkerchief, Brockley tells us, originally belonged to Benny's grandfather. It had significance to him. You, too, would have recognised it, the instant you saw it.'

Joe scowled. '*Benny's* grandfather? He was my granfer too. And I am the eldest son. But it was all "Benny, Benny".'

He seemed not to realise how revealing was his reaction. As an afterthought, he said, 'So what if I did recognise it? Benny ran away to sea. He was always losing things. I thought someone had put the neckerchief on that there corpse and I didn't want you upsetting Father with it. That's all.'

Hughes looked uneasy. This did not seem a wholly implausible explanation. He waited for Gabriel to press the question of the identity of the corpse.

But Gabriel did not press Joe further. As though satisfied, he shifted tack.

'I believe you had visited the vaults before ever you entered them with Wright and me. And you knew that a body was in there, preserved by the heat from the kitchen oven. And I am very much afraid, Joe, that you removed from that corpse a hand, foot, toe and ear. You sent them to members of the Inn with whom you felt you had some sort of score to settle.'

'No, I never! You can't prove that.'

Gabriel opened his desk drawer and took out the carving knife and the Delphinium cigarette card. 'These arrived the very morning after Constable Wright here had told you that I wished to appoint a gardener above you.'

'That ain't my doing,' Joe blustered. 'And I can't help what you think. I ain't had nothing to do with that or with any parcels. And you can't say I did! You getting that after Wright spoke to me in private, that ain't no proof of anything!'

Beside Gabriel, Hughes made an uneasy movement. It seemed to him that this was only too true. Oh, Sir Gabriel's little trick had been a clever try, but there was no doubt that the timing of the threat to Delphinium *could* have been a coincidence. He couldn't see a jury thinking it proved anything beyond a reasonable doubt. And why had Sir Gabriel just left the identity of the body in the air like that? He needed to pin it all down. This was beginning to seem like a job for a policeman. He wondered if he should intervene.

But Gabriel shifted tack again.

'Do you have a scar on your knee, Joe?'

Joe Brockley looked confused. 'Yes,' he said begrudgingly.

'You knew Frank Holloway, the journalist who was killed in Fleet Street, did you not?'

'No,' said Joe, unwisely.

'Yes, you did,' said Gabriel. 'You and Frank Holloway were childhood friends. You were both born in South Rising, the village in Norfolk owned by Lord Somerton. Constable Wright here had occasion to make a visit there—'

Wright gazed fixedly at the wall and avoided his superior's eye. He was glad he no longer had a bandage around his fist.

'—and in conversation with the landlord of the local public house, discovered the link. So, I asked your father about it. He told me about your family's early years. Frederick Sewell, the boy from the big house, he told us, would give his governess the slip and come and play with you. Brockley said Sewell would *"side up with the agent's son, both of them always wanting to be top. Top of the group, top climbing the wall, fastest on their bicycles, and Joe tagging along behind, always trying to keep up."* Holloway was the agent's son, wasn't he? He told me himself his father was a land agent.'

Joe scowled. 'I reckon there are a lot of land agents in Norfolk,' he said. 'And a lot of them have sons.'

'Not,' said Gabriel politely, 'with a badly broken ankle, leaving them with a permanent limp. Fortunately, a lifetime of listening to evidence in court has left me with a very good memory for conversation. Your father told me: *"Joe and Benny were out there all the time with young Pat, and the other children of the village; the son of the Somerton Estate land agent and the son of the cook at the big house, and the vicar's two little daughters, and the blacksmith's twins. Young Frederick Sewell too... Young Sewell and the agent's son used to chase the little 'uns on those bicycles, Joe running behind, to give them a fright. Not in play; over and over, to make them fall and hurt themselves. Mind you, they were the ones who got into trouble. Both lads fell off their bicycles, Sewell cut his head open and the other boy broke his ankle and it never healed straight. My Joe just tripped over and cut his knee bad."* And he said that afterwards he told you: *"Let that be a lesson, Joe, that's what happens if you chase your little brother."*

'And that conversation gave me cause to think. Holloway told me at the dinner given for the press that he had not visited the Inner Temple before. I knew that to be a lie. I knew he had been into the garden because he referred to the hydrangeas. They cannot be seen from anywhere else. If he was known to be visiting one of our servants, the porters would let him into the Inner Temple without question. But if you wish, we can summon the head porter to confirm that.'

There was a short pause.

'Don't bother,' said Joe. And now any trace of deference had quite gone from his voice. 'You think you have been very clever, don't you? All right, me and Frank Holloway had known each other since we were lads. So what? Is it a crime? Are you going to have me arrested for chasing after snivelling little Benny?'

'Joe, I deduced a couple of days ago that you were the sender of these horrible parcels, but I have since been looking for two other people. One of them might have been you also, but I was certain the other was not.'

The two police officers both leaned forward; now, they both thought, surely it was all coming together.

'One was the man who was feeding Frank Holloway all the details of this horrible business so that he could publish it; his "source", as journalists call it. That could have been you. The other person was not you. It was the man, a barrister I first suspected, who had composed the notes that were sent with the parcels. This kind of word play, I told the police, was very characteristic of a lawyer's mind.

'But I now realise that Holloway was not a journalist with a source, either you or anyone else. He *was* the source. No one had to tell him about those parcels. *He* wrote the notes that accompanied them. Helped you to work off your grudges. Neither of you cared for the distress you caused, nor for the fragility of poor old Vernon-Osbert's heart. Holloway was, I suspect, quite indifferent to any slight you felt you had suffered. But at the same time, the parcels gave him what *he* wanted: sensational stories to discredit the Inner Temple. And of course he liked the risk involved. Such is the insularity of my life, I thought only of barristers in connection with word play. But of course journalists love words too.'

Joe Brockley folded his arms and rolled his eyes to the ceiling. Then he addressed the listening policemen.

'He ain't got no evidence! Frank Holloway is dead. Dead men can't give evidence. You knows that!'

Gabriel fumbled in his desk drawer and from it drew the white cards that had arrived with the parcels. In the silent room he laid them out in his careful way, like a man with all the time in the world, playing a game of Patience.

Can I give you a hand?; Don't put your foot in it; Toe the line; A word in your ear.

The assembled company gazed at them, transfixed.

Gabriel bent down again to his drawer and drew from it a crumpled piece of paper covered in untidy notes: '*Topsy pure as the driven snow.*' '*I know girls…*'

'I watched Holloway drop these notes in court. Future copy for the *Nation's Voice*, reporting on the trial. I was unable to give him back the sheet of paper and, as it only contained rough notes, I put it in my pocket and forgot it. It was only later that it dawned on me to compare the handwriting with these.' He put it next to the cards on his desk.

'There is your evidence, Joe.'

There was no mistaking it: the handwriting on notes and cards was identical.

Joe burst into speech.

'You snobby lot, you think you can do what you like! Always being pushed around by one or the other of you, we were. Speak respectful – no matter what was said to me! – sweep the paths, work harder, go to church every Sunday like a good boy! Well, I had had enough. We give you all a fright, didn't we? And why shouldn't Frank help me? The body was there, all shrivelled up, so we used it! Well, now you know the worst and you can do what you bloody like with it, that's all I can say.'

'No,' said Gabriel, and he said it very sadly. 'That is *not* the worst. The worst is still to come, Joe. You knew all too well that the body from which you took the parts was that of your younger brother. Benny was your father's favourite. Your father said he had green fingers, a magical talent with plants that you could not emulate. Your brother loved the garden, as you did. You could not bear to share it with him. And so you struck him a terrible blow.'

Once more, Gabriel produced the wooden mallet.

'With this. You had already discovered the vaults years ago while you were gardening and worked out that there was an entrance from the Reverend Master's house. I suspect you explored on a Sunday, the one day the whole household would be absent. You, as we know, have never been a regular church attender. It was the perfect hiding place for a body. No one even suspected its existence. I think you killed your brother in the Reverend Master's garden. And when you had done so, you dragged his body into the vaults when the household was sleeping on the upper floors of the house. As for the mallet, Constable Wright led me to realise the truth. Anyone could have taken it and used it; but as he said, surely the murderer would have got rid of the weapon after he had used it, all those years ago. It seemed to me the murderer must therefore be a person who for some reason could not risk getting rid of it. I remembered you telling me the shovel you were using in the snow had been given to you by your father. And he has now confirmed he gave you a set of his treasured old tools. Your father would have noticed if you had got rid of that mallet. It was safest hidden in plain sight and used regularly by you.'

Joe Brockley made a violent movement and then stilled again, sitting tense in his chair.

'I do not know what made you go back, all those years later, and discover that the body you thought would long-since have decayed and hidden its secrets, was in fact desiccated and preserved by the heat. But you told your old friend Frank Holloway and so you both made the plan to mutilate your brother's corpse for your own spiteful ends.'

'No,' said Joe defiantly. 'No. You have gone mad. Benny ran away to sea and wrote my father postcards regular.'

Gabriel leaned across his desk and picked up the package brought to him by Brockley that afternoon. It seemed unbearably poignant that on the surface where it had lain were grains of earth from the Inner Temple garden left by the gardener's old hands when he had put the package down. Gabriel opened it, and inside were the postcards that he had last seen displayed on Brockley's chimneypiece. He laid them on the desk, garish pictures upwards, from cities all over the world; and underneath the pictures, messages about places and voyages, plants seen, enquiries as to Brockley's and Joe's health, and each card concluding: '*Gdbye father, your son, Benny*'. And the handwriting on them all was identical to that on the cards that had accompanied the boxes and to Holloway's courtroom notes.

'You told Holloway, your childhood friend, what you had done, when you did it, eight years ago. And you chose the right man to confide in, didn't you? Games-playing, risk-taking, control... It was all there for Frank Holloway, wasn't it? A cruel game that went on and on and shaped the future. Holloway created this wicked plan to avert suspicion from you. He wrote these messages home, carefully drafted by someone who knew how to write, to keep your father satisfied and his hope alive. Oh, yes, he did it very convincingly; and the foreign stamps were easily obtainable. Your father, as I recall from a conversation about the labels on the daffodils, has not learned to read so he relied on you. He would not have questioned the locations on the postcards nor studied the postmarks. He simply cherished them.'

In the deathly quiet that followed these accusations, Joe Brockley leaped to his feet, all control lost. 'I hated bloody Benny!' he yelled. 'Father's little favourite with the green fingers! I'm glad I done it, do you hear?'

Sending his chair crashing to the floor, he scrambled for the door. Wright stepped aside as Joe raised his fist to him and opened the door. Outside it stood four more uniformed policemen, blocking the exit. Wright thrust him back into his chair. There was no escape.

'Joseph Brockley,' said Hughes, 'I am arresting you on—'

'Wait, please, Detective Inspector Hughes,' said Gabriel. 'I am not yet finished.'

At the same moment, a deferential knock indicated the return of Chapman, the door opened once more and Sir Vivian Barton KC was ushered in. He assimilated the varied group before him and raised his eyebrows at the presence of the two police officers.

Seeing Joe, he nodded to him with the breezy affability he adopted when greeting servants: 'Afternoon, Joe', and then to the police officers with a nod, 'Gentlemen' (in a tone of voice that made it plain he did not really think they were), and to Gabriel, 'Well, Ward, dear boy, what can I do for you?' He hitched up his immaculate trousers and sat down in the chair proffered.

'I will come straight to the point, Barton,' said Gabriel. 'I am told that Brockley and Joe along with two porters did a clearance of the trees and shrubs overhanging the Embankment pavement?'

'Indeed yes. At five o'clock in the morning, if you please! Sometimes I do wonder about our dear Treasurer,' said Barton, relaxing at the innocuous question and forgetting for a moment that a servant was present. 'Obsessed with the smooth running of it all... Didn't want to upset the Corporation of the City... Essential it was done when the morning traffic had not begun... so there we were in the pitch dark and freezing cold. Not why I volunteered to be Master of the Garden! I thought it was all garden parties, dear boy!'

'And why was Hopkins present?'

'Well, I was there to check on the servants.' He winked at Gabriel. 'And Hopkins, the Treasurer's little helper, was there to check I actually got up at that hour and did as I was told.'

'How was the job carried out?'

Barton shrugged. 'Well, they hacked it all back. Nothing much to it, except they had to get the cut branches back into the Temple for burning. A lot of tedious journeys in the pitch dark from the Embankment up Temple Avenue. Whole thing was a ridiculous amount of effort but there we are. What the devil is this all about, Ward?'

'And the date?'

'Early morning, around five o'clock on the fourteenth of January,' said Barton promptly. 'My wife's birthday. She took a very dim view of my crack-of-dawn departure.'

'The morning after my trial finished,' observed Gabriel, as though inconsequentially. 'Barton, did all the men work under your eye all the time?'

'What on earth *is* all this? Yes, they did; back and forth like busy ants. Though Joe had had enough of it at one point, I seem to remember, and got a telling-off from his father when he got back. Sneaked off for fifteen minutes. A cigarette in the gardener's hut, eh, Joe? Can't say I blame you.'

The panic in Joe Brockley's eyes was plain to see. They darted around as though he was seeking escape from the accusation he knew was to come.

It came, delivered in Gabriel's quiet measured voice, gentle, almost wheedling.

'Come, Joe. This is the end of the road. You strangled Frank Holloway in that fifteen-minute absence, in the darkness and confusion. Five minutes up to Fleet Street; five minutes to accost him and strangle him; five minutes back. You knew when he arrived at work; he would not be expecting a ferocious attack; and you were by far the stronger and bigger man. And, of course, you had killed before. Why did you do it this time? Was he threatening you with exposure?'

'No!' shouted Joe, and fear and anger mingled in his voice so that in its high pitch it seemed to Gabriel he could hear the little boy again, running around Inner Temple gardens.

'No! I never! I never!'

In the end it was Constable Wright who broke him. Leaning forward, he said, man to man, as though the two of them were alone, 'Come on, mate. You will hang for the killing of your brother. You knows that. They can't hang you twice so tell us about Holloway. Better off your chest.'

Joe Brockley shuddered and speech flooded out of him, unstoppable.

'Frank was a friend. He'd always helped me in the past. But he got funny. Said to do as he told me. He said *he* was the clever one of us. He said that I needed him. Then, the night after that little trollop's trial, he said he was in trouble at his paper. He taunted me then. Said if he had to, to keep his job, he might try to get back in favour by saying he had a big story about the Temple. He said he might publish in his paper all about Benny's body being in the vaults and how he was my brother and I murdered him and how we was both Temple servants and our guv'nors never knew nor cared.'

Gabriel intervened. 'But, Joe, surely he realised if he did that, you would reveal the part he had played?'

'Of course I said that! I'm not stupid, whatever he said,' said Joe bitterly. 'But he had thought it all out, hadn't he? He said he would say I asked him to write them postcards to my father because Benny had run away and never bothered to keep in touch. To make Father happy like. And he would say he wrote the notes in the boxes to begin with because he thought I was playing jokes after I found some old bones when I was digging a trench in the garden. He would say he never knew what bones they were or about Benny's dying or the body or the vaults or nothing! He said he would say he had just reported a story about the parcels as I told it to him. He'd get off scot-free, or with a telling-off at worst, and I would get all the blame.'

Joe covered his face with his hands and continued to speak in a tone of muffled anguish.

'I thought all night. He was seeing that Sullivan bloke in the morning. I didn't know what he was going to do then and I was desperate like!'

Gabriel sighed, and then, as ever, inner lawyer involuntarily to the fore, he murmured to Barton, sitting next to him, 'That story might have worked as a defence for Holloway with a clever enough counsel.'

'It might indeed,' said Barton soberly.

Gabriel nodded to Hughes. 'Go ahead, please, Detective Inspector.'

And Hughes completed what he had already begun. 'Joseph Brockley, I am arresting you on suspicion of the murder of Benjamin Brockley and of Francis Holloway and the manslaughter of Reverend Master Hugh Vernon-Osbert.'

After he had been taken away, followed by a shaken Barton, only Gabriel, Hughes and Wright remained. There was a brief silence. Gabriel looked at his pocket watch. It was five o'clock.

Politely, he said, 'May I offer you both a cup of tea, gentlemen?'

32

When Chapman had performed that soothing ritual, Detective Inspector Hughes said gruffly, 'We are grateful for your help, Sir Gabriel. I have been a policeman a long time but never would I have believed such wickedness. Killing his own brother and then cutting him up? It doesn't bear thinking about. And not one lead had I been able to find on Holloway's murderer.'

'They were bad men,' said Gabriel, 'influenced by one another since childhood. Joe was the brawn and Holloway the better brain. They had corrupted each other, both fundamentally driven by the same two emotions.

'One was burning ambition: Joe to be the only and best in the garden where he wanted to spend the rest of his life, and Holloway to create sensational headlines for the *Nation's Voice* and so advance his career as a journalist. Joe was prepared to resort to terrible violence to achieve his end. And Holloway, of course, was a born gambler, who loved the risk and the thrill and the manipulative control; loved it until, in the end, after years of it, he overstepped the mark.

'We will never know if Holloway would have played the card he threatened Joe with, particularly with the risk to himself that that would entail. My guess is he would not have had to. Sullivan would probably have forgotten and forgiven the Topsy debacle. After all Holloway was very valuable to him, a master of manipulation to gain sensational headlines.

But manipulating Joe — that was one game too far by Holloway.'

'And the second emotion?' said Hughes.

'Wright will tell you about the second. He will express it better than I.'

Wright looked bashful. 'I think they both thought they were judged to be inferior, sir. That they were treated bad by people what thought they were better and higher up than them. Holloway and Joe wanted to hurt them and make fools of them in return.'

'Exactly,' said Gabriel, very sadly. 'We, too, have lessons to learn from this whole tragic business.'

'How did you arrive at the solution, Sir Gabriel?'

'Through my latest case, Detective Inspector Hughes. It is always, ultimately, because of what my cases teach me. The Honourable Frederick Sewell, Joe Brockley, Frank Holloway: all childhood friends in Norfolk. Sewell and Holloway a nasty pair, Joe Brockley admiring, running along behind, learning to emulate them. Constable Wright provided the key when we saw Holloway engaged in street betting. Being an intrusive, unpleasant reporter is one thing; but I suddenly realised just how much the man liked to bet, and that led me to think he had played an active part in the one that led to the dreadful betrayal of Miss Tillotson. He did not want to win that one of course; it was a highly effective way of challenging Sewell to attempt the deception. He knew Sewell could not resist a bet, any more than he could himself. But it seemed to me that if Holloway had been wicked enough to dream up that cold-blooded complicated manipulation, he was wicked enough to do pretty much anything to create his newspaper headlines.

'Then his role in colluding with Joe slipped into place for me. Joe would never have been able to compose the cards that went with the body parts, nor carry out the deception of his father, without Holloway. And, of course, it explains the other matter that was puzzling me; although the story of the body parts appeared in the newspaper, the discovery of the corpse from which they had been removed did not. That was a story Holloway did not want to advertise to the world, lest it led to the discovery of the body's identity and the part he had played, both in covering up the murder and, later, in playing games with the body parts.

'But in the end, if he needed to reveal that story, he thought he had a way round what he himself had done. He could regain favour with a sensational story for his editor while lying his way out of his own involvement in the Temple case. That was the final horse he told me that he had to run.'

'Well, he lost his race,' said Hughes sombrely. 'And now Joe will hang for the murders of both his brother and Frank Holloway.' He thought of something else. 'You did well there, Wright,' he said gruffly. 'You got to Joe somehow, the way you spoke to him. We'll make a detective of you one day.'

Wright blushed scarlet.

'As for Reverend Master Vernon-Osbert,' Gabriel said sadly, 'the whole Temple knew he had a fragile heart, poor old man. Joe and Holloway may not have set out to kill him — they just didn't care if that was the result of settling their score. I suppose it will be a kind of justice for his death, a verdict of manslaughter.'

He got up from his desk. 'Speaking of old men, I must go to Brockley.' And he felt a sinking of his heart, a shrinking from what he feared to face above all else: the suffering and vulnerability of others.

Hughes looked shrewdly at him. 'Shall we do it together, sir?'

Gabriel hesitated then shook his head. 'Thank you, Inspector,' he said. 'But Brockley has known me a long time. It is my duty.'

He met Mrs Bugg outside the kitchen, fetching provisions from the larder.

'He's in there by the fire with a scone,' she said comfortably. 'Waiting for you like you asked him to, Sir Gabriel. Are you all right, sir? You look rather pale.'

'It is cowardice, Mrs Bugg,' said Gabriel ruefully. 'I have to tell Brockley news so terrible that I cannot bear to do it. Yet I must.'

She looked sympathetic and uncomprehending.

Gabriel took a deep breath. How did you tell a man he had lost both his beloved sons? That one was long-dead and the other a murderer who had deceived the father who loved him and was now destined for the gallows?

He opened the kitchen door and went in.

When he emerged an hour later, he stood dazed for a moment. Fumbling for his pocket watch, he discovered to his astonishment that it was still not yet six o'clock. It felt as though hours had passed. He could not bear to think of the grief he had left behind him.

From the shadows of the buildings, a familiar burly figure emerged and came towards him.

'I thought I would just wait for you,' said Wright.

'Thank you.'

'I will walk back to King's Bench Walk with you, sir.'

They did so in silence.

At last, Wright said, 'I once had to tell a lady her husband had died, kicked by a horse in the Strand. I had only been a policeman for a week. I went home and I— I was very upset. My mother, she said to me, "Maurice, if you are truly sad for someone else, then you take a bit of their sadness away with you when you leave them. That is how you know you have helped them."'

'Everything I hear of your mother makes me think she is a very kind and sensible woman. You are fortunate indeed.'

They walked on. As they approached 4 King's Bench Walk, Wright felt, in some obscure way, that he was handing Sir Gabriel over.

'Delphinium will be safe inside waiting for you. I will say goodnight, sir.'

'Goodnight, Wright. And thank you again.'

Wright watched him go on slowly, across the Terrace and up the steps to King's Bench Walk.

33

The next morning, Gabriel reported the whole story to Sir William Waring, who reacted with predictable priorities.

'I am appalled. Disgraceful story! Those vaults must be closed, no word spread about them, and hopefully they will soon be forgotten. As for Holloway, this confirms all my views. I will never allow Fleet Street through these gates again. Thank God Joe Brockley is one of the servants and the culprit did not turn out to be a member of the Bar. Of course, the hanging will cause a stir, but we can weather that. His father had better be asked to leave.'

'Joe's father has been a good and faithful member of this community.' Gabriel's tone was repressive. 'He has suffered the most grievous loss it is possible to imagine. I have told him that after he has claimed Benny's body and arranged for his proper burial, he may remain here as long as he wishes and find whatever solace he can in the garden. Ultimately, I believe he will go home to South Rising in Norfolk where he tells me his sister still lives.'

The Treasurer, well aware that Gabriel had undertaken a duty which was in reality his own, said grudgingly, 'Well, I suppose we must thank you, Ward, for bringing all this to a discreet conclusion. And for speaking to Brockley. I confess, I should not have relished the task.'

Gabriel looked at him in some astonishment. He could not recall Sir William ever before thanking him for anything, nor admitting to weakness. Looking closer, he saw that the man did not seem to be his usual self-confident self. He wondered if the news he had just imparted had upset the Treasurer more than he had conveyed.

'Are you feeling unwell, Sir William?'

The Treasurer scowled at him. 'I am quite well, thank you, Ward. I will, however, tell you that I have had a personal disappointment which is causing me great distress. And not just me. Lady Waring has had to take to her bed and Raymond has gone back to Cambridge in some disgust.'

Gabriel waited. He wondered what was coming and feared it with a sinking heart. But when it did come, after the silence had lengthened and Sir William had revolved on his desk chair and back again and fiddled with a pencil until it broke, it was surprising.

'Amelia has broken off her engagement to Gibson. Just like that, if you please.'

'I am sorry to see you so upset, Sir William,' said Gabriel cautiously. He felt unable to say he was sorry at the news. 'And I am sorry if Miss Amelia is unhappy.'

'Unhappy? She is not the least bit unhappy! Quite the contrary. She has always known it was what we wished for her and yet she is positively defiant. When she first told us, her mother took her off for a little – a little talk. We wondered if she was nervous about – oh, you know,' he said impatiently as Gabriel listened inscrutably. It then occurred to the Treasurer that perhaps Gabriel did not know, and he hastened into further speech.

'Anyway, Amelia was downright pert to her mama. So, we spoke to her together and all she would say was that she had changed her mind. She tossed her head and said, "Girls are allowed to change their minds, aren't they? Well, I have changed mine." Not a word more. And when her mama pointed out to her that she was twenty and she might find herself a spinster, Amelia giggled!'

'Well,' said Gabriel, even more cautiously, 'perhaps it is for the best, Sir William, if that is how Miss Amelia feels.'

'It is not for the best as far as young Gibson is concerned,' said Waring shortly. 'She has broken that young man's heart. I spoke to Sir Leopold Gibson last night. Young John has told his father he is so devastated that he must go far away. Lady Gibson has taken to her bed. I am most embarrassed and distressed about the whole business. And the Archbishop of Canterbury's special licence for the marriage has just arrived!'

He seemed to recover himself with a jolt. 'Well, well, this will not get the work done.' He nodded a clear dismissal.

Gabriel made for the door. When he reached it, he paused.

'Will you remember me to Miss Amelia, Sir William, and – and give her my respects?'

Walking back, he reflected on the interview. How typical of the little world in which he lived that Miss Amelia Waring's broken engagement had taken up far more of Sir William's time and attention than Brockley's tragedy, than Joe's unimaginable iniquity, than the loss of young Benny's life.

Back in King's Bench Walk, the reality of Gibson's plan to leave was apparent. The porters were already moving his belongings down the stairs. Two of them were carefully carrying one of the Wardian cases, the little fern a-tremble inside it. Gabriel gave it a nod of fellowship as he passed by. On the stairs he met Rupert Brandish carrying a packing case.

'I would like to talk to you, Sir Gabriel,' he said.

'Of course,' said Gabriel. 'Let us walk around the garden.'

And so they did, around the Inner Temple garden that had heard centuries of confidences exchanged, reflecting every emotion from extreme grief to extreme joy and everything in between.

'We want you to know that John did what you advised—'

'No, no,' Gabriel interrupted in some alarm, 'not *advised*, Brandish.'

'Well, *hinted at* then,' said Rupert Brandish with a smile. 'And it was very difficult. John did not know if she would... would know about... well, understand. But she did. Or he thinks she did. Miss Amelia Waring is *a brick*, Sir Gabriel.'

'I had gathered that,' he said drily. 'I had an interview with Sir William this morning. I am told Mr Gibson is leaving the Bar with a broken heart.'

'John is to join a collecting expedition with members of the Royal Horticultural Society. They are to bring back ferns from Chile for Kew Gardens. He will be away two years. There are other plant-collecting trips planned all over the world. When he comes home, now and again over the years, he will lodge at the Reverend Master's house with me, an old Cambridge friend. *My* house. The Wardian cases will be there to welcome him and others will join them. And in between our meetings, we will both have immensely rewarding and fulfilling work, Sir Gabriel.'

'Will it be enough?' Gabriel said sadly.

'It will have to be enough. It is all we can have.'

Returning home, it seemed to Gabriel that these three young people had faced and dealt with their dilemma with dignity and courage and resourcefulness. He thought of his own life. He had never faced its difficulties with such shining gallantry. He had been fifty-five at Christmas. He wondered whether perhaps, in this last year, he, too, had gone a little way towards confronting the human emotions from which he had always tried to shield himself. But even as he thought it, he felt the now familiar aching in the back of his throat and still could not bring himself to resist ensuring that no part of his foot impinged on the lines of the familiar paving stones of the Terrace.

One loose end remained.

'I believe, Delphinium,' said Gabriel the next day, 'there are such things as cat doors. Chaucer mentions them, you know, and there is some evidence Isaac Newton had one, not to mention many cathedrals. It is a most interesting subject. I have never given it proper thought. I must research it further.'

Delphinium yawned.

'I am going to ask Sugden to create such a door, thus ensuring that you are able to make a quieter and more ladylike entrance and egress.'

He put on his overcoat. Delphinium followed him out of number 4 and down the long Walk to Sugden's workshop, an Aladdin's cave of pieces of timber removed over centuries of renovation around the Temple, of old locks and door handles and bolts, immaculate jars of carefully graded nails, chaotic piles of pails and ropes, and large pots of the black paint used for the signwriting over all the doors in the Temple. And amidst it, the steady-handed magician, Sugden.

Gabriel made his request.

Sugden, who missed nothing, had a twinkle in his eyes.

'I had a feeling she would get round you. Coming to live with you, is she, sir?'

'Certainly not,' said Gabriel. 'Her home is now with Mrs Bugg in the kitchen. I have frequently had occasion to remind Delphinium of that. But she will keep thumping at my door when I am reading. She must have a quieter way of getting in and out.'

'Would you like me to paint her name above it, sir?'

'Certainly not,' said Gabriel again. 'That would be a step too far, Sugden.' But he made his little snuffle of amusement.

Sugden fumbled around in an overflowing box and produced his loved and well-worn tape measure, curled within its leather case.

'I will have to measure round her middle, sir. She is such a whopper.'

'It might be wise,' said Gabriel.

Delphinium submitted grimly to this indignity. After it, they returned together along the Terrace.

From his elegantly curtained study window, Sir William Waring watched the scene with strong disapproval and a complete lack of appreciation of its subtlety. All thoughts of Gabriel's tactful handling and admirable detecting on behalf of the Inner Temple had now fled.

Really, he thought to himself disagreeably, sometimes I do wonder about Sir Gabriel Ward KC. Now he has taken to walking about the Temple with that objectionable cat at his heels! A lawyer of his seniority and distinction. One of our King's Counsel! In public! I shall have to speak to him.

AUTHOR'S NOTE: WHAT IS REAL AND WHAT ISN'T

IMPORTANT: THIS HISTORICAL NOTE CONTAINS
INFORMATION WHICH WILL SPOIL THE PLOT

The area of London called the Temple, situated between Fleet Street and the Embankment on the north bank of the Thames between the West End and the City of London, houses two of the four societies of barristers: the Middle Temple and the Inner Temple. The other two societies, Gray's Inn and Lincoln's Inn, are housed a short distance away on the other side of Fleet Street, and have their own ancient historical backgrounds. The four are collectively known as the Inns of Court.

To this day the Temple, Inner and Middle, holds the extraordinary status described in my novel. Although within the boundaries of the City of London, it is a little world of its own, similar in some respects to the Vatican in Rome. It is free from the jurisdiction of the Mayor and Corporation of London, exempt from all other civil and ecclesiastical jurisdictions, governed by its own parliaments and policed by its own porters in conjunction with, by consent of the Temple, the City of London Police. Nowadays, of course, many of these peculiarities are purely technical and some, after over 600 years, still said to be arguable.

The Temple Church is jointly owned and cared for by the Inner and Middle Temple.

The governance of the Inner Temple, even in 1902, was rather more complex than described in my novel. It has been simplified for the sake of the story.

The Temple was heavily bombed during the Second World War and so its layout today is different from that described in this book. Those interested in seeing how it looked then can consult the map provided. I have taken a few authorial liberties with the location of doors and windows and generally with the layout. The Gardener's Cottage at the bottom of King's Bench Walk did once exist there but in real life was demolished long before 1902. The descriptions are otherwise as accurate as I could make them, as is the way of life described.

There really are vaults for both Inner Temple and Middle Temple under the Reverend Master's garden, next door to the church, where many senior members of both Inns have been interred. The names I have used upon the coffins are fictional.

In reality, the vaults under the garden only contain senior members of the Inn – that is, lawyers and judges – but there are in addition many burials in the Temple Church and the surrounding churchyard and the records indicate that these were egalitarian, as in my story: butlers, gardeners, laundresses (an Inn term for cleaners, whose duties are not confined to laundry), washpots and other servants of the Inns, lie in close proximity to the barrister members and judges. I have used some artistic licence to extend this egalitarianism to the vault, and I hope none of its occupants will mind.

They lay undisturbed for longer as well, as the vaults were in fact not rediscovered until forty years after the time of my story, when they were revealed by bombing damage. The discovery caused quite a stir, and investigations of the Temple archives did ultimately reveal the note referred to in my book; in 1684 the Inner Temple paid £60 'to Horne the bricklayer' to make a burying vault.

The vaults are now closed and inaccessible.

The law relating to body parts in those days was indeed as obscure as in Gabriel's expostulation, and it really was arguable that it was not a criminal offence to send someone parts of a corpse in privately delivered parcels.

Topsy's theatre and all those connected with it are fictional, although based on similar West End theatres and productions of the period. While I borrowed the location of the Theatre Royal for Topsy's Drury Lane Theatre, the two should not be confused.

Keen collectors of cigarette cards will know that the series used to convey the threat to Delphinium was not in fact issued until several years after 1902. I apologise for the anachronism. I have used some poetic licence.

All the human characters are fictional, as is the entire story, and any resemblance to any real person is coincidental.

Over the centuries there have been many Inner Temple cats. But none, so far as I am aware, has ever been quite like Delphinium.

ACKNOWLEDGEMENTS

My thanks to my dear Inner Temple for my inspiration.

My husband Roger, to whom this novel, like the first, is dedicated, has been a rock of support, as always.

I also thank my sister Pippa for her unfailing encouragement.

As these books progress I realise more and more the skill of the contributions of the many people that bring them to fruition. I am hugely indebted to my agent, Anne Marie Doulton at The Ampersand Agency, and to my editor, Therese Keating at Bloomsbury, Raven Books, and all the rest of the team at Bloomsbury. Also to Jessica Buckman of The Buckman Agency, who has guided me through the labyrinthine-world of foreign rights. I could not have been luckier with all of them. They are making my second career as interesting and satisfying as the first (which is saying a great deal) and I am very grateful.

A NOTE ON THE AUTHOR

Sally Smith spent all her working life as a barrister and later KC in the Inner Temple. After writing a biography of the Edwardian barrister Sir Edward Marshall Hall KC, she retired from the bar to write full-time. Her series of mystery novels starring the reluctant sleuth Sir Gabriel Ward KC is inspired by the historic surroundings of the Inner Temple in which she still lives and works, and by the rich history contained in the Inner Temple archives.